Sarah Anderson's Travel Companion

Acknowledgements

Thanks especially to Richard Adams, Sam Adams, Elisabeth Anderson, Rose Baring, Alexander Fyjis-Walker, Simon Gaul and the Travel Bookshop, Sarah Quill, Meg Richardson and Barnaby Rogerson - all of whom rescued me with their various skills and expertise when this sometimes seemed to be becoming an impossible project.

Sarah Anderson's Travel Companion

Sarah Anderson

Portobello Publishing
London
2004

© Sarah Anderson 2004

Published by Portobello Publishing,
13 Blenheim Crescent,
London, W11 2EE
March 2004

A new, revised and updated version of
Anderson's Travel Companion
Scolar Press 1995

Production
Cover design: Nicola Murray
Design and typesetting: Sarah Anderson
Printed in the UK by
Antony Rowe Ltd
Chippenham

The moral right of the author has been asserted.

A catalogue record for this book is available from the British Library.

ISBN: 0 9542624 0 9

Contents

Introduction

This book was first published in 1995 as *Anderson's Travel Companion* - a volume which covered the whole world. When I got the rights back, and decided to publish it under my own imprint, the 'whole world' seemed too daunting a prospect, so I opted to do it continent by continent.

The idea behind this book is very much the same as the idea behind the Travel Bookshop, which I started in 1979. It seemed to me then, and still does now, that when you travel you often want to know more about a country than can be found in a guide book: reading about a place makes any trip, however short, more worthwhile, and reading widely about a country and finding out about its art, history and natural history makes travelling far more interesting. I have often found that a place comes most alive through reading fiction set there, and for this reason I have included many novels and short stories by both local and foreign authors.

But it is not always easy to find out what literature exists on a country without having a great deal of time and access to a good library - I hope that this book will provide a short cut. I am not claiming to have produced a definitive and comprehensive guide to books about countries, but rather I have made a personal choice, which the reader can sift through and, I hope, find the kind of book which will make his or her trip more enjoyable. Some people might disagree with my choices and think that I have left out essential reading: I would welcome ideas for the next edition.

I hope that the book will appeal to all kinds of different people, especially since it covers such a wide range of books. I would like to feel that not only travellers and armchair travellers, but also journalists, diplomats, business people and aid workers will benefit from discovering more about the literature of the country of their choice.

SA

Guide Book Series

It is possible to give only an approximation of what each guide book series is like, since each book within the series will have a different author and the quality therefore varies enormously. The odd guide from a series appears in the text as a one-off and these are not mentioned below.

Blue Guides

Over the last few years the Blue Guides have updated their rather musty image and have become the guide of choice for many serious travellers. Good for in-depth information.

Bradt

Bradt are quick off the mark in publishing guides to places where other guides don't go (e.g. Iraq), continuing in the tradition started by Hilary Bradt who was a pioneer in publishing off-the-beaten-track guides. Basic information.

Cadogan

As a series the Cadogan guides are somewhat patchy, but the ones to North Africa are particularly good, being full of historical descriptions as well as practical information.

Everyman

The kind of guide which can help you make a choice about where to go: Everyman guides are in the same style of format as the Eyewitness series.

Eyewitness

Crammed full of information and illustrations - some people love them, some people hate them.

Footprint

The first in the series was the legendary *South American Handbook*. With more than eighty handbook titles now in print, Footprint have begun to be a serious contender to the other major series.

Insight

Insight guides cover countries, areas and themes. Filled with colour pictures, they also have interesting anecdotal material. Good pre- and post-trip.

Lonely Planet

Lonely Planet celebrated their 30th anniversary in 2003 and have come a long way since Maureen and Tony Wheeler published *Across Asia on the Cheap* - they now produce more than 600 titles. One of the downsides of being so successful is that so many people use the Lonely Planet guides that 'a quiet taverna' is unlikely to have retained its charm.

Rough Guides

Rough Guides have gone decidedly upmarket since their inception as a series for youth 'travelling rough'. They have evolved along with their clientele and are now one of the best series on the market.

Vacation Work

Targeted primarily at students and full of ideas on what to do either on short vacations or for longer periods abroad. Their guides are called *Travellers' Survival Kit*, confusingly similar to the Lonely Planet name but much more budget-oriented.

Africa

AFRICA

Anthropology

Black Skin, White Masks
Frantz Fanon 1967 (1952)
This book was not published in England until after Fanon's death in 1961. He uses psychoanalysis and psychology to explain his theory about the feelings of dependency and inadequacy that black people experience in a white world. *The New York Times* wrote "One feels a brilliant, vivid and hurt mind walking the thin line that separates effective outrage from despair" and *Newsweek* described the book as "A strange, haunting mélange of existential analysis, revolutionary manifesto, metaphysics, prose, poetry and literary criticism".

The Africans
David Lamb 1990
The author tries to try to cram too much into this book making it a somewhat muddled overview.

Art, Archaeology and Architecture

African Traditional Architecture
Susan Denyer 1982
A survey of architecture in sub-Saharan Africa; the text is broken down into Rural Settlements; States and Towns; Sacred, Ceremonial and Community Buildings; Defence; The Building Process; Decoration; a Taxonomy of House Forms; Distribution of Styles; The Impact of Modernization. Thorough, but accessible to the general reader; detailed line drawings and photographs make this a useful book.

A Short History of African Art
Werner Gillon 1988 (1984)
A concise and comprehensive history of African art illustrated with many black and white photographs. Gillon examines the worldwide influences on African culture through the ages and includes an invaluable bibliography at the end. Very useful for reference and for a general appreciation of the many different art forms in Africa.

Archaeology Africa
Martin Hall 1996
Methodology and achievements of archaeology in Africa.

The Dance, Art and Ritual of Africa
Jean-Louis Paudrat; photographs Michel Huet 1978
More than 260 photographs of dances recorded during thirty years in sub-Saharan Africa. The significance of the ritual and dances is explained in the text.

African Textiles
John Picton and John Mack 1991 (1979)
A book showing how textiles are produced in the different countries of Africa. The mostly black and white photographs show the processes of preparing the raw materials, dyeing, appliqué and embroidery etc. Sixty colour illustrations show the finished result.

Africa Explores
Susan Vogel 1991
An exploration of the major themes in 20th century African art. Susan Vogel divides the sub-Saharan African art of today into five main themes: Traditional art, New Functional art, Urban art, International art and Extinct art. Many people have contributed a variety of essays to the book and it is well illustrated with colour photographs throughout.

African Art
Frank Willett 1991 (1971)
A very good introduction and survey of African art which shows the variety and power of the different forms of art. The book is easy to use and has many colour illustrations.

3

Biography

The Devil Drives
Fawn Brodie 1990 (1967)
A riveting biography of Richard Burton, the explorer, botanist, swordsman, zoologist, geologist, pornographer, author of forty three books and speaker of forty languages.

Frantz Fanon – A Life
David Macey 2000
A worthy biography of Fanon, one of the great figures of Third World revolutions.

The Arabs
Peter Mansfield 1992 (1976) (see Middle East)

Fiction, Poetry

African Short Stories
eds. Chinua Achebe & C.L. Innes 1985
A collection from writers from all over Africa including Jomo Kenyatta.

In The Shadow of Islam
Isabelle Eberhardt (2003) (1993)
A collection of stories collected by Isabelle Eberhardt. An ideal starting-point from which to discover more about her life and North Africa.

Leaf and Bone
ed. Judith Gleason 1994 (1980)
An anthology of spoken poetry in Africa.

General Background

A Passage to Africa
George Alagiah 2001
As a child Alagiah moved from Sri Lanka to Ghana with his family and as the BBC's Africa correspondent has travelled widely and witnessed much.

Fishing in Africa
Andrew Buckoke 1992
A guide to war and corruption in Africa.

Where There is No Vet
Bill Forse 1999
Invaluable for helping people keep healthy animals in remote places.

Inside Africa
John Gunther 1955
A classic - inevitably dated but nevertheless interesting.

Africa. Dispatches from a Fragile Continent
Blaine Harden 1993 (1991)
Harden, an American reporter, writes controversially about the reality of Africa today.

Belly Dance
Tina Hobin 2003
Written by a dance expert, teacher and performer, this is an introductory history and practical guide.

Brothers under the Skin
Christopher Hope 2003
The author observes tyranny around the world.

The Shadow of the Sun
Ryszard Kapuscinski 2001
Kapuscinski first arrived in Africa in 1957 and over the next 40 years travelled widely. His interpretation of the complex continent is well-worth reading.

The Soccer War
Ryszard Kapuscinski 1991 (1990)
Among the revolutions and coups that Kapuscinski covered were incidents in Algeria, the Congo and Ghana.

People on the Edge in the Horn
Gaim Kibreab 1996
An in-depth study of land use in Africa.

The Aquarian Guide: African Mythology
Jan Knappert 1995 (1990)
Comprehensive overview of beliefs,

4

myths and cosmology of African peoples. An alphabetical cross-referenced guide.

The Invention of Africa
V. Y. Mudimbe 1988
Gnosis, philosophy and the order of knowledge.

Aspects of Africa
David Robbins 1996 (1995)
Travels through Namibia, Zimbabwe, Zambia, Malawi, Zaire, Tanzania, Kenya, Rwanda and Uganda.

Traveller's Literary Companion to Africa
Oona Strathern 1994
An invaluable book to African literature which includes quotes from many writers and their biographies.

Where There is No Doctor
David Werner 1994
A village healthcare handbook for Africa.

The White Tribes of Africa
Richard West 1965

Guides
Bradt:Africa by Road 2001

Lonely Planet: Africa on a Shoestring 2004

Lonely Planet: Read this First
An essential pre-departure guide 2000

History
The History and Description of Africa
Leo Africanus1896 (done into English in 1600 by John Pory. Hakluyt Society)
Born in Grenada in 1491, Leo Africanus went to Africa as a child when the Moors surrendered to Ferdinand and Isabella. Morocco was in a period of disintegration and decay, with the exception of Fez, a great centre of Arab learning, where Leo went and studied. He went on various pilgrimages and undertook diplomatic missions, travelling to Tunis, Timbuktu, Central Africa, Constantinople, Egypt, Algiers, along much of the Niger and to much of Arabia. He was captured by Christians and taken as a present to Pope Leo X (a Medici), who converted and renamed him. He spent many years in Rome, but when the pope died he returned to Tunis where in 1552 he died as a Muslim. He was very adaptable and "at home" everywhere - explaining his easy transitions to different religions. He wrote in Arabic and Italian, but interestingly does not mention his contemporaries Columbus, Vasco da Gama and Cortes. There was nothing known about Africa at the time, which makes his detailed descriptions of the shops and artisans of 16th-century Fez and other places especially fascinating. He writes about the different religions in Africa at the time. An important and neglected work.

Tales from the Dark Continent (Images of British Colonial Africa in the 20th century)
ed. Charles Allen 1979
A distillation of the experiences of fifty British men and women who lived and worked in Africa in the days of colonial rule. They originally went to Africa as traders, missionaries, soldiers and policemen and here tell their candid and often funny reminiscences.

Africa in History
Basil Davidson 1968.
A very clear introduction to Africa's past. Davidson uses interviews in the text as well a wide variety of other sources making this a far ranging and useful book.

Moslems in Spain
Reinhart Dozy
Published in 1861 and first translated in 1913 this important work has now been published in facsimile.

5

Africa Explored
Christopher Hibbert 1984 (1982)
Subtitled *Europeans in the Dark Continent 1769-1889;* this is a very readable account of the exploits of the white explorers in Africa before colonial times. The book is arranged chronologically and Hibbert writes about lesser known people as well as the more famous names of Park, Stanley and Livingstone. Most of his research is based on the diaries, letters an books of the explorers themselves.

In Quest of Spices
Sonia E. Howe c.1946.
A history of the explorers and discoverers who in pursuit of spices ended up by discovering new countries. Alexandria, West Africa, Zanzibar and Madagascar were all important in the development of the spice trade; Sonia Howe charts the journeys of the explorers who visited these places and shows how for example seeds and seedlings from cloves and nutmeg were sent from the Moluccas and ended up in Zanzibar and Madagascar which today supply the world with cloves.

The Exploration of Africa. From Cairo to the Cape
Anne Hugon 1993 (1991)
A small profusely illustrated book about some of the great explorers of Africa: Burton, Speke, Grant, Baker and Kingsley.

History of North Africa from the Arab Conquest to 1830
Charles-André Julien 1970
An in-depth but readable history of Tunisia, Algeria and Morocco. Translated from French with an extensive bibliography.

Europe's Myths of Orient
Rana Kabbani 1986.
An intriguing reassessment of why Europeans travelled and travel to the east. The majority of travellers come from societies which exercise a high degree of political power; inevitably they take their preconceptions with them and their observations and writings are geared to their fellow countrymen. Through the writings of Naipaul, Blunt, Canetti, Thesiger, Burton, Galland, Doughty and Lawrence among others, Rana Kabbani makes a fascinating case as to why there was and is the great pull to the east.

The Blue Nile 1984 (1962) and The White Nile 1973 (1962)
Alan Moorehead
The Blue Nile is a compelling historical narrative of the events on the Nile from 1798-1869. Alan Moorehead traces the course of the Blue Nile through its history starting from the Ethiopian Highlands, through the Sudan and Egypt, to the sea. Four ambitious and powerful people dominated the period: James Bruce, Napoleon, Mohammed Ali and Emperor Theodore of Ethiopia. They are all vividly described here. *The White Nile* continues the history and takes the period from 1856-1900, with descriptions of its early explorers, including those brave pioneers who were searching for the source.

A Short History of Africa
Roland Oliver & J.D. Fage 1995 (1962)
The authors draw on much classic work written about Africa.

The Scramble for Africa
Thomas Pakenham 1992 (1991)
The last twenty years of the nineteenth century saw a mad 'scramble' for Africa. Between 1880 to 1902 five European powers had grabbed most of Africa and divided it up between them; the rush started after Livingstone had exposed the horrors of the slave trade and said that what Africa needed was Commerce, Christianity and Civilisation. Thomas Pakenham has written a fascinating book on this huge subject.

The History of the World
Pliny (translated by Philemon Holland) 1962
Pliny was writing in the first century AD

6

and this translation first published in 1601 was the one probably read by Shakespeare. Pliny was insatiably curious; he lived in a permanent state of astonishment, accumulating sensational 'facts' to emphasise the extraordinary world in which he lived. Book Five deals briefly with Africa: the inhabitants of Aethyopia, the Source of the Nile and Alexandria which he compares to a "Macedonian cloak, full in the skirts"

Africa - A Biography of the Continent
John Reader 1998 (1997)
Wide ranging and all-encompassing.

Natural History

The Fate of the Elephant
Douglas H. Chadwick 1994 (1992)
Everything about elephants in both Africa and Asia.

Collins Guide African Wildlife
1996
A well-illustrated compact guide.

A Field Guide to the Larger Mammals of Africa
Jean Dorst and Pierre Dandelot 1990 (1970)
Full of colour photographs, line drawings and detailed descriptions of the animals, including their measurements, colour, markings, habitat, behaviour and habits. The book also has distribution maps making it an invaluable, but rather dated reference work.

The Safari Companion
Richard D. Estes 1999
A Guide to watching African mammals.

Field Guide to the Mammals of Africa including Madagascar
T. Haltenorth & H. Diller 1992 (1977)
The guide covers every species of mammal found in continental Africa. Each family of species has its own introduction

and this is followed by detailed descriptions and illustrations of each species.

African Wildlife and Livelihoods
eds David Hulme & Marshall Murphree 2001
Conservation policies.

Field Guide to African Mammals
Jonathan Kingdon 1997
Every known mammal in Africa is mentioned with identification and distribution charts. The author is a respected biologist.

Africa. A Natural History
Chris & Tilde Stuart 1995
Also *The Larger Mammals of Africa* (1997) – a handy pocket guide for travelling.

Where to Watch Birds in Africa
Nigel Wheatley 1995
Self-explanatory.

Field Guide to the Butterflies of Africa
John Williams 1969.
A general guide which covers all of Africa except Madagascar. Colour illustrations and line drawings and descriptions of over four hundred of the most common butterflies.

Photographic

Wildest Africa
Paul Tingay 1995
Mostly wildlife photographs.

Visions of a Nomad
Wilfred Thesiger 1993 (1987)
A selection of Thesiger's black and white photographs from Africa, the Arab World and Asia.

Travel Literature

From the Niger to the Nile
Boyd Alexander 1907
The expedition which took place between 1904-7 ended in the death of two of

7

Alexander's companions including his brother. He succeeded in reaching the Nile doing a lot of mapping and wild-life investigation en route.

Passing Through
Don Bloch 1988
"Passing Through has all the virtues of an excellent travel book with much more thrown in" *(Financial Times)*

Behind God's Back
Negley Farson 1983 (1941)
Just before the Second World War Negley Farson, an American journalist, spent four months crossing Africa overland. He gives a very good account of colonial Africa.

From the Cape to Cairo
Ewart S. Grogan 1900
(The First Traverse of Africa from South to North). Grogan was a Cambridge undergraduate at the time of his expedition which he undertook on foot; in the introduction Cecil Rhodes writes how 'humorous' it is that a "youth from Cambridge during his vacation should have succeeded in doing that which the ponderous explorers of the world have failed to accomplish".

Native Stranger
Eddy L. Harris 1994 (1992)
Eddy Harris is a black American who travelled throughout Africa in order to understand just how little and yet how much it had to do with himself. He went to Tunisia, Algeria, Morocco, Western Sahara, Mauritania, Senegal, The Gambia, Guinea-Bissau, Mali, Ivory Coast, Liberia, Burkina Faso, Togo, Benin, Nigeria, Cameroon, Central African Republic, Zaire, Rwanda, Burundi, Zambia, Zimbabwe and South Africa.

No Man's Land
John Heminway 1983
A personal memoir in which Heminway travels through Africa focusing on the expatriates who cannot call Africa home

and yet cannot leave it. "A literary gem that belongs on your shelf beside the best of Isak Dinesen and Elspeth Huxley, Ernest Hemingway and Laurens van der Post, or currently Edward Hoagland and Peter Matthiessen" (*Los Angeles Herald Examiner).* Heminway has also written *African Journeys* (1990), a personal guidebook and *The Imminent Rains* the account of a car journey from South Africa to Kenya with Mary Ann Fitzgerald.

Mr Bigstuff and the Goddess of Charm
Fiona Sax Ledger 2001 (2000)
The author was an editor and producer on the BBC African service; the book is well informed and amusing.

Fantastic Invasion
Patrick Marnham 1988 (1979)
Patrick Marnham went on many trips to Africa in the 1970s including one in which he wrote a report on the Nomads of the Sahel after a drought. This book, which had much trouble finding a publisher, was widely acclaimed when it was published; Paul Theroux said of it "An absolutely horrifying chronicle which, better than any book I know, explains Africa and finds a pattern in what has baffled every other observer up to now. It is a courageous and brilliant effort".

African Silences
Peter Matthiessen 1992 (1991)
Matthiessen travels through Senegal, Gambia, the Ivory Coast, Zaire and the Central African Republic, examining the fate of African wildlife.

And Mother Came Too
Joy Viney 1996
The author started travelling to Africa when 'no-longer-young'.

When the Going Was Good
Evelyn Waugh 1992 (1946)
A collection of abridged travel writing which includes a train trip from Djibouti to Abyssinia en route for Haile Selassie's

coronation; an expedition to Aden, Zanzibar, Kenya and the Congo; and a return trip to Addis Ababa to report on the war between Abyssinia and Italy. He was a perceptive traveller: "That merciless eye illuminated all it saw with a brilliant and lurid light" *(TLS)*. Originally published in full as *Remote People* (1931).

NORTH AFRICA

Algeria and the Sahara

Man eats you; the desert does not. Arab proverb quoted by Richard Burton.

Anthropology
The Tuareg
Jeremy Keenan 2002 (1997)

Among the Berbers of Algeria
Anthony Wilkin 1900

Art & Archaeology
A Guide to the Archaeological Sites of Israel, Egypt & North Africa
Courtland Canby and Arcadia Kocybala 1990
Over three hundred sites are covered, but the black and white photographs are disappointing. The book is divided into three sections: each begins with a history of the area and is followed by a fairly detailed gazetteer of each site.

The Art and Architecture of Islam 650-1250
Richard Ettinghausen and Oleg Grabar 1991 (1987) (see Middle East)

Africa Adorned
Angela Fisher 1996 (1984)
Jewellery and body adornment are collected here in over four hundred stunning

photographs. Angela Fisher travelled through North Africa looking out for different kinds of decoration; the ingenuity and diversity of what she found is interesting as much for what it means as for its beauty.

Islamic Architecture of North Africa
Derek Hill and Lucien Golvin 1976
A photographic survey with notes on the monuments.

North Africa: Islamic Architecture
Anthony Hutt (1977)
A brief introduction, illustrated with copious well-annotated plates to Islamic architecture in Morocco, Algeria, Tunisia and Libya.

The Search for the Tassili Frescoes. The Story of the prehistoric rock-paintings of the Sahara
Henri Lhote 1959
The rock-paintings of the Sahara were not discovered until 1933, but due to the Second World War, no real expedition to explore the Tassili frescoes was mounted until 1956. Lhote faithfully copied the hundreds of paintings of people and animals that he discovered, providing a new understanding of eight millennia of life in the Sahara.

Rome in Africa
Susan Raven 1993
An interesting book - updated and reprinted.

Islamic Art
David Talbot Rice 1991 (1965) (see Middle East)
Only a few chapters refer to North Africa and Morocco in particular, but this is definitely a book worth perusing, since it is interesting to be able to place Islamic art in North Africa into context.

9

Autobiography/Biography

My Life Story
Fadhma Amrouche 1988 (trans. Dorothy S. Blair)
The author was married aged 16, and writes convincingly about what it felt like to be suddenly in her in-laws' house.

The Sword and the Cross
Fergus Fleming 2003
The story of two adventurers - Charles de Foucauld & Henri Laperine who helped conquer the Sahara for France. Both men found their vocations in the desert. For Foucauld it was religion and self-negation, whereas Laperine formed a camel-corps for the long-range pursuit of the Tuareg.

The Life of Isabelle Eberhardt
Annette Kobak 1991
A biography of Isabelle Eberhardt who became part of the Saharan legend.

The Private Life of Islam
Ian Young 1992
An Algerian diary of 1970 of a medical student in a provincial maternity unit.

Fiction

The Golden Ass
Apuleius. (trans. Robert Graves) 1976
Apuleius was born in Madaurus (Soul Ahras in Algeria) and trained as a lawyer in Carthage. This novel is set in Greece where the hero got involved with witch-craft.

L'escargot entêté (1982)
Le Désordre des Chose (1991)
La Pluie (1987)
Le Vainqueur de Coupe (1981)
Rachid Boudjedra
In French only.

Everything is Nice
Jane Bowles 1989
The collected stories of Jane Bowles were put together by her husband Paul Bowles after her death. The indications are that she would have been reluctant to publish them, but the stories, some of which are set in North Africa, although strange, are full of precision and wit. Unlikely things happen - a true reflection of life.

Sheltering Sky
Paul Bowles (see Paul Bowles, fiction, Morocco)
Probably Bowles' most famous book is The Sheltering Sky 1990 (1949) - now a major feature film. He describes it as "a novel just like any other novel: a triangle laid in the Sahara", but of course it is much more than 'just a novel' and it is the Sahara, which helps make it so different. The power of the desert is tangible in his work and raw emotion is powerfully near the surface.

The Plague
Albert Camus 1989 (1947).
Albert Camus (1913-1960) was born in Algeria. The Plague is ostensibly set in a French port in Algeria, but the destruction of the town could as easily be an analogy for the sufferings of France, under German occupation in the Second World War. The Immoralist 1986 (1902) is about a young man, newly married, who goes to live in Algeria; he discovers he has tuberculosis and while recovering goes through a voyage of self-discovery. He realises in Gide's words "To know how to free oneself is nothing; the arduous thing is to know what to do with one's freedom". Also The Outsider (1961).

Tea in the Harem
Mehdi Charef 1989 (1983)
The author was born in Algeria; this novel is set in the Paris suburbs and is about a young boy growing up split between two cultures: at home Arab culture and at school the French culture.

Mimoun
Rafael Chirbes 1992 (1988)
The slow, hypnotic story of a Spaniard's slow breakdown in North Africa.

The Alchemist
Paulo Coelho 1995 (1988)
An Andalulusian shepherd boy in search of treasure, travels to Tangier and into the Egyptian desert where he meets an alchemist.

L'Espèce Errante
Afsaneh Eghbal 1983
In French only.

The Mysteries of Algiers
Robert Irwin 1993 (1988)
Set in 1959 in Algiers when the French were making a last stand against the FLN liberation army. It was described in the *Listener* as "Entertaining and very nasty, this calculatedly intellectual comedy succeeds well as an unheroic quest starring Philippe, an interesting monster of disarming honesty".

The Ogre's Embrace (1990)
La Fleuve détourné (1982)
The Honour of the Tribe (1993)
Une Paix à vivre (1983)
Rachid Mimouni
Most of Rachid Mimouni's books have not yet been translated into English.

Desert Love
Henry de Montherlant 1960 (1955)
Extracts from the novel called *La Rose de Sable* which de Montherlant wrote in Algiers between 1930 and 1932 and which has its subject the colonial question seen through the eyes of the people of North Africa. The translation leaves out the politics and concentrates on the love story in which a stupid, but sensitive young French lieutenant who is stationed at a remote oasis in French North Africa, becomes obsessed by a young Arab girl Ramie, who has to remain a virgin. Graham Greene described it as "Fascinating, brilliant and aseptic in its analysis of lust."

The Little Prince
Antoine de Saint-Exupéry 1982 (1945)
A parable which tells of an air pilot who after making a forced landing in the Sahara Desert meets the little prince who tells him wonderful stories about the planet where he lives. The book was written a year before St. Exupéry died.

Desperate Spring
Fettouma Touati 1987 (trans. Ros Schwartz)
A novel which describes the lives of many Algerian women.

Food
Tastes of North Africa
Sarah Woodward 2001
Food of Morocco & the southern Mediterranean.

General Background
Camel Tracks
eds. Debra Boyd-Briggs & Joyce Hope Scott 2003
Critical perspectives on Sahelian literatures.

Selected Essays and Notebooks
Albert Camus 1979
Included in this collection are essays entitled *The Wind at Djemila, Summer in Algiers* and *Ruins at Tipasa*.

Algerian White
Assia Djebar 2003 (2000)
"A hymn to friendship & the enduring power of language, *Algerian White* is also a requiem for a nation's unfinished literature" *(New York Times Book Review)*.

A Dying Colonialism
Frantz Fanon 1980 (1959)
Fanon had worked as a psychiatrist in an Algerian hospital during the Algerian revolution. Here he identifies the justice of

11

the Algerian cause and analyses the relations between colonial and subject peoples. He also shows how this nationalist struggle altered traditional attitudes to family, women, technology and medicine.

The Wretched of the Earth
Frantz Fanon 1990 (1961)
A study of the Algerian revolution which has served as a model for other liberation struggles. Fanon exposes the economic and psychological degradation of imperialism and points the way forward (through violence if necessary) to socialism.

The Sierra Club Desert Reader
ed. Gregory McNamee 1995
A Literary Companion.

Algeria
J.R.Morell reprint 1984
Fascinating pen-portraits of the inhabitants of Algeria, their customs, beliefs and daily lives.

The Battlefield - Algeria
Hugh Roberts 2002 (1988)
Studies in a broken polity.

The Sahara
Jeremy Swift (1975)
A survey of the Sahara through contemporary photographs, history and fascinating text. As an overall view of this vast area of North Africa, there is no better introduction.

Guides

Sahara Handbook
Simon Glen 1990 (1987)
Invaluable as a practical guide for anyone intending to travel across the Sahara. There is information on the climate, how to choose and maintain a vehicle as well as detailed routes. Since the last edition, crossing the Sahara has become very dangerous; few tour operators risk the journey because of outbreaks of violence among the Tuareg and banditry 'liberation' actions. Be warned!

Desert Biking
Chris Scott 1998
A guide to independent motorcycling in the Sahara.

Sahara Overland
Chris Scott 2000
Off-piste routes into the Akakus.

History

Modern Algeria: A History from 1830 to the Present
Charles-Robert Ageron 1991 (1964)
A balanced political, social and economic account of the colonial period in Algeria from the beginning of the French conquest in 1830 up until 1962.

The Golden Trade of the Moors
E.W. Bovill 1968 (1958)
This book shows what an important part the Sahara played in linking the sophisticated cities of North Africa with the great markets to the South. Bovill argues that Berbers, Arabs, Jews and Christians all drew on the wealth and industry of the Sudanese and that it was the routes through the Sahara that made this possible. Both areas gained from this interchange of merchandise, salt and above all differing cultures.

Alamein to Zem Zem
Keith Douglas 1979 (1966)
Keith Douglas was one of the few poets who wrote about the North African campaign during the Second World War. He had been a pacifist as a student, but against orders drove a truck to El Alamein and reported for duty in the Sherwood Rangers. He portrays his experiences in vivid prose; he was both curious and detached.

A Savage War of Peace. Algeria 1954-1962
Alistair Horne 1987 (1977)
Around a million Muslim Algerians were killed in the savage colonial war and as many Europeans were made homeless. Alistair Horne's book documents the

12

course of the war and includes an excellent bibliography.

The Hunt for Zerzura
Saul Kelly 2003 (2002)
The lost oasis and the Desert War.

Exterminate all the Brutes
Sven Lindqvist 1996 (1992)
A study of Europe's dark history in Africa, written as a Saharan travel diary.

African Trilogy
Alan Moorehead 2000 (1944)
The Desert War 1940-43. An account of the prolonged battles between the Allies and the Axis powers.

The Conquest of the Sahara
Douglas Porch 1986 (1984)
A history which describes the French attempt to colonise the Sahara in the late nineteenth century. The men who attempted it were often driven mad by the adverse conditions of heat, thirst, insects and sandstorms which they encountered, but they were driven on by dreams of grandeur and imperialist policy.

A Traveller's History of North Africa
Barnaby Rogerson 1998
Morocco, Tunisia, Libya and Algeria are covered in this short, readable yet comprehensive history of the Maghreb.

Tomorrow To Be Brave
Susan Travers 2000
Travers was the only woman to join the Foreign Legion. This is her story.

Natural History
Birds of Britain & Europe with North Africa and the Middle East
H. Heinzel, R.F.Fitter & J.Parslow 1994 (1972)
The birds are arranged by family; all the illustrations are in colour and the text indicates the points most useful for identification.

The Flowers of the Mediterranean
O. Polunin & A. Huxley 1990 (1965)
The whole of the Mediterranean, including Morocco, is covered with over three hundred colour illustrations and over two hundred line drawings. The descriptive text makes the plants easily identifiable.

Complete Mediterranean Wildlife 2000

Photographic
Sahara. Magic Desert
Jean-Marc Durou 1986
A series of evocative images of land, life and ecology in the Sahara, with a short introduction and text by Theodore Monod.

Inside Algeria
Michael von Graffenried 1998
Award-winning Swiss photographer's view of the civil strife in Algeria in black and white photographs.

13

Travel Literature
Impossible Journey
Michael Asher 1989 (1988)
Michael Asher embarked on the crossing of the Sahara from west to east, by camel, with his wife of five days. This is one of the most punishing journeys left for man to make and Asher tells of how he and his wife Mariantonietta made the 4,500 mile trek, An honest account from which he emerges with credit.both as a traveller and as a writer

Travels in North and Central Africa 1845-55
H. Barth
A scholar and traveller of the Sahara, he mapped the ruins of Tunisia.

Ibn Battuta. Travels in Asia and Africa 1325-1354. 1984 (1929)
Ibn Battuta was born in Tangier and as a good Muslim made a pilgrimage to Mecca. As both pilgrim and theologian he

was warmly welcomed along the route and discovered the joys of travel for its own sake. He spent seven years in India amassing both wealth and fascinating memories about life in a medieval Muslim court.. He was eventually sent as an envoy to China but to get there he took a circuitous route via the Maldives and Sumatra, finally arriving in Peking. He was known as 'The Traveller of Islam' and is the only known person to have visited the lands of every Muhammadan ruler, as well as many others, covering about 75,000 miles.

Esto Perpetua: Algerian Studies and Impressions
Hilaire Belloc 1906

Their Heads Are Green
Paul Bowles (see Morocco)

Grains of Sand
Martin Buckley 2001 (2000)
Buckley realised that you could circumnavigate the world without ever leaving the desert – this is his journey through deserts worldwide.

Difficult and Dangerous Roads
Hugh Clapperton 2000
Clapperton was one of the first British explorers to go to the central Sahara. This is the first time his journals – written between 1822-25 - have been published.

Tangier to Tunis
Alexandre Dumas 1959
A tour of the North African coast undertaken by Dumas while he was waiting for the return of the governor of Algiers. The English translation is an abridged version of the original, but concentrates on all the exciting parts including a visit to the bey's palace in Tunis.

The Passionate Nomad
Isabelle Eberhardt 1987 (1944)
Isabelle Eberhardt was born in 1877 near Geneva, the illegitimate daughter of an ex-pope of the Russian Orthodox Church and a Prussia/Russian mother. She and

her mother went to North Africa, where they both converted to Islam. When her mother died she started her desert wanderings, dressed as a man and known as Si Mahmoud. *The Passionate Nomad* is the collection of her journals found in notebooks after she was killed by a flash flood in 1904. She suffered from constant illness and poverty, but through her writing shines a real love of the desert and Arab culture. She also wrote an unfinished novel *Vagabond* 1988 (1922) and a collection of short stories, *The Oblivion Seekers*, set in North Africa. Isabelle Eberhardt is one of the four women referred to in Lesley Blanch's *Wilder Shores of Love*.

Between Sea & Sahara
Eugene Fromentin 2004
Fromentin visited Algeria three times in the 1850s and kept journals which he made into a book. He also sketched and painted.

The Lands of Barbary
Geoffrey Furlonge 1966
Furlonge travelled through North Africa in 1960 and 1964. He writes convincingly about all the different landscapes, people and scenery that he encounters.

Amyntas
André Gide 1988 (1906)
These North African journals were written over a seven year period at the turn of the century. Gide's descriptions of Tunis and Algiers are an "articulation of consciousness" and mark an interesting evolution in his writing, as he said "Few realise I have never written anything more perfect than *Amyntas*".

'Twixt Sand and Sea
C.F. & L. Grant 1986
A keenly-observed study of the coastal region of North Africa, written at the turn of the century and centred on Algiers. An entertaining account of Arab life.

Desert Encounter
Knud Holmboe 1994 (1936)
A Danish journalist who embraced Islam and spoke fluent Arabic records his experience of life in North Africa under colonial rule. He drove through North Africa dressed as an Arab, collecting much information, and was eventually arrested as a spy.

The Book of Roger
Al Idrisi
A geographical account written for Roger II of Sicily in the mid-12th century.

In the Glow of the Phantom Palace
Michael Jacobs 2000
Jacobs, a readable and authoritative writer, follows the trail of the Moors who were exiled from Granada in 1492.

Desert Divers
Sven Lindqvist 2000
Part travel, part literary history – an original and imaginative book about the European writers who were drawn to the Sahara during the first half of the twentieth century.

Auto Nomad in Barbary
W. McArthur 1950
A drive from Tangier to Alexandria.

Travels with a Tangerine
Tim Mackintosh-Smith 2001
A journey in the 'footsteps' of Ibn Battutah who had set out in 1325. In this volume Mackintosh-Smith travels through North Africa, Syria, Oman and parts of Turkey. The next stage is eagerly awaited.

North African Notebook
Robin Maugham 1948
Robin Maugham travelled through the countries of North Africa to see what the politics in each country were like. He also gathers much information about the social climate in each place.

The Fearful Void
Geoffrey Moorhouse 1974
A personal odyssey of a journey across the Sahara west to east.

Purchas His Pilgrimes
The French diplomat Nicholas Nicholay wrote *Navigations at Peregrinations Orientales* with descriptions of sixteenth century Algiers.

People of the Veil
Francis Rennell Rodd 1926
A nine-month journey made in 1922 to the mountains of Air in the Central Sahara. Little was known about the Tuareg at the time.

North Africa Travel
ed. Barnaby Rogerson 2001
An annual collection of travel-writing from North Africa and the Sahara, from the Atlantic to the Nile, from the Mediterranean to the Niger and from Herodotus to yesterday's postcard. Jeremy Keenan on the Tuareg is particularly recommended.

Desert Travels
Chris Scott 1996
The narrative companion to his *Desert Biking*.

Travels and Observations in Barbary
T. Shaw 1757
Written by an early Scottish antiquarian.

In Search of Sheba
Barbara Toy 1961
Barbara Toy started her journey in northern Libya, crossed the Central African Republic, the Sudan, Tanganyika, Uganda and into Ethiopia. She was eager to discover for herself the people and the country about whom so much myth had been written.

Forbidden Sands
Richard Trench 1978
Trench sets out across the Sahara by

15

camel caravan ostensibly to try and find out what was happening at the notorious salt mines in Mali. In fact he found himself attracted to the desert with a desire to pit himself against its difficulties. He endured great hardship, but recounts his journey with humour.

The Great Sahara
H.B.Tristram 1985 (1860)
The author went to Algeria to recuperate from ill health but, unable to suppress his wandering spirit, wandered into the desert regions south of the Atlas Mountains.

By Bus to the Sahara
Gordon West 1996
Gordon and Mary West travelled to the Sahara by bus with their paints in the 1930s.

EGYPT

Egypt is an acquired country, the gift of the river. Herodotus *History*

Anthology
The Nile. A Traveller's Anthology
Deborah Manley 1996
Deborah Manley opens her book with a quote by G.W. Steevens "Egypt is the Nile" and proceeds to trace travellers' age old fascination with the river. She begins with a section of short biographies of the travellers and continues geographically through the country introducing each section with a short description. The diverse quantity of people who travelled in Egypt is staggering and reading what they wrote would certainly enhance a present day trip to Egypt.

Egypt - An Anthology
C.Pick 1991
Extracts ranging from the nineteenth to the twentieth centuries.

Anthropology
Shahhat: An Egyptian
R. Critchfield 1978
Based on many years' research in the Nile Valley.

Bedouin Life in the Egyptian Wilderness
Joseph Hobbs 1989
About the Bedouin Khushmaan clan of Ma'aza.

Art & archaeology
He who wants to see his time rightly, must look upon it from a distance. How great a distance? Quite simply, just far enough away so that he cannot discern Cleopatra's nose. (Ortega Y. Gasset.)

The Encyclopaedia of Ancient Egyptian Architecture
Dieter Arnold 2002
More than 600 entries and 350 illustrations.

Egyptian Antiquities in the Nile Valley
James Baikie 1932
This book 'confines' itself to descriptions of objects of Egyptian architecture and art, leaving out Roman, Coptic and Arab culture only describing objects *in situ* in Egypt. It is wonderfully detailed and although somewhat dated is well worth trying to find from a library. Surprisingly Baikie never went to Egypt.

Gods, Graves and Scholars
C.W. Ceram 1984 (1949)
An entirely fresh approach to archaeology which was quite revolutionary when it was first published; the stories of Schliemann, Evans, Champollion, Belzoni, Petries, Howard Carter, Grotefend, Rawlinson, Layard, George Smith, Stephens and Thompson.

Early Muslim Architecture (1969 2nd edn) and *Muslim Architecture of Egypt* (1951-9)
K.A.C. Cresswell
Massive and well-illustrated volumes: *Early Muslim Architecture* covers the first three centuries of Islam in all countries and *Muslim Architecture of Egypt* starts with Egypt where the previous volume left off.

Religion and Magic in Ancient Egypt
Rosalie David 2002
An historical overview of the beliefs of the Ancient Egyptians.

The Pyramids of Egypt
I.E.S. Edwards 1991 (1947) (revised edn.)
One of the classic books on Egyptian archaeology, the revised edition includes recent discoveries and scholarship. Dr Edwards uses a combination of his own and other peoples research, ensuring a comprehensive whole.

Archaic Egypt
W. Emery 1991
Aimed at the general reader; not much detail about the archaeological sites.

The Hidden Tombs of Memphis
Geoffrey T. Martin 1991
A detailed and illustrated account of recent discoveries.

Architectural Guides for Travellers: Ancient Egypt.
Delia Pemberton 1993 (1992)

The Art of Ancient Egypt
Gay Robins 1997
A well-illustrated survey of Egyptian art.

Art & Archaeology of Ancient Egypt
W. Stevenson Smith 1984 (1958)
Over 400 illustrations accompany a detailed text to the monuments of Ancient Egypt. Copious notes at the end provide those who want to pursue a particular area with many further sources.

The Search for Ancient Egypt
Jean Vercoutter 1992 (1986)
One of a series translated from the French, this little book is crammed full of photographs, pictures and snippets of fascinating information. The kind of appetite wetter which could lead you into all kinds of other avenues.

Mamluk Art: the Splendour and Magic if the Sultans
Salah Ahmed El-Banasi 2001
An illustrated account of three centuries of near stability during the Mamluks.

Biography
Out of Egypt
André Aciman 1997 (1994)
An evocation of life in Alexandria over three generations.

Akhenaten, King of Egypt
Cyril Aldred 1991 (1968)
Trustworthy biography.

Leisure of an Egyptian Official
Lord Edward Cecil 1996 (1921)
Edward Cecil well known at the time for his wit, wrote these sketches for his family. They give a rather irreverent but highly amusing account of his eighteen years spent serving in Egypt. Many of his observations are hilarious; he is especially acute at analysing people's characters.

Tutankhamen: Life and Death of a Pharaoh
Christiane Desroches-Noblecourt 1984 (1965)
The boy king and his times.

Sadat
David Hirst and Irene Beeson 1981
A revealing political biography.

17

Tutankhamun: the Untold Story
Thomas Hoving 1980 (1978)
A look at archaeological back-biting.

Oleander, Jacaranda
Penelope Lively 1995 (1994)
An autobiography about growing up in
Cairo in the 1930s and 40's.

Henry Salt
Deborah Manley and Peta Rée 2001
Salt (1780-1827) was an artist, traveller,
diplomat and Egyptologist.

Amelia Edwards
Joan Rees 1998
A short biography of the founder of the
Egyptian Exploration Society.

Writings on the Nile
Joan Rees 1995
Short biographies of Harriet Martineau,
Florence Nightingale and Amelia
Edwards.

The Boss
Robert St John 1961
A racy biography of Nasser.

Nefertiti and Cleopatra
Julia Samson 1990 (1985)
A fascinating account of these two
famous queens.

Harem Years: Memoirs of an Egyptian Feminist 1879-1924
Huda Shaarawi 1986
A riveting document from the last generation of upper class women who lived in a
harem.

Travellers in Egypt
eds. Paul Starkey & Janet Starkey
2001
Essays written by a wide range of travellers to Egypt, starting in the seventeenth
century.

Fiction

The Golden Chariot
Salwa Bakr 1995
Absorbing novel set in a women's prison
near Cairo.

A Woman of Cairo
Noel Barber 1985 (1984)
Set in Farouk's Cairo; westernised
Egyptians mingle with ex-patriots.

From Sleep Unbound
Andrée Chedid 1987 (1976)
An Egyptian girl of 15 is forced into a
loveless marriage and becomes even
more isolated when she gives birth to a
daughter.

Death on the Nile
Agatha Christie 1937
Agatha Christie stayed in Aswan while
she wrote this book about a murder on
the Nile which was solved by Hercule
Poirot.

City of Gold
Len Deighton 1993 (1992)
A thriller set in 1941.

The Alexandria Quartet
Lawrence Durrell 1991 (1962)
Justine (1957), *Balthazar* (1958),
Mountolive (1958), *Cleo* (1960)
The quartet intended to be read as a con-
tinuous novel has the rich background of
Alexandria in the 30's and 40's. It is easy
to get completely enmeshed in the exotic
world created by Durrell.

The Key to Rebecca
Ken Follet 1998 (1980)
A thriller based on the true story of the
German spy, Eppler.

Incidents in Zafraani Alley
Gamal al-Ghitani 1986
Al-Ghitani is a journalist who has cov-
ered all the major recent conflicts in the
Middle East. Very readable and darkly

18

humorous read. Also *Zayni Barakat* – an historical novel

Beer in the Snooker Club
Waguih Ghali 1987 (1964)
Ram and Font both lived in England and drank pints of Bass from two mugs which now hang in a bar in Cairo where there is no Bass. The Bass is a symbol for their longing to leave a country where there is a revolution and where they feel stranded between two cultures.

Zainab
M.H. Haikal 1989
This story of an Egyptian farm worker, who tries to come to terms with an arranged marriage she does not want, explores the customs and traditions of rural Egyptian society.

The Cheapest Nights
Yusuf Idris 1978
A collection of short stories by a fine writer of short stories as is *Rings of Burnished Brass* (1984). Also *A Leader of Men* (1988).

The Arabian Nightmare
Robert Irwin 1987 (1983)
A brilliant, paranoid fantasy set in the Cairo of Sultan Qaitbey.

Unreal City
Robert Liddell 1993 (1952)
Set in wartime Alexandria. *The Rivers of Babylon* is set in Cairo prior to Suez.

Moon Tiger
Penelope Lively 1987
This and *Cleopatra's Sister* are novels set in Egypt.

The Search
Naguib Mahfouz 1991 (1964)
Naguib Mahfouz (1911-) is one of the most widely read authors in the Arab world and was the winner of the Nobel Prize in 1988. He has written more than thirty novels which are now beginning to be translated into English. *The Search* is a compelling and lyrical account of a man's search for his father which moves from Alexandria to Cairo. *The Cairo Trilogy* composed of *Palace Walk,*1991 (1956) *Palace of Desire*, 1991 (1957) and *Sugar Street* 1993 (1957) is a rich family saga set at the beginning of the century. Other books by Mahfouz include *Midaq Alley*, *Wedding Song* 1984 (1981) and *Autumn Quail* 1985 (1962).

The Levant Trilogy
Olivia Manning 1996 (1982)
Wartime Cairo is the setting for Olivia Manning's trilogy, *The Danger Tree, The Battle Lost & Won* and *The Sum of Things*. Guy and Harriet Pringle have their own problems as well as those of rumours of a bloody desert campaign. A compelling read which was made into a television serial.

Journey to the Orient
Gérard de Nerval 1973 (1851)
De Nerval, poet, visionary and dreamer, made his first voyage to the East in 1843 visiting Cairo, Alexandria, Lebanon, Syria, Cyprus, Rhodes, Constantinople and Malta. He was encouraged to write this collection of exotic tales by his doctor as therapy: "I feel the need to liken myself unto the entire universe of nature... foreign women...memories of having lived there".

Woman at Point Zero
Nawal El Saadawi 1983 (1975)
Nawal El Saadawi is an Egyptian novelist and militant writer on women's issues. She became Egypt's Director of Public Health. Her novel *Woman at Point Zero* is based on the true case of a woman sentenced to death for murder in Cairo. The story of her life as a prostitute is simply and directly told and is very powerful. She also wrote *God Dies by the Nile* (1974), *The Hidden Face of Eve* (1980), *The Circling Song* (1989), and *Searching* (1991).

Antony and Cleopatra
William Shakespeare

19

Birds of Passage

Robert Solé 2001 (2000)
A family saga about sophisticated Greek Catholic French-speaking Syrians who live in a Muslim Cairo run by the British. Also *The Photographer's Wife* 2000 (1996) set in nineteenth century Cairo. And *The Alexandria Semaphore* 2001 (1996) - Solé has an intimate knowledge of the tensions between Muslims & Coptic Christians.

The Map of Love

Ahdaf Soueif 2000 (1999)
Set between America and Egypt, this gripping love story spans a century. Also *Aisha, In the Eye of the Sun* and *Sandpiper* (1996) – a collection of short stories.

Aunt Safiyya and the Monastery

Bahaa 'Taher 1996
Novella set in a village in upper Egypt.

Desiring Cairo

Louisa Young 1999
Novel about love and fantasy.

20

Food

Apricots on the Nile

Colette Rossant 2001 (1999)
A memoir with recipes.

General Background

The Bible
Book of Exodus
The descriptions of the desert in Exodus are well worth reading.

The Garden in Ancient Egypt

Alix Wilkinson 1998
An examination of the evidence for ancient Egyptian gardens, using archaeology, texts and paintings.

Culture Shock Egypt

Susan L. Wilson 1998
A guide to the customs and etiquette.

Guides

The Little Book of Egyptian Hieroglyphs

Lesley & Roy Adkins
How to recognise gods and pharaohs.

Baedeker Egypt

The 1929 Baedeker to Egypt is the most sought-after, as it includes the discovery of Tutankhamun's tomb. These old Baedekers are full of maps, plans and diagrams and advice to travellers; although of course well out of date, they are always worth reading.

The Nile. Notes for Travellers in Egypt and in the Egyptian Sudan

E.A.Wallis Budge 1910
The book was written for people who had only a few weeks to spend in Egypt and concentrates almost entirely on the Ancient Egyptians excluding almost everything to do with the Persians, Ptolemies, Romans, Arabs and Turks. It is, however, very much more detailed than almost any guide available today and well worth trying to find.

Cadogan Guide: Egypt 2000

Everyman Guide: Egypt 2000

Eyewitness Guide: Egypt 2003

Egypt Handbook 2003

Cairo Insight Guide 2002

Egypt Insight Guide 2002

The Nile Insight Guide 2002

Lonely Planet: Cairo 2002

Lonely Planet: Egypt 2004

Rough Guide: Egypt 2003

History

The Egyptians
Cyril Aldred 1998 (1961)
A readable account of ancient Egypt.

Cairo
James Aldridge 1969
A history of the city from ancient times up until the mid-1960s.

The Rise of Modern Egypt
George Annesley 1994
From Napoleon's invasion to the Suez crisis.

Egypt in Late Antiquity
Roger S. Bagnall 1993
Society, information and culture from Diocletian in 284 to the middle of the fifth century.

Sadat and After
Raymond William Baker 1990
Heavy-going but fascinating.

The Orion Mystery
Robert Bauval 1994
The theory that the Giza pyramids corresponded to the three stars in Orion's belt.

Black Athena
Martin Bernal 1991 (1987)
The author argues that classical civilization has its roots in Afro-Asiatic cultures. He followed it up – after much debate – with Black Athena Writes Back (2001).

The Dwellers on the Nile
E.A.Wallis Budge 1977 (1926)
(The Life, History, Religion and Literature of the Ancient Egyptians). The book begins with a history of ancient Egypt and follows this with descriptions of the Ancient Egyptians' everyday life from birth to death. Budge writes about their work, their manners, their schools, their food and drink, their literature and writing methods and finishes with what they did with their dead and their beliefs about the afterlife. Very informative and interesting.

The Vanished Library
Luciano Canfora 1990 (1987)
The library at Alexandria was one of the wonders of the Ancient World; the ambition of the Ptolemaic kings of Egypt was to house all of the books ever written under one roof. In 196 B.C. the library in Pergamum was established and became its great rival but by the 4th century A.D. all of the great libraries, Rome, Pergamum, Alexandria, Antioch and Athens had been destroyed. The history of what happened is unravelled here.

The Tomb of Tutankhamen
Howard Carter 1963
Howard Carter discovered the first evidence of Tutankhamen's tomb in 1922.

Cairo in the War 1939-45
Artemis Cooper 1989
A look at Cairo society during the war especially through the eyes of writers there at the time.

The Mountains of Pharaoh
Leonard Cottrell 1955
In this book the pyramids are approached from the viewpoint of explorers and adventurers to Egypt starting with Herodotus in the 5th century B.C. Cottrell concentrates on little known anecdotes such as Colonel Howard-Vyse in 1837 who was so desperate to find hidden chambers within the pyramids that he used gunpowder.

Monarchs of the Nile
Aidan Dodson 1995
The lives and times of some those who ruled Egypt for 3000 years from 3000BC.

Letters from Egypt 1863-1865
Lady Duff-Gordon 1865 (2nd edn.)
Informal letters like the ones written by Lady Duff-Gordon are an extremely good way of learning about a country. She combines domestic details "A number of camels sleep in the yard under my verandah; they are pretty and smell nice, but they growl and swear at night abominably", with observations about the

21

country "One must come to the East to understand absolute social equality". The unfortunate lady seems to have suffered from a variety of ailments, but in one instance perked up considerably when she was finger fed pigeons and rice by her loyal servant Omar.

Egypt. Land of the Valley
Robin Fedden 1977
Robin Fedden gives an interpretation of Egypt through its history and makes a special point of how important both the Nile and the Nile Valley were to its development. Despite the many attempted conquests of Egypt, Fedden concludes, as did Herodotus, that Egypt is averse to being anything but Egypt.

Alexandria. A History and Guide.
E.M.Forster 1986 (1922)
Forster had thought Alexandria worthy but dull until he encountered Cavafy who supplied him with the link "The 'sights' of Alexandria are in themselves not interesting, but they fascinate when we approach them through the past". The book was written during a hiatus in the writing of *A Passage to India* (1924) and was described by Lawrence Durrell: "The whole historical perspective of the city in all its variety, has been captured and fixed in a series of short essays brightly starred with all the virtues of this fine artist...It is a work of deep affection and a noble monument raised to this most haunting of cities". Also *Pharos and Pharillon (1923).*

The Rape of Egypt
Peter France 1991
Background to the early archaeologists.

A History of Ancient Egypt
Nicholas Grimal 1992
A reign by reign account.

Lovers on the Nile
Richard Hall 1981 (1980)
Samuel and Florence Baker were lionised in Victorian England as national heroes and explorers. Florence was the first

white woman to have sailed to the source of the Nile, but her dubious origins, she was bought by Samuel from a slave market in Bulgaria, reached Queen Victoria's ears and she refused ever to meet her, despite Samuel's friendship with the Prince of Wales. They remained a devoted couple for the whole of their lives.

Fingerprints of the Gods
Graham Hancock 2001 (1995)
Also *The Message of the Sphinx, The Mars Mystery* and *Heaven's Mirror* – Hancock postulates that all ancient sites were created by a lost civilization propagated by Martians.

A Dictionary of Egyptian Gods and Goddesses
George Hart 1986
Guide to the deities and myths of Ancient Egypt.

The Histories
Herodotus c. 460 BC (see Turkey)
Book 2 describes the Nile in flood, and the Pyramids.

How the Pyramids were Built
Peter Hodges 1993
Written by a stonemason.

Cleopatra
Lucy Hughes-Hallett 1991 (1990)
The myth and fantasy that have been woven around Cleopatra over the years are here brilliantly described and analysed. A fascinating look at the historical Cleopatra and the many different portrayals of her throughout the ages.

Egypt the Living Past
T.G.H.James; photographs by Graham Harrison 1992
T.G.H. James was Keeper of Egyptian Antiquities at the British Museum and his book is an authoritative look at the continuity which exists between Ancient Egypt and the Egypt of today and the importance that the Nile plays in this continuity. The text is accompanied by

115 colour illustrations. Also *Pharaoh's People – Scenes from Life in Imperial Egypt* (2002)

Egypt. A Short History
James Jankowski 2000
A history which focuses on the last two centuries.

Cavafy's Alexandria
Edmund Keeley 1977
An analysis of everything that Alexandria meant to Cavafy (q.v.). The book is divided into 'metaphoric', 'sensual' and 'mythical' Alexandria, the World of Hellenism and the Universal Perspective.

An Account of the Manners and Customs of the Modern Egyptians 1833-5
Edward William Lane 1836
Lane was well placed to study the 'modern' Egyptians since he spoke Arabic and lived as an Egyptian Muslim while he was compiling notes for this book. Lane got to know the Egyptians better than any other European of his time and has detailed chapters on charms, magic, the bath and marriage, as well as every other aspect of life.

The History of the Suez Canal
Ferdinand de Lesseps 1876
De Lesseps, a French diplomat, built the Suez canal.

The Library of Alexandria
ed. Roy MacLeod 2002
The history of this mysterious and wonderful institution from its foundation up until its destruction.

The British in Egypt
Peter Mansfield 1971
The British remained in Egypt for a period of seventy four years from 1882; the relationship between the two countries was unique, Britain saw Egypt as a stepping stone to India and did not view it as an imperial mission. A readable account of the period.

Monks and Monasteries of the Egyptian Desert
Otto Meinardus 1989
A history of the Coptic monasteries.

Egypt's Belle Epoque: Cairo 1869-1952
Trevor Mostyn 1989
An account of the ex-patriot community in Cairo from the time of Ismail to the overthrow of King Farouk.

Cairo – the City Victorious
Max Rodenbeck 1999 (1998)
A lively and entertaining biography of one of the world's great cities.

Lifting the Veil: British Society in Egypt 1768-1956
Anthony Sattin 1988
Anthony Sattin realised on a trip up the Nile that very little had been written about the foreigners who had been visiting the Ancient Egyptian sites for hundreds of years; he decided to tell the story of why and how those visitors came. Many had left graffiti as evidence of their being there and he quotes at length from these voices from the past.

23

Egyptian Legends and Stories
M.V. Seton-Williams 1998 (1988)
An introduction to Egyptian legends and stories, told in a very readable form.

British Museum Dictionary of Ancient Egypt
Ian Shaw & Paul Nicholson 1995
Well-illustrated, coffee-table sized dictionary.

The Rosetta Stone
Robert Solé & Dominique Valbelle 2002 (2001)
The story of the decoding of hieroglyphics.

Daughters of Isis
Joyce Tyldesley 1995 (1994)
About the women of Ancient Egypt.

Judgement of the Pharaoh
Joyce Tyldesley 2000
Crime and punishment in Ancient Egypt.

The Pyramids: Their Archaeology & History
Miroslav Verner 2002 (1997)
Knowledge about the pyramids has increased in recent years.

Alexandria: City of the Western Mind
Theodore Vrettos 2001
The story of the birthplace of the western mind.

Coptic Egypt
Barbara Watterson 1988
Coptic history and culture up to the present.

Serpent in the Sky: The High Wisdom of Ancient Egypt
John Anthony West 1993 (1979)
A new-age interpretation. Also *The Traveler's Key to Ancient Egypt.*

The Complete Temples of Ancient Egypt
Richard H. Wilkinson 2000
Illustrated - the most extensive catalogue of Egyptian temples to be published in one volume. Maps, plans and 535 illustrations - 173 in colour.

Natural History
The Butterflies of Egypt
T.B.Larsen 1990
The author, although trained as an economist, has spent most of his life investigating and writing about butterflies. The book contains ample descriptions of the butterflies and their habitat, followed by several pages of colour plates.

Photographic
Egypt. Antiquities from Above
Marilyn Bridges 1996
Black and white photographs.

The Great Pyramids of Giza
Alain D'Hooghe & Marie-Cecile Bruwier 2000
A large book with black and white photographs.

Egypt from the Air
Max Rodenbeck 1991
Glossy aerial photographs of Egyptian sites.

Philip's Egypt
Peter Stocks, photos David Couling 1992
The book includes Egypt both ancient and modern.

Poetry
Collected Poems
C.P.Cavafy (translated by Edmund Keeley & Philip Sherrard) 1984
The Greek poet Cavafy (1863-1933) was born in Alexandria and lived there most of his life; during his lifetime he only circulated his poems to a select few people. It was not until after his death that he won international acclaim; today he is considered as "one of the greatest writers of our times" *(TLS)*. His rich use of history, myth and eroticism and his commitment to Hellenism and cynicism about politics combine to make his poetry relevant today, while giving us an understanding of history and of the times in which he lived.

Religion
Daily Life of the Egyptian Gods
Dimitri Meeks & Christine Favard-Meeks 1997 (1996)
A scholarly study of the rituals and beliefs surrounding the gods.

A Test of Time: The Bible – From Myth to History
David Rohl 1996
An argument for revising the chronology of ancient Egyptian and Biblical history.

Travel Literature

Libyan Sands. Travel in a Dead World. (Jordan, Egypt, Sudan, Libya)
R.A.Bagnold 1987 (1935)
In the 1920's, Brigadier Ralph Bagnold and a group of young officers, used all their free time from the army to explore the Libyan Desert in a Ford Model T. They drove the car along camel tracks and so were able to cover huge distances in a short amount of time finding places which had probably not been explored since the Stone Ages. An energetically written and interesting book.

Sinai: The Great and Terrible Wilderness
Burton Bernstein 1980 (1979)
Mixture of travel writing and history.

Egyptian Diaries
J-F Champollion 2001
Champollion decoded the Pharaoh Ramesses' name from the Rosetta Stone in 1822, electrifying the scientific world.

A Thousand Miles Up the Nile
Amelia Edwards 1993 (1877)
Amelia Edwards arrived in Egypt unexpectedly in 1873 and stayed on to become an eminent Egyptologist.

The Oases of Egypt
Ahmed Fakhry 1973
Fakhry only finished two of a projected three volumes on the Western Desert Oases before he died. Vol 1 covers Siwa and Vol 2 Bahariya and Farafra.

In an Antique Land
Amitav Ghosh 1998 (1994)
The author moved into a chicken-coop on the roof in a Delta village.

Egyptian Journal
William Golding 1989
An account of the author's travel down the Nile on a felucca and the story of Egypt past and present.

Beyond the Pyramids
Douglas Kennedy 1995 (1988)
A journey through contemporary Egypt, with much emphasis on the characters Kennedy met, with a look at what happens behind the pyramids of tourism.

The Travels of Sir John Mandeville
trans. C.W.R.D. Moseley 1983. (see Middle East)
During his travels Mandeville reputedly served with the Sultan of Egypt.

Pearls and Arms and Hashish
Henri de Monfried 1930
A smuggler's tale. The swashbuckling author smuggled hashish on the Red Sea during the 1920s after having spent time in a Djibouti jail. Collected and written by Ida Treat.

Cairo: Behind the Pyramids
Jan Morris in Destinations

Cleopatra's Needle
Anne Mustoe 2003
The ex-headmistress cycled from the Thames Embankment in London to Heliopolis in Egypt via France, Italy, Greece, Turkey, Syria & the Lebanon.

Letters from Egypt: a Journey on the Nile 1849-50
Florence Nightingale 1987
Florence Nightingale wrote a prodigious amount of letters during her five month journey in Egypt. This edition is well illustrated with paintings and sketches contemporary with her travels.

Flaubert in Egypt
Francis Steegmuller 1983 (1972)
An amalgamation of Flaubert's diaries and letters written in Egypt during the years 1849-50. Flaubert arrived in Egypt as a Romantic and he and his friend, Maxime Du Camp, spent much time photographing Egyptian antiquities. However, much of Flaubert's time was devoted to sensual pursuits and pleasure and within a year of returning to France,

as a Realist, he wrote *Madame Bovary* the novel which was to have such a profound effect on literature.

The Other Nile
Charlie Pye-Smith 1986
Several journeys made along the length of the Nile in Sudan, Ethiopia and Egypt between 1975-1985. Much changed in Africa during those years - famine and civil war prompted him to quote Evelyn Waugh "There is no room for tourists in a world of displaced persons".

The Pharaoh's Shadow
Anthony Sattin 2001 (2000)
An investigation into how the ancient and the modern sit side by side into today's Egypt. Sattin writes with authority and a love of the country.

Old Serpent Nile
Stanley Stewart 1997 (1991)
A journey to the source from the Nile Delta to the Mountains of the Moon. A winner of the Thomas Cook/Daily Telegraph Travel Book Award.

The Innocents Abroad
Mark Twain 1988 (1869)
A record of a pleasure-trip, which as Jonathan Raban points out in the introduction is ironic, since the fashionable thing to do now-a-days is to mock package tours and those who take them. What we need suggests Raban is a "Twain - or a Waugh - to chronicle them". Twain visited Egypt towards the end of his cruise and writes "We were very glad to have seen the land which was the mother of civilisation".

Islands of the Blest: A Guide to the Oases and Western Desert of Egypt
Cassandra Vivian
The guide covers all the oases in detail.

LIBYA

The land of Libya ... because of over mickle heat is barren and bears no man-

ner of fruit. John Mandeville - *The Book of John Mandeville* c.1360

Anthropology
The Sanusi of Cyrenaica
E.E. Evans-Pritchard 1949
The author was Political Officer to the 3rd British Military Administration of Cyrenaica. He spent two years in the country among the Bedouin studying the development of the Sanusiya order among the Bedouin tribes.

Art & Archaeology
The Antiquities of Tripolitania
D.E.L. Haynes 1965
An archaeological and historical guide to the pre-Islamic period. Published in Tripoli.

Fiction
The Bleeding of the Stone
Ibrahim al-Koni 2003
Asouf, a solitary Bedouin, goes in search of the legendary moufflon.

General Background
The Book of Mordechai. A Study of the Jews of Libya
Mordechai Hakohen 1993 (1980)
A fascinating record of Jewish life written in the early years of this century by a Talmudic scholar who was also a teacher, itinerant peddler and amateur anthropologist.

Tripoli the Mysterious
Mabel Loomis Todd 1994 (1912)
The author recounts life as she remembered it in a Tripoli whose peace was shattered in 1911.

Guides
Libya Handbook 2000

Lonely Planet: Libya 2002

Green Mountain
Gwyn Williams 1963
(An informal guide to Cyrenaica and its Jebel Akhdar).The author lived in Libya for six years and wrote this book as a series of itineraries. Although it is out of date, it has worthwhile descriptions of the sites, the history and peoples who were subjected to so many administrations: Greek, Roman, Byzantine, Arab, Turkish, Italian and British. Gwyn Williams even discovered that the Celts had been there.

History& Politics
The Maverick State
Guy Arnold 1996
Gaddafi and the New World Order; a book charting the history of Libya's external relations.

Qadhafi's Libya
Jonathan Bearman 1986
The transformation of Libya from a tribal society to a wealthy oil state.

Piracy & Diplomacy in Seventeenth Century North Africa
C.R.Pennell 1989
Academic book on piracy in Tripoli.

Libya since Independence
Dirk Vandewalle 1998
Essential for anyone wanting to understand modern Libya.

Libya, Chad and the Central Sahara
John Wright 1989
Ethnic, cultural and economic links between Libya and Chad and how these links contribute to present rivalries.

Photographic
Libya – the Lost Cities of the Roman Empire
Antonino Di Vita & Robert Polidori (photographs) 1999
Leptis Magna, Sabratha, Cyrene & Apollonia.

Travel Literature
A Vicarious Trip to the Barbary Coast
Mary Berenson 1938
A journey taken when Italy ruled Libya.

The Gateway to the Sahara
C.W. Furlong 1985
The American visited Tripoli in 1904 and made several journeys into the adjacent desert.

Adventures in Tripoli
E.H. Griffin 1984
The author was on a medical mission to Tripoli in 1912 where he set up aid for the Muslim casualties of the Italian occupation.

A Narrative of Travels in Northern Africa
G.F.Lyon 1985
The author's first expedition into the little-known interior of the Libyan desert.

South from Barbary
Justin Marozzi 2001
Having read a nineteenth-century account of crossing the Sahara, Marozzi vowed to cross the Libyan Sahara by camel. He set off from Tripoli on a 1500 mile journey.

A Cure for Serpents
The Duke of Pirajno 1985(1955)
(Libya, Eritrea, Ethiopia & Somaliland)
The Duke of Pirajno arrived in North Africa as a doctor in 1924 and stayed for eighteen years. A doctor gets to see facets of life hidden to most other people and as Cyril Connolly says "Doctors who are good raconteurs make wonderful reading". This collection of reminiscences and stories does make wonderful reading.

Wind Sand and Stars
Antoine de Saint-Exupéry 1990 (1939)
Much of Saint-Exupéry's flying takes place in the Sahara. His plane crashed in Libya. Also *Southern Mail* and *Night Flight* (1971).

27

A Fool in the Desert
Barbara Toy 1956
Barbara Toy was driven back to Libya by the desert which she had glimpsed from Egypt "for the desert means different things to different people. Men have cursed it, come to love it and died in it". She realised that there was no escape once you had come under its spell and that the magic would always draw you back. She had fallen party to this spell and embarked on a journey through the Libyan desert.

MAURITANIA

But Mauretania's giant-shadows frown From mountain-cliff to coast descending sombre down. **Lord Byron** *Childe Harold's Pilgrimage.* 1812.

Travel Literature

The Songlines
Bruce Chatwin 1987
An extract includes Mauritania.

Travels in Mauritania
Peter Hudson 1991(1990)
Very little has been written about Mauritania, so Peter Hudson was able to approach it with few preconceptions. The result is an engaging and descriptive account of his journey.

The Fearful Void
Geoffrey Moorhouse 1974
A personal odyssey of a journey across the Sahara west to east.

Barefoot in Mauritania
Odette du Puigaudeau 1937
A journey by camel through an unknown Mauritania.

Mauretania: Warrior, Man, and Woman
Sacheverell Sitwell 1951 (1940)
The first part is about Morocco, the second the oases of the Sahara, the third Tunisia and the fourth Libya.

MOROCCO

If you like your romance dark, Fez is probably the most romantic city on earth. It might have been dreamed up by Edgar Allan Poe - almost sinister in its secretiveness, a twisted city, warped and closed. John Gunther *Inside Africa*

Anthology
Morocco: the Traveller's Companion
Margaret and Robin Bidwell 1992
A collection of excerpts from writers taken from the last five centuries.

Anthropology
The Berbers
Michael Brett and Elizabeth Fentress 1997
An overview of the Berber people.

A Street in Marrakesh
Elizabeth Fernea
An anthropologist's account of her experiences in Marrakesh.

Saints of the Atlas
Ernest Gellner 1969
An in-depth study of a group of Zaouia villages in the High Atlas.

Tribe and Society in Rural Morocco
David Hart 2000
A collection of essays about tribalism and Berberism.

Beyond the Veil
Fatima Mernissi 1975
(Male-Female Dynamics in a Modern Muslim Society)
Fatima Mernissi asks whether there is a nascent female liberation movement in the Morocco of today similar to those in the West. She describes the politics of Islam, the traditional Muslim view of women and the effect that the modern world has had on traditional views. Also

Doing Daily Battle – a collection of interviews.

Reflections on Fieldwork in Morocco
Paul Rabinow 1977
The author finds it hard to find anyone he can trust.

Ritual and Belief in Morocco
Edward Westermarck 2 vols 1926
Westermarck made twenty one journeys to Morocco between 1898 and 1926, spending a total of seven years. His work is still recognised today as one of the most authoritative on the country. He travelled throughout Morocco with a Moorish friend Shereef 'Abdsslam I-Baqqâli which enabled him access and assistance in places which otherwise it would have been difficult to visit. Westermarck wrote many articles on Morocco and *Marriage Ceremonies in Morocco* (1914).

Art and Architecture

Andalusian Morocco: Islamic Art in the Mediterranean 2002
The account of how Morocco became such a centre of Islamic civilisation.

Majorelle – A Moroccan Oasis
Pierre Bergé & Madison Cox 1999
Laid out in the 1920s by Louis Majorelle who gave his name to the shade of blue, the site has recently been restored by Yves Saint Laurent and his partner Pierre Bergé.

The Moors. Islam in the West
Michael Brett 1980
A well illustrated book which relates the rise of the Moors, their achievements, the society they lived in, a general picture of the world at that time and their eventual decline.

Fez; City of Islam
Titus Burckhardt 1992 (1960)
The author went to Morocco in 1933/4 and "Seeking a spiritual master, settled in Fez, where I divided my time between this search and the study of Arabic". He returned twenty five years later, and the book, an illustrated history, personal interpretation and description of Fez was published in Germany in 1960, but not in England until very recently.

Matisse in Morocco
Jack Cowart et al 1990
The paintings and drawings of Matisse in Morocco between 1912-1913. Matisse visited Tangier twice and made full use of the exotic environment. This large book was published to coincide with the large travelling exhibition which was held in the nineteen nineties.

Moroccan Interiors
Lisa Houatt-Smith 1995

Islamic Monuments in Morocco
R.B. Parker 1985 (1974)
Over 200 monuments to Islamic sites which are often neglected in favour of Pharaonic Egypt. Detailed sketch maps.

Moroccan Carpets
Brook Pickering et al 1994
The best book on the subject.

Morocco Modern
Herbert Ypma 1996
Traces the artisan traditions of Morocco.

Biography

The Track
Arturo Barea 1984 (1943) (see Spain)
The Track is the second volume in Barea's autobiographical trilogy in which he records his life in the army during the Spanish war in Morocco in the 1920s. It is, at times, a very shocking account dealing with the sordid life of conscript soldiers in North Africa and vividly describing the vermin, disease, brothels and foul food which were part of that life.

For Bread Alone
Mohamed Choukri 1987
The first volume of Choukri's autobiogra-

29

phy is relevant to a whole generation of North Africans. The second volume is *Streetwise*.

The Tangier Diaries 1962-1979
John Hopkins 2003 (1997)
A powerful and captivating account written by a young American of life in Tangier and roundabout.

Look and Move On
Mohammed Mrabet 1989 (trans. Paul Bowles)

An Invisible Spectator
Christopher Sawyer-Lancanno 1990 (1989)
A biography of Paul Bowles who was an enormously successful composer and novelist before going to live in Tangier where he became a cult figure and spiritual icon of the Beat movement.

Messaouda
Abdelhak Serhane 1986
Semi-autobiographical novel about growing up in Azrou during the 1950s.

Fiction

A Woman of My Age
Nina Bawden 1997 (1991)
A couple who have been married for 18 years go on holiday to Morocco and the wife assesses her marriage.

Wedding by the Sea
Abdelkader Benali 1999
The first novel of a writer who lives in the Netherlands. Magic realism.

My Sister's Hand is Mine
Jane Bowles 1978
Collected works.

The Spider's House.
Paul Bowles 1985 (1955)
Paul Bowles was a great traveller and composer, spending chunks of time living in different countries, until he came to Morocco, which rarely left. He made

Tangier his home in the late 40's and wrote, translated and become an expert on Moroccan folklore and magic. His best Moroccan novel is probably *The Spider's House* set in Fez.; *Let it Come Down* (1952) is set in Tangier and *Too Far from Home* (1991) is set in the desert. He wrote several collections of short stories: *Collected Stories 1939-76, Call at Corazon* 1989 (1939), *Points in Time* 1990 (1982), *100 Camels in the Courtyard* 1991 (1962). Travel books include *Their Heads are Green* 1990 (1963) (which includes a superb piece on the Sahara) *Two Years Beside the Strait - Tangier Journal 1987-9.* 1990 (1989). He translated much of Mohammed Mrabet's work.

Earthly Powers
Anthony Burgess 1980
Includes descriptions of life in 1950's Tangiers.

Naked Lunch
William Burroughs 2001 (1959)
Written in a Tangier hotel room between 1954-7.

Tales and Legends of Morocco
Elisa Chimenti
The author travelled with her doctor father in the 1920s and 30s.

Mimoun
Rafael Chirbes 1992 (1988)
A Spanish teacher is based south of Fez; this is the story of his slow breakdown.

Jean Genet in Tangier
Mohamed Choukri 1990
Paul Bowles translated this, *For Bread Alone* and *Tennessee Williams in Tangier* also by Mohamed Choukri.

Heirs to the Past
Driss Chraïbi 1971
Chraïbi left for Paris where he studied chemical engineering. *Heirs to the Past* is about a man who returns to Casablanca after 16 years in France. Also *Flutes of Death*.

30

Destination Unknown
Agatha Christie 1977 (1954)
Mrs Betterton's scientist husband disappeared from a conference in Paris. A young woman intent on committing suicide in Casablanca is recruited instead to try and solve the mystery.

Mr Narrator
Pat Gray 1989
A portrayal of 'a Morocco ... colonized by surrealism.'

The Marrakesh One-Two
Richard Grenier 1984 (1983)
A racy thriller which includes an attempted coup against the King of Morocco, an encounter with Gaddafi and an aeroplane hijack.

The Process
Brion Gysin 1985 (1969)
A novel which was written in Tangier between 1965-8. The American character, on a Fulbright fellowship, smokes his way through various encounters in the Sahara in prose reminiscent of Burroughs.

Body of Contention
John Haylock 1999
Adventures among the expat community in Tangier in 1957.

In the Lap of Atlas
Richard Hughes 1979
In the Lap of Atlas is an article about Hughes' own experiences in Morocco, the rest of the book is Hughes' retelling of some traditional Moroccan stories.

The Sand Child
Tahar Ben Jelloun 1988 (1985)
The shame felt by a father of eight daughters made him bring up his youngest daughter as a boy. The fear of being found out and the pain suffered by the child makes this a haunting book. The solitary life at home contrasts with the bustle of the Marrakesh bazaar. Other books by Jelloun include *Silent Day in*

Tangier 1991 (1989), *The Sacred Night* 1989 (1985), *Solitaire* (1989) and *With Downcast Eyes* (1991)

Honor to the Bride Like the Pigeon that Guards its Grain Under the Clove Tree
Jane Kramer 1970
Fictionalised account of a true story of a Berber woman's kidnap.

Yesterday and Today
Larbi Layachi 1985
Layachi, who now lives in America, was born in 1937 in a small town in Morocco. He moved to Tangier when he was three years old and in 1961 he met Paul Bowles; he told Paul Bowles many Moghrebi stories which Bowles then translated. Other titles include *A Life Full of Holes* and *The Jealous Lover*.

Leo the African
Amin Maalouf 1994 (1988) (trans. Peter Sluglett)
A novel closely based on the life of Leo Africanus (q.v.). It is narrated in the first person, starts in Granada and moves on to Fez, Cairo and Rome.

31

The Wrong People
Robin Maugham 1986 (1967)
Arnold Turner, a repressed English schoolmaster on holiday in Tangier, meets Ewing Baird, a rich Anglo-American expatriate who sets himself up with everything he desires, ultimately for his own plans.

The Beach Café and The Voice
Mohammed Mrabet 1980
Paul Bowles taped and translated this and other works by Mrabet including *Marriage with Papers* (1986) and *Love With a Few Hairs* (1986). Also *The Boy Who Set the Fire & Other Stories, The Lemon, The Big Mirror.*

The Age of Flowers
Umberto Pasti 2003 (2000)
A scandalous and alarming novel set in Tangier.

The High Flyer
Nicholas Shakespeare 1993
Thomas Wavery arrives in Gibraltar en route to take up his post as HM Consul General in Abyla in North Africa. The variety of people he comes into contact with is brilliantly observed.

Food

Taste of Morocco
Robert Carrier 1987
Robert Carrier lived in Marrakesh for several months each year.

Street Café Morocco
Anissa Helou 1998
A sumptuous cookery book.

Lonely Planet World Food Morocco 2000

Good Food from Morocco
Paula Wolfert 1989 (1973)
The author lived in Morocco for two years and indulged her love of the adventurous and exotic life. Some of the recipes included in this book are: couscous, Moroccan bread, fish tagine, chicken stuffed with almond paste and briouats (pastry stuffed with almond paste and dipped in honey.)

General Background

Places
Colette 1970
Colette went to Morocco in 1926 and writes sensually about Moroccan food.

The Caves of Hercules
Rupert Croft-Cooke 1974
The author's aim was to love and identify with people of 'strange callings' and those antithetical to natural associations. He lived in Tangier although the people of Morocco "did not stir any vital interest" in him.

Cinema Eden: Essays from the Muslim Mediterranean
Juan Goytisolo 2003
Essays by Spain's master novelist and long-term resident of Morocco.

The Dream at the End of the World
Michelle Green 1992
The literary life and people of Tangier.

In Touch: The letters of Paul Bowles
ed. Daniel Halpern

Culture Shock – Morocco
Orin Hargraves 1999

Second Son
David Herbert 1972
Herbert the second son of the Earl of Pembroke had a devouring curiosity. He was left a house in Tangier and went to live there; he loved it but said that his life there was not so very different from what it would have been at Wilton. Also *Engaging Eccentrics* (1990).

Marrakech - the Red City
eds. Barnaby Rogerson & Stephen Lavington 2003
The city through writers' eyes - arranged in chapters themed by mood.

Tangier, a Writer's Notebook
Angus Stewart 1977
Over 13 years Stewart often visited Tangier, about which he had conflicting views: "A violence of happiness. The loneliness is obscene". He also made excursions into other parts of Morocco.

Guides

Blue Guide: Morocco 2002

Cadogan Guide: Morocco 2004

Marrakech Handbook 2003

Morocco Handbook 2002

Insight: Morocco 2002

Lonely Planet: Morocco 2003

Rough Guide: Morocco 2004

Time Out: Marrakech & Best of Morocco 2004

History

History of the Maghreb in the Islamic Period
J.M. Abun-Nasr 1987
Morocco seen in the wider context of North Africa.

Morocco
Nevill Barbour 1965
Morocco, unlike its neighbouring North African countries, has a long and interesting history and unlike the rest of the Arab world was never subject to the Turks. Barbour writes about it from the earliest times right up to the twentieth century in an accessible and easy to read manner.

Black Sunrise, The Life and Times of Moulai Ismail, Emperor of Morocco 1646-1727
Wilfred Blunt 1951
A Moorish villain Mulai Ismail (1646-1727), succeeded his brother al-Rashid to the kingdom of the Filalis in 1672. He is said to have built his kingdom with the life blood of Christian slaves.

Tangier. City of the Dream
Iain Finlayson 1992
Tangier has a long and exotic history and in recent years has attracted many writers: William Burroughs, Jack Kerouac, Allen Ginsberg, Tennessee Williams, Joe Orton, Paul Bowles and Truman Capote are among those who have lived there. Finlayson's book tells how all these and many more came to be in a city which was full of the kind of drugs and sex banned in Europe.

El Raisuni, the Sultan of the Mountains
Rosita Forbes 1924
His life as told to the author. Superficially Raisuni's life appears as one of wild adventure, war cruelty and political ambition. His own story reveals him as a man of single purpose with a considerable breadth of judgement. He was a warrior, philosopher, saint, tyrant and psychologist.

The Muqaddimah. An Introduction to History.
Ibn Khaldun 1987 1967)
The Muqaddimah was written in 1377 by the Arab scholar Ibn Khaldun as an introduction to a history of the world. It is the summing up of the achievements of Islam and is remarkable for its insights; the abridged version contains the essence of all he wrote. He was the first person who attempted to find a pattern in the changes that occur in man's political and social organisation.

33

Fez in the Age of the Marinides
Roger Le Tourneau 1981
A scholarly study of the Merenid capital of Morocco.

Lords of the Atlas
Gavin Maxwell 1991 (1966)
The history of the Glaoua family who rose and fell from power in Morocco from 1893-1956. Gavin Maxwell draws on Walter Harris (q.v.), but writes an exciting and bloodthirsty account of this once obscure tribe who within a few years had become frighteningly powerful and controlled Morocco until Independence in 1956.

Morocco since 1830
C.R. Pennell 2000
The first general history of Morocco.

The Conquest of Morocco
Douglas Porch 1986 (1982)
The French conquest of Morocco took from 1844-1934. The meeting of Islam and Christianity make it a compelling story. Douglas Porch concentrates here on what happened at the beginning of the century when Hubert Lyautey, an eccentric and colonial soldier played such an important part in events, but who has, nonetheless, been ignored by biographers in France. An illuminating historical account.

Leisure Activities
Trailblazer: Trekking in the Moroccan Atlas 2001
(Includes Marrakech city guide)

Natural History (See North Africa)
Complete Mediterranean Wildlife 2000

Photographic
Morocco Seen from the Air
Yann & Anne Arthus-Bertrand 1994

'How Could I Send a Picture into the Desert?'
Paul Bowles 1994
Bowles was a talented photographer as well as writer.

The Berbers
Alan Keohane 1991
A well-illustrated book about the Berbers.

Medinas: Morocco's Hidden Cities
Jean-Marc Tingaud & Tahar Ben Jelloum 1998
Behind the doors in Fez, Marrakech and other cities.

Travel Literature
Morocco Its People and Places
Edmondo de Amicis 1982 (1885)
A fresh, original and lively account of Morocco in 1882, which was popular when it was published and is now considered a classic.

The Voices of Marrakesh
Elias Canetti 1982 (1967)
Canetti, who won the Nobel Prize for Literature in 1981, uses a series of sketches to convey his impressions of Marrakech. Each scene that he selects is so vivid and so full of imagery that the rich diversity of life in a bazaar-town shines through.

Saints and Sorcerers
Nina Epton 1958
Good on background history and interesting anecdotes: Nina Epton's journey covered much of Morocco from Tetuan to the High Atlas including a meeting with the magicians of Sous. An easy and enjoyable read.

Hideous Kinky
Esther Freud 1992
Esther Freud, aged five, was taken by her hippy mother to Morocco during the sixties. The book brilliantly conveys how a five year old thinks and feels about travelling. The shock of having her hair hennaed and turn orange is balanced by 'magic' sugared almonds appearing out of nowhere. The relationship between her and her sister Bea who was two years older is sensitively drawn. The book which is an extraordinary feat of memory rings true and is by turn both funny and sad.

Mogreb-el-Acksa
R.B.Cunninghame Grahame 1988 (1898)
Cunninghame Grahame, much opposed to imperialism, disguised himself as a Turkish doctor to enable him to travel and find out about Moorish life. He was arrested on the way to Taroudant; this is

the account of that episode. His book was praised by Joseph Conrad for its "skill, pathos, wit, indignation".

Morocco That Was
Walter Harris 1983 (1921)
Walter Harris arrived in Tangier in 1886 and became the *Times* correspondent there until his death in 1933. He approached his work seriously but always with a certain amount of humour. Morocco was virtually unknown to Westerners when Harris arrived - a closed country; his descriptions may seem excessive, but they were representative of life in the then wild and primitive country.

Western Barbary: its Wild Tribes and Savage Animals
John Drummond Hay 1846
Drummond Hay was to become British consul in Tangier. This is the account of a journey from Tangier to Larache.

Tangier Journals 1962-79
John Hopkins 1997
Amusing journals of Tangier life.

See Ouarzazate and Die
Sylvia Kennedy 1992
The author spent twelve months and three different trips travelling round Morocco on buses, trains and coaches with a variety of travelling companions in order to write this gutsy and amusing book. She describes many local customs in detail and you get the feeling that she really threw herself into whatever she was seeing or doing.

Kasbahs of Southern Morocco
Rom Landau 1969
The first kasbas (qasbas) – the walled in section of the ruler's capital - which included the palace, mosque and college - were built in the 13th century. Landau writes about those in the High Atlas which he visited over 20 years.

Morocco and the Moors
Arthur Leared 1985 (1876)
(Being an Account of Travels With a General Description of the Country and its People). The author kept prolific notes while travelling and talked at length to people who were resident there. The country was relatively unknown to outsiders when he was there and he decided that with its excellent climate it was a very desirable place for invalids.

Journey into Barbary
Wyndham Lewis (ed. C.J. Fox) 1983
Wyndham Lewis went to Morocco in 1931 for a few months, writing two books from his experiences, *Filibusters in Barbary* (1932) and *Kasbahs and Souks* which seemingly has not been published. He was fascinated by the Berbers and their energy and did many drawings of them; it is interesting to note the different ways he translated what he observed as a writer and as a painter. He read about Morocco in depth before he went "I always desire the fullest information regarding any habitation or work of man, strange to me, which I propose to approach and interrogate ...before I set foot in the Maghreb I knew more about the inhabitants of, say, the hinterland of Tetouan than they know themselves".

Into Morocco
Pierre Loti 1889
Loti makes no pretence of trying to write about the politics of Morocco, indeed he makes a point of trying not to offend anybody. He does however immerse himself in the culture of the Moghreb having always felt himself half Arab at heart, thrilling "to the sound of the little Africa flutes, of the tam-tams and the iron castanets".

A Year in Marrakesh
Peter Mayne 1990 (1953)
Peter Mayne lived much of his life in India and Pakistan and so had a fundamental understanding of Muslim life by the time he moved to Morocco. He lived in a small house in Marrakech and wrote

35

this book (originally published as *The Alleys of Marrakesh)* from his observations. The style is simple and easy to read and shows what everyday life was like.

Life in Morocco and Glimpses Beyond
Budgett Meakin 1986 (1905)
Sketches and observations gathered from many visits by an enthusiast. "Nothing ... elsewhere excels Morocco in point of life and colour save Bokhara." Meakin's style is somewhat over the top, but he is good on detail and gives fascinating insights into Moorish domestic life. His most interesting book is *The Moors: A Comprehensive Description* . Also *The Land of the Moors.*

Blue Nile and White Nile
Alan Moorehead (see Egypt - history)

Valley of the Casbahs
Jeffrey Tayler 2003
A journey across the MNoroccan Sahara.

In Morocco
Edith Wharton 1920
Rather patchy but with some good insights into harem life.

TUNISIA

Carthage had not desired to create, but only to enjoy: therefore she left us nothing. Hilaire Belloc *Esto Perpetua* 1906

Anthropology
Cave-Dwellers of Southern Tunisia
D. Bruun 1985 (1898)
Bruun was one of the first Europeans to live with the cave-dwelling people of Matmata and Haddej.

Change at Shebika
Jean Duvignaud 1970
This report from an African village was written in the 1960s when Chebika was an isolated village.

Medicine and Power in Tunisia 1780-1900
Nancy Elizabeth Gallagher 1983 (1974)
The author's interest, written as a dissertation, was in the social history of North Africa and the interplay of cross-cultural medical ideas. The long struggle between Arabic and European medicine accelerated with European economic expansion.

Art & Archaeology
The North African Stones Speak
P. MacKendrick 1980
Four chapters on Tunisia.

The Life and Death of Carthage
Gibert Charles-Picard and Colette Charles-Picard 1968
Until this book it was thought that Western Phoenician society evolved very little during the six or seven centuries of its existence. This book written by authoritative French archaeologists takes a different view.

Ifriqiya
2002
13 centuries of art and architecture in Tunisia.

Biography
Confessions
Augustine 1970
St. Augustine's spiritual autobiography - invaluable for an insight into his times.

Augustine of Hippo
Peter Brown 1969
Brown writes very interestingly about the Africa of Augustine's time.

Milk for the Orange Tree
Gisèle Halimi 1990
An autobiography of a child of impoverished highly Orthodox Jewish parents who was self-educated and went to Paris to study law.

Albert Memmi
Judith Roumani 1987
Memmi, born in 1920 into a modest family of artisans; Tunisian, Jewish and a resident of France, was a multi-dimensional writer: a novelist, sociologist and poet. One of the founders of modern Maghrebian literature, he was recognised as a major psychologist of the dynamics of colonialism.

In the Boy's Palace
M. Williams 1990
Memoirs of a British consul's wife during the struggle for Tunisian independence.

Fiction

The Golden Ass (1998)
Apuleius (see Algeria)

Return to Thyna
Hedi Bouraoui
The only work that has been translated by this well-known novelist.

Salammbo
Gustave Flaubert 1977 (1862)
A visually rich and exotic novel set in North Africa after the first Punic War with Rome. Flaubert was criticised for making the history surrounding the passionate story too accurate, but it is through this kind of book that you can really imagine life in the time of the Carthaginian army under Hamilcar.

The Tremor of Forgery
Patricia Highsmith 1969
Set in 1960s Hammamet. Very creepy.

Waiting in the Future for the Past to Come
Sabiha Khemir 1993
Written in English by a Tunisian author.

Strangers
Albert Memmi 1958.
Memmi, a Tunisian Jew, tells the story of a Tunisian Jew who marries a French Catholic girl while he is studying in

Paris. She returns to Tunisia with her husband but finds it impossible to settle down and to adapt to the new society in which she finds herself. Her husband is torn between her needs and the needs of his family and when she decides to return to France, the suggestion is that such a mixed marriage cannot work. Other books by Memmi include *The Pillar of Salt* (1992), *Colonizer and the Colonized* (1990) and *The Scorpion* (1975).

Lion Mountain
Mustapha Tlili 1998
Tragic events of tourism on a remote Tell village.

General Background

The Diaries of Paul Klee 1898-1918
Paul Klee 1965
In 1914 Klee went to Tunisia and was much taken with the country: "Color possesses me. I don't have to pursue it. It will possess me always. I know it. That is the meaning of this happy hour: color and I are one. I am a painter ... The evening is deep inside me forever".

Guides

Tunisia
Nina Nelson 1974
More of a travel narrative than a guide and by now somewhat out of date; there are however some good descriptions of the country.

Blue Guide: Tunisia 1996

Tunisia Handbook 2002

Insight Tunisia 2000

Lonely Planet: Tunisia 2004

Rough Guide: Tunisia 2001

37

History

The Tunisia of Ahmed Bey
Leon Carl Brown 1837-1856
An interesting look at 19th-century
Tunisia.

Pagans and Christians
Robin Lane Fox 1986
The Mediterranean spiritual world 2nd-
4th century AD.

The Muqaddimah
Ibn Khaldoun (See Morocco)

Tunisia
Wilfred Knapp 1970
An introductory history and background.

The War with Hannibal
Livy 1934
Flaubert used this as one of his sources.

The Rise of the Roman Empire
Polybius (1979)

The Vandalic War
Procopius

Habib Bourguiba, Islam and the Creation of Modern Tunisia
N. Salem 1985

The Jugurthine War
Sallust 1969
An amusing account of war and morality.

The Aeneid
Virgil 1991
The Aeneid includes the tragic love story
of Queen Dido, founder of Carthage and
Aeneas, founder of Rome.

Carthage
B.H. Warrington 1964
For both expert and amateur.

Tunis: The Land and the People
Chevalier de Hess Wartegg 1899
The last years of Beylical rule.

Natural History

Mediterranean Wildlife. The Rough Guide
Pete Raine 1990
Includes Morocco and Tunisia.

Poetry

Songs of Life
Abu el Kacem al Shabbi 1987
An insight into the modern heart and soul
of Tunisia.

Travel Literature

About Tunisia
John Anthony 1961
Anthony lived in Sidi Bou Said for five
years and during that time travelled widely throughout Tunisia; the book is an
account of his experiences and the people
he met.

To Kairwan the Holy
Alexander A. Boddy 1985 (1883)
A lively account of a visit to the sacred
Tunisian city – the centre of Western
Islamism.

East from Tunis
R. Carrington 1957
A trip from Tunis to Cairo.

Fountains in the Sand
Norman Douglas 1986 (1912)
Norman Douglas bravely set out into the
deserts of Tunisia, but sadly for such a
widely travelled person, never shook off
his prejudices about the aridity of Arab
culture. However, worth reading for the
descriptive passages.

Tangier to Tunis
**Alexandre Dumas (see North Africa
general)**

Amyntas
Andre Gide (see Algeria)

Travels in Tunisia
Alexander Graham and Henry
Spencer Ashbee 1887
The account of three visits to Tunisia in
1883 and the spring and winter of 1885.
The controversy about invention in travel
writing was obviously an issue in the
19th century: "To write what is popularly
known as an entertaining volume of travel, much fiction and very little fact would
seem to be requisite. This plan we have
declined to adopt". A massive 74-page
bibliography.

The Olive Tree
Aldous Huxley 1973 (1936)
A travel piece in this collection called *In
a Tunisian Oasis* is about a trip Huxley
took to Tunisia.

*A Journey through the Tunisian
Sahara*
Sir Harry Johnston 1898
Johnston was one of the first European
travellers to attempt to understand the
people among whom he travelled in the
Sahara.

Among the Faithful
Dahris Martin 2001 (1937)
Dahris Martin, a young American, arrived
in Kairouan in the late 1920s and was
welcomed into the roguish Kalifa's family. She was therefore able to witness life
in Tunisia from within.

Tunis, Kairouan and Carthage
Graham Petrie 1985 (1908)
The author visited these three towns at
the beginning of the century and writes
interesting descriptions of the life that he
encountered there.

Letters of Rainer Maria Rilke
Rainer Maria Rilke 1933
Rilke travelled to Kairouan in 1910-11
and wrote letters to his wife in Austria.

Excursions in the Mediterranean
Sir Grenville Temple 1835
An early travel account.

WEST AFRICA - General Biography

*Mary Kingsley. Imperial
Adventuress*
Dea Birkett 1992
There is no one better qualified to write
about Mary Kingsley than Dea Birkett.
She first wrote about her in an undergraduate essay and since then has written
many articles and followed her routes all
over West Africa. Dea Birkett 'creates'
Mary Kingsley in this biography, showing her to have been a complex character
who took on many roles.

Fiction

The Crystal World
J.G.Ballard 1993 (1966)
A forest area in West Africa is gradually
becoming crystallised - everything has to
keep moving to ensure that they too do
not get trapped.

A Good Man in Africa
William Boyd 1982 (1981)
William Boyd was born in Ghana and
lived there and in Nigeria and set this
very funny novel in tropical 'Kinjanja'.
Morgan Leafy, the not very successful
and overweight British Government representative, finds himself involved in all
kinds of local bribery, which he has to
use all kinds of guile to deal with.

Water Music
Thomas Coraghassen Boyle 1998
(1983)
Very long but often very funny fictional-
ization of Mungo Park's explorations.

Men at Arms
Evelyn Waugh 2001 (1952)
The first in the *Sword of Honour* trilogy
tells of Guy Crouchback and his first
campaign - an abortive affair on the West
African coast.

39

General Background

East and West Africa. Travel Resource Guide
Louis Taussig 1994

Guides

Lonely Planet:West Africa 2002

Rough Guide: West Africa 2003

History

A History of West Africa 1000 - 1800
Basil Davidson, F.K.Bush & J.F.A. Ajayi 1990 (1965)
A new edition of a clear and all-encompassing history.

Griots and Griottes: Masters of Words and Music
Thomas A. Hale 1998
A comprehensive look at the griots of Niger, Mali, Senegal and the Gambia.

An Economic History of West Africa
A.G. Hopkins 1993 (1973)
The standard text on economic history of the whole of West Africa which ranges from prehistoric times up to independence.

The Revolutionary Years. West Africa Since 1800
J.B.Webster et al 1992 (1967)
A new edition of a classic text on West African history from 1800.

Natural History

Birds of West Central and Western Africa
(2 vols.) by C.W. Mackworth-Praed and C.H.B.Grant 1973
This large and comprehensive work is of use as a reference book, but can also be used 'in the field.' It took twenty years to compile and is full of maps, sketches and detailed descriptions, as well as many colour photographs.

Illustrated Check List: Birds of Western & Central Africa
Ber van Perlo 2002

Collins Field Guide: Birds of West Africa
W. Serle, G.J. Morel, & W. Hartwig 1992 (1977)
Over 500 species of bird are illustrated and described with their identifying characteristics, distribution, habitat and eggs etc.

Photographic

African Canvas
Margaret Courtney-Clarke 1990
Every year, after the harvest, the women of West Africa get together to restore and paint their houses. This is a beautifully coloured photographic book which records the event in Nigeria, Ghana, Burkina Faso, Ivory Coast, Senegal, Mauritania and Mali.

Religion

A History of Islam in West Africa
J. Spencer Trimingham 1962
An historical background into the penetration of Islam into West Africa; by understanding how a religion gets into a country it is easier to understand its implications in contemporary society.

Travel Literature

One Dry Season. In the Footsteps of Mary Kingsley
Caroline Alexander 1989
Caroline Alexander was intrigued by Mary Kingsley's travels and decided to follow her journey to the Gaboon (Gabon) as closely as possible.

French Lessons in Africa
Peter Biddlecombe 2001 (1994)
An often hilarious account of the author's travels through French speaking West

40

Africa – Benin, Burkino Faso, Cameroon, Congo, Côte d'Ivoire, Mali, Niger, Senegal, Togo and Zaire.

Jella
Dea Birkett 1992
Dea Birkett was the only woman on a cargo ship going from Lagos to Liverpool. She was nicknamed 'Jella', meaning small boy, and dressed in blue overalls, as this somehow made her more acceptable to the male crew. An interesting look at life in a confined community, with reflections about West Africa.

Wanderings in West Africa
Richard F. Burton 1991 (1863)
In 1861 Richard Burton joined the Foreign Office as consul in Fernando Po, an island off the coast of West Africa. Using that as his base he made many expeditions on to the mainland amassing a huge quantity of information which he later used in his books of travel and exploration. He wrote very good descriptions of the people he encountered, which anthropologists have found invaluable.

Zanzibar to Timbuctoo
Anthony Daniels.1989 (1988)
Anthony Daniels worked for years as a doctor in Africa - in Zimbabwe, South Africa and Tanzania. He decided to travel back to Europe overland, disillusioned about Africa after two years in Tanzania. His journey takes him through Burundi, Rwanda, Zaire, Gabon, Equatorial Guinea Cameroon, Nigeria, Niger and Mali. Inevitably he encounters much corruption poverty and ignorance en route, but overall he reckons that most Africans have an ability to enjoy life which we have largely lost.

Africa Dances
Geoffrey Gorer 2003 (1935)
Gorer went to West Africa with Feral Benga, a dancer from Paris, in order to study music and dance. This book ends up as much more than that: he describes everything with which he comes into contact so that we learn about fetish,

magic, wrestling, dancing, marriage and the military.

Four Guineas. A Journey Through West Africa
Elspeth Huxley 1954
Elspeth Huxley was aware of the disadvantages of travelling by car to the Gambia, Sierra Leone, The Gold Coast and Nigeria, however she manages to capture the atmosphere and is good on background.

Mali Blues
Lieve Joris 1998
Joris travelled in Senegal, Mauretania and Mali meeting people and writing four stories about them.

Travels in West Africa 1982 (1897) and West African Studies 1901 (1899)
Mary Kingsley
Mary Kingsley first went to Africa in 1893. Ostensibly she chose Africa to continue her father's natural history research -West Africa was one of the few places he had not visited - but desolate with grief after her parents' death she probably wanted a complete change of life. She was very sympathetic to and about the Africans she lived among "As it is with the forest, so it is with the minds of the natives. Unless you live among the natives, you never get to know them. If you do this you gradually get a light into the true state of their mind-forest". This was an extraordinarily enlightened view in an age when Africa was known as the 'dark continent.' She considers her Travels in West Africa an 'interim report' and was amused by being called 'an intrepid explorer.' In West African Studies she used some of the material collected on her first trip, but most of it is as a result of further reflection and research. She died in 1900 in South Africa of heart failure after a fever and was buried, at her request, at sea.

41

Captain Clapperton's Last Expedition to Africa
Richard Lander 1967 (1830)
Lander agreed to join a British government party under Clapperton to go in search of the Niger. Many people urged him not to go because of the danger and because of what had happened to Mungo Park (q.v.). Here he describes the trip via the Madeiras, Canaries and Cape VerdeIslands, the arrival in Sierra Leone and the departure into the interior. Clapperton died of fever during the trip but Lander continued to Badagry which was a market for the sale of slaves to European merchants. He was picked up here by an English vessel and returned to England.

Travels in the White Man's Grave
Donald Macintosh 2001 (1998)
Posted to Nigeria as a forester in 1954, Macintosh spent the next 30 years travelling through the forests of West and Central Africa.

42

Travels into the Interior of Africa
Mungo Park 2003 (1799)
Mungo Park, a young Scottish doctor, made his first journey in 1795, in search of the Niger, into what was the almost uncharted territory of inland West Africa. Although he found the river he accomplished little else and a year later returned to Scotland exhausted. In 1805 he went on a second expedition which ended in death for all forty six Europeans, including himself. He documented what he did see diligently, but brought back little new information. The account of his travels appeared in 1799 and show him to have been a tough and resolute explorer who according to Joseph Banks had "opened a gate into the interior of Africa".

Lake Chad
Sylvia K.Sikes 1972
Lake Chad is situated in the southern part of the Sahara where Tchad, Niger, Nigeria and Cameroon meet. It is now very shallow, but still vast and has a mass of fascinating lagoons and islands with tribes called the 'Yedina' (formerly called 'the pirates of the papyrus'), living on the floating islands.

Malaria Dreams
Stuart Stevens 1992 (1989)
(Cameroon, Chad, Niger and Mali). Stevens was almost completely unprepared for this trip and would probably make the most infuriating travelling companion; he has however written a very funny account of his journey from Bangui to Algeria, driving through Cameroon, Chad, Niger and Mali.

BENIN

Fiction

Snares Without End
Olympe Bhêly-Quénum 1981 (1978)
Probably the only novel from Benin translated into English. Anatou awakens a monster in Ahouna leading him to a motiveless murder.

The Viceroy of Ouidah
Bruce Chatwin 1982 (1980)
A poor Brazilian sailed to Dahomey, now Benin, in the early 1800's determined to make a fortune and to return triumphantly to Brazil. He never returned but managed to establish an outpost of Brazil in Africa by siring an enormous amount of children. Macabre and funny.

The Dogs of War
Frederick Forsyth 1975
A mountain of platinum is discovered in the remote African kingdom of Zangaro and a coup is plotted. A power game develops.

History

A Short History of Benin
Jacob Egharevba 1991 (1968)
A very slight history of the country from the founding of the Benin empire in about 900 A.D.

Travel Literature

A Mission to Gelele, King of Dahome
Richard Burton 1966 (1864)
Burton was Consul to West Africa, 'the white man's graveyard' and went to seek an audience with King Gelele.

Show Me the Magic: Travels Round Benin by Taxi
Annie Caulfield 2002
The scriptwrite author, went to Benin as an adviser and guide to Spice Girl Mel B.

The Best of Granta Travel 1991
The collection has a piece by Bruce Chatwin about the coup that installed Kérékou, entitled *A Coup*.

BURKINA FASO

Most of the little written about Burkina Faso is in French.

General Background

Benin, Congo and Burkina Faso
Joan Baxter & Keith Somerville 1989
In the Marxist regime series.

Burkino Faso: New Life for the Sahel
Robin Sharp 1990
Demonstrates the magnitude of the country's difficulties.

CAMEROON

Farewell, Camaroons! Farewell, beautiful heights! where so many calm and quiet days have sped without sandflies or mosquitoes, or prickly heat. Adieu! happy rustic wilds. Richard Burton *Abeokuta and the Camaroons Mountains* . 1863

Anthropology

The Innocent Anthropologist
Nigel Barley 1986 (1983)
The hilarious account of Barley's first field trip to the Dowayo in the Cameroons. All the theory he had learnt was seemingly completely useless in the field, but he managed to turn his experiences into a very revealing book. Also *A Plague of Caterpillars* (1986).

Leaf of Honey
Joseph Sheppherd 1988
An American anthropologist's delightful book about the Ntuumu people of Cameroon.

The Forest People
Colin Turnbull 1994 (1961)
An account of the Ituri forest Pygmies.

Biography/Autobiography

Mbella Sonne Dipoko
Autobiography – a piece in *African Writing Today* (1967)

Fiction

Agatha Moudio's Son
Francis Bebey 1971
Bebey is well known as a musician as well as a novelist.

The Poor Christ of Bomba
Mongo Beti 1971
A cynical novel which deals with political satire; a French priest tries to convert a whole village. Other books by Beti include: *Mission to Kala* (1957) and *King Lazurus* (1960). Also *Perpetua* and *The Habit of Unhappiness*.

The Sun Hath Looked Upon Me
Calixthe Beyala 1996 (1988)
A shocking novel, translated from French, about life in the African ghetto. Also *Your Name Shall Be Tanga*.

The White Man of God
Kenjo Jumbam 1980
Childhood in a strict Christian family in the early days of colonialism; a time mixed with both sorrow and happiness.

43

Man Pass Man
Ndeley Mokoso 1998
Darkly funny short stories.

Houseboy
Ferdinand Oyono 1990 (1956)
Satirical novel about colonialism. Also
Man and the Medal.

History

The Cameroons
Mark DeLancey 1989
A survey of politics, economics and his-
tory.

Natural History

The Overloaded Ark
Gerald Durrell 1987 (1953)
Durrell's first book is about an expedition
to the Cameroons to collect animals for
his zoo. "A delightful book ... you can
feel his bush-shirt sticking to his back ...
Bagging a monitor, smoking out a
Pangolin (scaly ant-eater), celebrating the
capture of the rare Angwantibo (small
lemur), bird liming for Giant King-fishers
on the warm milky waters of Lake
Soden: he communicates every detail of
his experiences with just the right degree
of zest." (*New Statesman*) His other
books about the Cameroon are *The Bafut
Beagles* (1954) and *A Zoo in My Luggage*
(1960).

Travel Literature

Behind God's Back
Negley Farson 1983 (1940)
The book, an account of a four month
drive across Africa by the author and his
wife, was an instant bestseller. Farson
was larger than life and this adventure
story is also a sweeping portrait of Africa.

Cameroon With Egbert
Dervla Murphy 1990 (1989)
Dervla Murphy trekked through Western
Cameroon with her daughter and a horse
named Egbert. She and her daughter were
intrepid travellers who got themselves

into all kinds of scrapes from which they
always seemed to emerge unscathed.

CAPE VERDE ISLANDS

*These Ilands are held to bee scituate in
one of the most unhealthiest Climates of
the world, and therefore it is wisedome to
shunne the sight of them, how much more
to make abode in them?* Sir Richard
Hawkins 1593 in *Purchas & His
Pilgrimes* 1625

Anthropology/Ethnology

*Atlantic Peeks – an Ethnographic
Guide to the Portuguese-Speaking
Islands*
Jean Ludtke 1989

Fiction/Literature

*Fire: Six Writers from Angola,
Mozambique and Cape Verde*
Donald Burness 1977

*Voices from an Empire: A History
of Afro-Portuguese Literature*
Russell Hamilton 1975
An in-depth look at some of the leading
writers and poets.

General Background

*The People of the Cape Verde
Islands*
Antonio Carreira 1982
Heavy going.

*The Fortunate Isles - a Study in
African Transformation*
Basil Davidson 1989
History as well as present day impres-
sions about these very unwritten-about
islands.

Atlantic Islands
T. Bentley Duncan 1972
About the history, importance and trading

of the Portuguese islands: Madeira, Azores and Cape Verdes.

Cape Verde: Politics, Economics and Society
Colm Foy 1988
One of few contemporary surveys of the islands.

Guide
Bradt: Cape Verde Islands 2001

History
No Fist is Big Enough to Hide the Sky: the Liberation of Guinea-Bissau and Cape Verde
Basil Davidson 1981
A history of the armed struggle.

Cape Verde: Crioulo Colony to Independent Nation
Richard Lobban 1995
A book with a wide-ranging look at the islands. Also (with Waltraud Berger Coli) *The Cape Verdeans in Rhode Island: A Brief History.*

A Guide to the Cape Verde Islands
C. Wilson 1856
Not much detail.

Leisure Activities
Atlantic Islands
Anne Hammick and Nicholas Heath. 1989.
A sailors' pilot with navigational charts which includes plenty on the Cape Verde Islands.

Natural History
The Birds of the Cape Verde Islands
Cornelis Hazevoet 1995

Travel Literature
A New Voyage Round the World
William Dampier 1937
Dampier visited the islands in 1683.

West African Islands
A.B. Ellis 1885
Adventures from Madeira to Ascension.

Black and White Make Brown: An Account of a Journey to the Cape Verde Islands and Portuguese Guinea
Archibald Lyall 1938
Lyall went to the Cape Verde Islands as they "are easily the least known of all the Atlantic islands." He discovered a wealth of bird life, but most of the natural vegetation and animal life had disappeared due to endless droughts, much changed since they were discovered by a captain of Prince Henry the Navigator in 1460 when they had been covered with trees.

Account of a Voyage to the Islands of the Canaries, Cape de Verde and Barbadoes
George Roberts 1887 (1721)
"The 4 Years Voyage of Captain George Roberts, being a series of uncommon events which befell him in a voyage to the islands of the 'Canaries, Cape de Verde and Barbadoes'. The manner of his being taken by three pyrate ships, the hardships he endured – with a description of the Cape de Verd Islands."

Six Years of a Traveller's Life in Western Africa
Francisco Travassos Valdez 1861
A positive report sent by a Portuguese about the islands.

CHAD
*Who holds Chad holds Africa.*French maxim, quoted by John Gunther *Inside Africa* 1955.

45

Fiction
Descent from the Hills
Stanhope White 1963
The Wakara tribe live above Lake Chad: leadership is passed down by secret rites and there has been an unbroken succession from Wakara, the founder, through the Gidigils (guardians). This story is set in 1890 and documents the disintegration of the tribe through three generations.

Travel Literature
Travels in the Congo
André Gide 1986 (1927)
Gide travelled as a special envoy of the Colonial Ministry to the Congo and Chad in 1925-6; he was appalled by the injustices of French colonialism and wrote a book which is part travel, but which is filled with reforming zeal. He dedicated it to Conrad.

EQUATORIAL GUINEA

Seen from the sea, or from the continent it looks like an immense single mountain that has floated out to sea. Mary Kingsley *Travels in West Africa* 1897 (about Fernando Po).

General Background
Equatorial Guinea
Randall Fegley 1991
More of a reference book.

Small is Not Always Beautiful
Max Liniger-Goumaz 1988
A monograph on Equatorial Guinea which was prosperous until 1968. The Nguema clan took power and the country is now one of the world's poorest.

GABON

The majesty and beauty of the scene fascinated me, and I stood leaning with my back against a rock pinnacle, watching it.

Mary Kingsley *Travels in West Africa* 1897 (about Sierra del Cristal from the Ogowe River)

Biography
Albert Schweitzer: A Biography
James Brabazon 2000
The second edition of this biography contains recently-discovered documents including correspondence with his wife, Helen Bresslau, ten years before their marriage.

My African Notebook
Albert Schweitzer 1938
Schweitzer, a German theologian, went to what is now Gabon after reading an article about the diseases in the area. He also wrote *On the Edge of the Primeval Forest* and *My Life and Thought*.

Albert Schweitzer: The Man and His Mind
George Seaver 1969 (1947)
Schweitzer was acclaimed as a genius with diverse talents: he was a musician, philosopher, theologian and most famously founded a hospital for lepers at Lambaréné.

Guide
Bradt: Gabon, Sao Tome & Principe 2003

Travel Literature
The Rainbird
Jan Brokken 1997
A journey through the jungles of Gabon.

In Search of a Character
Graham Greene 2000 (1961)
Greene's journals kept while writing the novels he set in Africa. *Congo Journal* was written in 1959 and *Convoy to West Africa* in 1941.

GAMBIA

Gambia is more English than England,

more English even than India. Richard West *The White Tribes of Africa* 1965.

Fiction

Chaff in the Wind
Ebou Dibba 1986
The author now lives in Britain, but here describes life in Gambia in the 1930s. Also *Fafa* (1989) and *Alhaji* (1992).

Roots
Alex Haley 1990 (1976)
The first part of this epic saga is set in the Gambia.

The Second Round
Lenrie Peters 1965
A young doctor returns home to the Gambia after several years of medical school in England and encounters family hate and disloyalty.

Guides

Bradt: The Gambia 2001

Insight Guide: The Gambia & Senegal 2000

Lonely Planet: The Gambia & Senegal 2002

Rough Guide: The Gambia 2003

History

History of the Gambia
J.M. Gray 1966
A rather turgid history which finishes before the Second World War.

A Political History of the Gambia 1816-1994
Arnold Hughes & David Perfect 1995
The most up-to-date history.

Photographic

Gambia
Michael Tomkinson 1991 (1987)
A rather slight, illustrated book which does give an idea of the place and which is accompanied by a fair amount of text.

Travel Literature

Our Grandmothers' Drums
Mark Hudson 1992 (1989)
Mark Hudson spent a year in Dulaba in the Gambia. For some, largely unexplained reason, he was allowed to be with the women of the village at times and in places where men were not allowed, so he spent much of his time with them gaining interesting insights into their lifestyle. The book is written with feeling and conviction.

GHANA

Accra ... is one of the five West Coast towns that look well from the sea ... What there is of beauty in Accra is oriental in type. Mary Kingsley *Travels in West Africa* 1897.

Anthropology

Onions are My Husband: Survival and Accumulation by West African Market Women
Gracia Clark 1994
About Kumasi market women.

Biography

All God's Children Need Travelling Shoes.
Maya Angelou 1991 (1986)
The fifth volume of Maya Angelou's autobiography has her emigrating to Ghana from the U.S. via Cairo. She discovers that 'you can't go home again' but finds untold riches in love and friendship, describing in her inimitable way her feelings about Africa.

Kwame Nkrumah: the Conakry Years
Kwame Nkrumah 1990
Correspondence from the exiled ex-president.

Fiction

The Dilemma of a Ghost and Anowa
Ama Ata Aidoo 1991 (1965)
Two plays which show very plainly the differences between Western culture and the traditions of Africa. In *The Dilemma of a Ghost* Ato returns to Ghana, having lived in North America bringing with him a sophisticated black American wife. Their idealism is soon shattered. *No Sweetness Here* (1995) is a collection of short stories. *Our Sister Killjoy* was Aidoo's first novel and *Changes* is a love story.

The Beautiful Ones Are Not Yet Born
Ayiu Kwei Armah 1968
A novel about politics, greed and corruption as told by a railway clerk. Armah also wrote *Fragments* (1970), *Two Thousand Seasons* (1979) and *The Healers* (1978).

This Earth, My Brother
Kofi Awoonor 1972
A young lawyer in Accra works within the confines of an inherited British law. Also *Night of My Blood* (1971).

Ethiopia Unbound
Joseph Casely-Hayford 1969 (1911)
Generally considered to be the first West African novel.

Beyond the Horizon
Amma Darko 1995
Story about a Ghanaian woman's prostitution in Germany.

Hurricane of Dust
Amu Djoleto 1987
Set in post-coup Accra. Also *The Strange Man* (1967) and *Money Galore* (1975).

Search Sweet Country
B.Kojo Laing 1987
Laing was born in Kumasi and educated in Ghana and Scotland. This was his first novel – also *Major Gentl and the Achimota Wars* (1992) and *God-Horse* (1989).

General Background

A View of the World
Norman Lewis 1987 (1986)
A collection of selected journalism which includes an essay called *A Few High-Lifes in Ghana.*

Guide
Bradt: Ghana 2001

History

History of Ghana
F.K. Buah 1980
Basic history.

African Eldorado. Ghana from Gold Coast to Independence
John Carmichael 1993
The book looks at the legend of ancient Ghana, the arrival of the Europeans and their quest for gold, the slave trade and the Ashanti wars, as well as examining the Ghana of today, the first Black African state to gain independence.

GUINEA

Fiction

Tropical Circle
Alioum Fantouré 1972
A novel set between the end of World War II and the reign of terror.

The African Child 1969 (1953)
A Dream of Africa 1968 (1954)
Camara Laye.
When his first book was published Laye soon became established as the leader of new African literature. His novels are full of the feeling of the spirit world enclosing the everyday world. Also *The Radiance of the King*

48

I Was a Savage
Prince Modupe 1969 (1958)
Modupe wrote this autobiographical novel after living for many years in the United States. He was born in French-speaking Guinea and here recounts his early life as a Sousou boy.

Travel Literature
In Search of Africa
Manthia Diawara 1998
The author returns to Guinea to shoot a documentary on Sékou Touré.

Meeting the Invisible Man
Toby Green 2001
Green became friends with a Senegalese photographer who swore that there were mystics in the West African hinterland who possessed the secret of how to become invisible and invulnerable.

GUINEA-BISSAU
General Background
Guinea-Bissau: Politics, Economics and Society
Rosemary E. Galli and Jocelyn Jones 1987
A rather heavy background survey.

History
No Fist is Big Enough to Hide the Sky: the Liberation of Guiné and Cape Verde
Basil Davidson 1981
An account of the war and its aftermath, by a sympathetic observer.

IVORY COAST
Grand Bassam ... is for connoisseurs of decay. Richard West *The White Tribes of Africa* 1965

Autobiography/Biography
Finding the Centre
V.S.Naipaul 1985 (1984)
The first part of the book recounts Naipaul's return to his native Trinidad, but the second part describes his exploration of African magic on the Ivory Coast and shows how far his writing grows out of his contact with other people.

Fiction
Climbié
Bernard B. Dadié 1971 (1953)
Largely autobiographical and reminiscent of Camara Laye (q.v.). A pre-independence Ivory Coast childhood. Also *The Black Cloth* (1987) and *The City Where No One Dies* (1986),

The Suns of Independence
Ahmadou Kourouma 1981 (1968)
Kourouma was born in the Ivory Coast in 1940. He was educated in Bamako, Mali, but was expelled. He did his military service in the Ivory Coast and was transferred to Indo-China. later becoming an actuary in Algiers. In the novel Fana is the last of the Dumbuya – the ruling dynasty of Horodugu but the colonial era deprived him of his chiefdom. He eventually discovers the beloved world of his youth has vanished, goes into politics and becomes aware of the reality. Full of imagery.

General Background
Trader Horn. The Ivory Coast in the Earlies
Aloysius Horn (1974) 1927
The Reader's Library edition had a foreword written by John Galsworthy. A Metro-Goldwyn-Mayer picture was based on the novel. The book was written by Mrs Ethelreda Lewis as the 'true story of a real man'.

African Silences
Peter Matthiessen 1991

49

LIBERIA

There is a distinctly Stuart air about the civilization of the Liberian Coast. Graham Greene *Journey Without Maps* 1936.

Biography

The Life of Graham Greene Vol 1 1904-39.
Norman Sherry 1989
Greene's time in Liberia is covered in several chapters.

Fiction

Love in Ebony: a West African Romance
Varfelli Karlee (pseudonym Charles Edward Cooper) 1932
There are very few works which deal with the hinterland of Liberia which is inhabited by Africans native to the area, rather than those who were sent from America to occupy coastal areas.

General Background

A View of the World
Norman Lewis 1987 (1986)
Selected journalism which includes an essay on Liberia called *Tubman Bids Us Toil*

The Colour Purple
Alice Walker 1993 (1990)
Part of this looks at the conditions that led to the creation of America's Liberian colony.

Travel Literature

Monrovia Mon Amour
Anthony Daniels 1992
Anthony Daniels arrived in Liberia in the aftermath of its civil war to find a country shattered by what it had gone through. The leaders Samuel Doe, Charles Taylor and Prince Y. Johnson had all in their turn resorted to brutal killings and laid trails of destruction. Daniels who has lived in Africa paints an accurate portrayal of what he found.

Too Late To Turn Back
Barbara Greene 1990 (1938)
The twenty three year old Barbara Greene accompanied her cousin Graham to the unmapped Liberia. She was used to a rather luxurious London life, missing the Savoy Grill and smoked salmon on her travels, but although she never meant this book to be published it is riveting to read it in conjunction with *Journey Without Maps* (q.v.). This was the first time that either of them had been to Africa and the portrait of Graham Greene through Barbara's book is fascinating. We learn an immense amount about him through her observations, while he only mentions her by name once in his book.

Journey Without Maps
Graham Greene 1980 (1936)
The journey across Liberia with his cousin Barbara was Greene's first book about Africa. It is interesting to read both of their books together: it is hard to imagine that they were on the same journey. Greene's acute observations of the differences in other cultures make him one of the best writers with whom to travel. Also *Ways of Escape.*

MALI

To that impracticable place Timbuctoo, where Geography finds no one to oblige her. With such a chart as may be safely stuck to. Lord Byron *Don Juan* 1819-24.

Most of what is written about Mali is in French.

Anthropology

Conversations with Ogotemmêli: An Introduction to Dogon Religious Ideas
Marcel Griaule 1977
This and *Pale Fox* (1986) are the two seminal works about the Dogon.

Autobiography/Biography

The White Monk of Timbuctoo
William Seabrook 1934
The biography of Pere Yakouba a white priest who married a woman from Timbuktu.

Fiction

Fortunes of Wangrin
Amadou Hampate Bâ 1999 (1987)
An administrative interpreter tells of the colonial period from 1900-45.

Segu
Maryse Condé

L'Assemblée des Djinns
Massa Makan Diabaté 1985
In Mali the 'griots' (wandering musicians) have kept power and influence; this novel tells of the struggle for that power. In French only. Also *Lieutenant de Kouta* (1984), *Boucher de Kouta* (1982) and *Comme une Pîque de Guêpe* (1980).

Sundiata: an Epic of Old Mali
D. Niane 1993 (1960)
Sundiata grew up to fulfil the prophecies that he would unite the twelve kingdoms of Mali into a powerful empire. The tale has been told by generations of griots (the guardians of African culture).

Bound to Violence
Yambo Ouologuem 1971 (1968)
An epic of a fictitious empire in which the author writes that three historical forces are responsible for the fate and character of the black African: African emperors, Arabs and Europeans.

God's Bits of Wood
Sembène Ousmane 1995 (1960)
Born in Senegal and self-educated. In 1947/48 the workers on the Dakar-Niger railway came out on strike. The novel is about that time. Also *Black Docker* (1956).

Gone to Timbuctoo
John Pearson 1967 (1962)
A non-violent thriller about a collection of odd characters who are involved in a journey from Dakar to the River Niger and up through remote parts of West Africa to Timbuctoo, where the climax of the book takes place. Vivid descriptions of the country as well as an exciting plot.

General Background

Mali: A Search for Direction
Pascal James Imperato 1989
The author was a young physician in Mali in 1966, working for the US Public Health Service. He made many return visits.

Guide

Bradt: Mali 2000

History

Historical Dictionary of Mali
Pascal James Imperato 1996
Broad historical background from prehistorical times to the present, with a comprehensive bibliography.

The Tuaregs
H.T.Norris 1975
Concentrates on the Tuaregs of Mali and Niger. It looks at the contribution Muslim scholars and leaders of the Tuareg have made to the cultural life of the Sahel.

The Gates of Africa
Anthony Sattin 2003
Death, Discovery and the Search for Timbuktu. The story of the African Association - the world's first geographical society.

Photographic

Seydou KeWta: African Photographs 1997
Black and white studio photographs of Bamako people between 1950s and 1970s.

51

Masked Dancers of West Africa: the Dogon
Stephen Pern & Bryan Alexander
1982
A well illustrated book with ample text in the Time Life series.

Travel Literature

Seasons of Sand
Ernst Aebi 1993
A loft-renovator from New York transformed the desert settlement of Araouane into what he thought a nice place to live.

Travels Through Central Africa to Timbuctoo 1824-28
Réné Caillié 1992 (1830)
Caillié was the first European to penetrate to Timbuktu and to return with information. 3000 miles of his 4500 mile journey were previously uncharted.

The Quest for Timbuktoo
Brian Gardner 1968
A collection of biographies of explorers to Timbuktu.

Timbuctoo
Leland Hall 1927
Good descriptive writing.

Two Rivers: Travels in West Africa on the Trail of Mungo Park
Peter Hudson 1991
A journey through West Africa following Mungo Park who had arrived there in 1795. Park was the first known European to travel deep into West Africa. Hudson went through Gambia, Senegal, Guinea-Bissau and Mali to explore the Niger River.

Mali Blues
Lieve Joris 1998
Joris travelled in Senegal, Mauretania and Mali, meeting people and writing four stories about them.

Frail Dream of Timbuktu
Bettina Selby 1993
A bicycle journey from Niamey to Bamako.

NIGER

Most books about Niger are in French.

Anthropology

Sufi Mystics of the Niger Desert: Sidi Mahmud and the Hermits of Aïr
H.T. Norris 1990
Islamic mysticism, *tasawwuf*, refers to the spiritual life of man. " ... frees him from the pleasures of the world. Only then will man achieve the ultimate goal: total unification with his beloved, the almighty God". Aïr Massif is the central and southerly Sahara – the northern part of Niger. Barth (q.v.) was the first person to report on Aïr.

In Sorcery's Shadow: a Memoir of Apprenticeship among the Songhay
Paul Stoller 1989
Paul Stoller writes about mystery and magic in Niger. Another book is *Fusion of the Worlds: an Ethnography of Possession among the Songhay of Niger* (1987).

History

A History of Niger 1850-1960
Finn Fuglestad 1983
Tough going.

Photographic

Nomads of the Niger
Carol Beckwith 1983
A glorious photographic account of eighteen months spent with the Wodaabe of Niger, following a herdsman, his wife and kinsmen on a year's migration. The text is ample and readable.

52

Travel Literature

The Strong Brown God: The Story of the Niger River

Sanche de Gramont 1991 (1975)
The story of a handful of obsessed explorers who wanted to find and open the Niger River.

NIGERIA

Nigeria is a place where the best is impossible but where the worst never happens. Old saying, quoted in *The Economist* 18th April 1953.

Anthropology

Return to Laughter

Elenore Smith Bowen 1954
"Smith Bowen is a pseudonym for an American woman academic, an anthropologist, who conducted fieldwork amongst the Tiv people of central Nigeria in the 1950s. Fearing that writing an account which included her own personal reactions and problems would dent her academic reputation, Smith Bowen wrote fiction under a pseudonym. *Return to Laughter* is an agonising account of a woman's struggle to be accepted in a society which is governed by principles other than her own. It is the story of her attempt to hold on to who and what she is when surrounded by strangeness. She does this through small things, such as dressing for dinner and reading Jane Austen in the bush. Without these simple gestures, she soon realises, she does not become 'one of the Tiv', but simply a nobody, a person without any principles at all, neither governed by their rules nor hers. It's a warning to all of us." (Dea Birkett)

Art

Yoruba: Nine Centuries of African Art and Thought

Henry J. Drewal & John Pemberton 1990
Lavish and well-illustrated.

The Art of Benin

Paula Girshick Ben-Amos 1995
The ancient kingdom of Benin is one of the most sophisticated in Africa. The book examines the role of art in every aspect of Benin life.

Autobiography/Biography

The Life of Olaudah Equiano

Olaudah Equiano 1997 (1789)
One of the earliest West African books.

A Month and a Day

Ken Saro-Wiwa 1995
The moving account of Ken Saro-Wiwa's period of detention in 1993.

In the Shadow of a Saint

Ken Wiwa 2001 (2000)
The biography of his father Ken Saro-Wiwa with whom, at times, he had a turbulent relationship.

Ake

Wole Soyinka 1982
An autobiographical account of Soyinka's childhood in Abeokuta.

Ibadan

Wole Soyinka 1995
A memoir from the years1946-1965. Also *The Open Sore of a Continent: A Personal Narrative of the Nigerian Crisis* (1996).

Fiction

Anthills of the Savannah

Chinua Achebe 1988 (1987)
Achebe was born in Eastern Nigeria. He writes movingly and powerfully about the troubled recent history in West Africa by making 'His Excellency', a defeated officer, into a dictator. Fact is woven with fiction creating an exciting novel. Other novels by Achebe include: *Things Fall Apart* (1958), *No Longer at Ease* (1960), *The Arrow of God* (1964) and *A Man of the People* (1966).

53

Orimili
Amechi Akwanya 1991
The author was born in Nigeria in 1952, became a priest and lived in Ireland before returning to Nigeria. His novel is set in pre-colonial Nigeria in a small but complex community which he uses as a structure for exploring human relationships.

A Virtuous Woman
Zainab Alkali 1984
A woman writer from the conservative north. Also *The Stillborn* (1988).

One Man, One Wife
T.M. Aluko 1967
A Yoruba village becomes disillusioned with the missionaries' God.

The Concubine
Elechi Amadi 1989
The first novel of a writer who has also been a land surveyor, a teacher, a fighter and a worker in the Ministry of Education. Also *Estrangement* (1986), *The Great Ponds* (1969) and *Sunset in Biafra* (1973).

Shaihu Umar
Tafawa Balewa 1989 (1968)
Written in Hausa by Nigeria's first prime minister.

Yoruba Girl Dancing
Simi Bedford 1994
A British Nigerian's depiction of early life in Nigeria.

Mister Johnson
Joyce Cary 1995 (1939)
Joyce Cary fought in the Nigerian Regiment during the First World War and subsequently rejoined the Nigerian Political Service. However he suffered from ill-health and was advised to retire. He left Africa and began to write. Mr Johnson is a minor government clerk at an outpost in Nigeria who has ideas of grandeur. Cary captures colonial life well

54

and manages to combine that with a real understanding of Africa and the Africans.

I Saw the Sky Catch Fire
T. Obinkaram Echewa 1993
Fictionalised accounts of war.

Jagua Nana
Cyprian Ekwensi 1987 (1961)
1950s life in Lagos. *Burning Grass* (1990/1962) is set in the north among the Fula. *Survive the Peace* is a political novel.

Slave Girl
Buchi Emecheta 1979
The theme of Buchi Emecheta's novels which include *Second Class Citizen* (1977), *Double Yoke* (1984) and *Bride Price* (1978) is about the struggle of being both a Nigerian woman and an independent person. Also *In the Ditch* (1988), *Head Above Water* (1986) and *Joys of Motherhood* (1988).

The Famished Road
Ben Okri 1992 (1991)
A lyrical and compelling book, full of flights of fancy, but also very instructive as to life in a West African village. After finishing it you begin to see the world around you in a different way. Okri's first novel was *Flowers and Shadows* (1980) and he has written collections of short stories including *Incidents at the Shrine* (1986) and *Stars of the New Curfew* (1988).

Loyalties
Adewale Maja Pearce 1987
Short stories about a society in disarray.

Lemona's Tale
Ken Saro-Wiwa 1996
Lemona was held in a Nigerian prison for a quarter of a century. Also *Sozaboy* (1994/1985), *A Forest of Flowers* (1995/1986), *The Prisoner of Jebs* (1988) and *Dumbrok's Prison* (1991).

The Interpreters
Wole Soyinka 1965
About a group of young intellectuals living in Lagos. Also *Isara* (1991/1989) and plays: *The Lion and the Jewel* (1963), *The Man Died* (1975) and *A Dance of the Forest* (1963).

The Palm-Wine Drinkard
Amos Tutuola 1977
A Yoruba and native of Abeokuta, Tutuola has a natural gift for story-telling. Also *My Life in the Bush of Ghosts* (1990) and *The Witch Herbalist of the Remote Town* (1990).

General Background
Home & Exile
Chinua Achebe 2003 (2000)
The inner workings of Achebe's mind - seen through the predicament of Africa.

The Trouble with Nigeria
Chinua Achebe 1983
The complexities of Nigeria are examined in a brief but informative book.

This House Has Fallen
Karl Maier 2002 (2000)
Nigeria in crisis. Invaluable read before a trip.

Politics and History
The Political Economy of Nigeria
ed. Claude Ake 1985
A critique by an outspoken academic.

Kingdoms of the Yoruba
Robert S. Smith 1988
Classic historical work.

Travel Literature
Equiano's Travels
ed. Paul Edwards (abridged)1969 (1789)
Olaudah Equiano was born in 1745 in what is now Nigeria. He was taken as a slave to the West Indies, managed to buy his freedom when he was twenty-one and in 1773 took part in Phipps' expedition to the Arctic. He was an ardent member of the Anti-Slavery movement. This book, which is an account of his life, was extremely popular going into seventeen editions in Britain between 1789 and 1827.

In My Father's Country
Adewale Maja-Pearce 1987
The author was revisiting his country for the first time in many years.

SÃO TOMÉ & PRÍNCIPE

General Background
São Tomé and Príncipe: From Plantation Colony to Microstate
Tony Hodges and Malyn Newitt 1988

Guide
Bradt: Gabon, Sao Tome & Principe 2003

SENEGAL
Dakar has been fittingly called 'the boomingest boom town on the continent'.
John Gunther *Inside Africa* 1955

Biography
Ambiguous Adventure
Cheikh Hamidou Kane 1972 (1963)
An autobiographical tale about a man torn between Tukolor, Islam and the West.

Fiction
So Long a Letter
Mariama Bâ 1982 (1979)
The novel deals with the problems of polygamy and social inequality faced by women in present-day Africa. Portrayed through the eyes of two women, both deserted by their husbands, whose lives take different courses. Also *The Scarlet Song* (1995).

A Dakar Childhood
Nafissatou Diallo 1982
The account of a middle-class girl growing up in Dakar in the postwar years.

The Wound
Malick Fall 1973
The author was a poet and diplomat.

The Music in My Head
Mark Hudson 1999
Inventive novel with good descriptive prose.

God's Bits of Wood
Sembène Ousmane 1960
The story of the 1947 rail strike by a political writer who can also be funny. Also *Xala* (1973) and *The Last of the Empire* (1981).

General Background

Senegal - An African Nation Between Islam and the West
Sheldon Gellar 1982
A very readable general survey of Senegal.

History & Politics

Muslim Brotherhoods and Politics in Senegal
Lucy C. Behrman 1970
Somewhat dated but interesting look at the marabouts at the turn of the twentieth century.

SIERRA LEONE

Sierra Leone, charming as it is, has a sort of Christy Minstrel air about it.
Mary Kingsley *West African Studies* 1899.

Biography

An African Victorian Feminist – the Life and Times of Adelaide Smith Caseley Hayford 1868-1960
Adelaide M. Cromwell 1992 (1986)
A biography of one of the Krio elite.

Fiction

Kossoh Town Boy
Robert Wellesley Cole 1960
A sort of autobiography. As the first-born he was promised to God and from early on his life implied a debt of service. This is about his schooldays in Freetown where his father was a Civil Engineer and head of his department – the first African in the 20th century to be so.

The African
William Conton 1960
Kisimi Kamara is awarded a scholarship to study in England where he meets a white South African girl; colour prejudice ends their affair, so he returns to Sierra Leone disillusioned and bitter, but turns his energies to politics.

The Heart of the Matter
Graham Greene 1992 (1948)
Graham Greene sets this novel in an imaginary West African country; he was stationed in Sierra Leone from 1941-43 and inevitably draws much from his experiences there. Scobie, a police officer, is passed over for promotion so has to borrow money in order to send his wife on holiday. While she is away he falls in love; the moral dilemma which this entails shows Graham Greene at his best. Also *The Ministry of Fear* (1970).

Road to Freedom
Yema Lucilda Hunter 1982
An historical novel about early Krio settlements.

*The Truly Married Woman &
Other Stories*
Davidson (Abioseh) Nicol 1965
The author is a poet, short story writer
and biochemist.

The Mocking Stones
Prince Dowu Palmer 1982
A mixed-race love affair takes place
among the Kono diamond business

History
A New History of Sierra Leone
Joe A.D. Alie 1990
An illustrated overall history of Sierra
Leone from early times up until the pres-
ent.

Travel Literature
Journey Without Maps
Graham Greene 1976
Greene's arrival in West Africa was at
Freetown.

View of Sierra Leone
F.W.H. Migeod 1926
A six-month trek through the country.
Eccentric.

TOGO
General Background
An African in Greenland
Tete Michel Kpomassie 1988
The author, from Togo, visits the Inuit.

The Village of Waiting
George Packer 1990
The experiences of a Peace Corps volun-
teer in Togo.

EAST AFRICA
General East Africa
Anthropology
Swahili Origins
James de Vere Allen 1993
A major study of the origin of the Swahili
and of their cultural identity.

Revealing Prophets
David M.Anderson & D H. Johnson
1995
The richly textured histories of prophets
and prophecies within East Africa.

The Tree Where Man Was Born
Peter Matthiessen 1984 (1972)
Difficult to classify as this is really a
book that feels and understands Africa in
all its many facets. Although Matthiessen
went to Africa primarily to see animals
he also writes in a compelling way about
the environment, history, politics, people
and the landscape. He feels that
"Something has happened here, is happening, will happen - whole landscapes
seem alert".

57

Biography
Tilda's Angel
Dick Hodges 1994
The man behind Safari Camp Services
and the Turkana bus.

Somebody Else
Charles Nicholl 1998 (1997)
Arthur Rimbaud's lost years in Africa
between 1880-91.

*Out of America: a Black Man
Confronts Africa*
Keith B. Richburg 1998 (1997)
The author was Nairobi bureau chief for
the Washington Times 1991-4, and cov-
ered many elections. Rather depressing.

Fiction

Henderson the Rain King
Saul Bellow 1990 (1979)
Bellow has created Henderson as a hero in the great tradition yet set in contemporary America and Africa. Very funny, punchy prose which has a thread of pathos running through it.

An Ice-Cream War
William Boyd 1983
Set in East Africa during the times of the campaigns in the First World War. The book is about the Europeans who took part, Africans seeming only to appear incidentally and in bizarre roles; the two cultures are seen here as stereotypes.

The Weather in Africa
Martha Gellhorn 1991 (1978)
Three novellas set in East Africa: *On the Mountain, By the Sea* and *In the Highlands*. All three are about Europeans who for one reason or another do not quite fit in Europe and so have either come or come back to East Africa. Their preconceptions of Africa are very different to the reality; all three are compelling stories.

The White Bone
Barbara Gowdy 2000 (1999)
The story of an infant elephant orphaned at birth.

The Year of the Lion
Gerald Hanley 1966 (1953)
An inexperienced but eager young man arrives from England to work on a farm in East Africa. He has to learn to cope with the heat and uncertainties of Africa as well as dealing with people and animals; by doing so he grows up. An exciting story which has wonderful descriptions of the hunt for a man-eating lion. Also Hanley's first novel *The Consul at Sunset* (1951).

58

The Snows of Kilimanjaro
Ernest Hemingway 1994 (1939)
Early stories including a drama on the snow-capped Kilimanjaro.

Fong and the Indians
Paul Theroux 1992 (1968)
Paul Theroux's perceptive and funny novel the 'first piece of fiction that satisfied him' is set in East Africa where a Chinese immigrant, Sam Fong, had been transplanted and where he had lived for thirty five years. Now in a collection called *On the Edge of the Great Rift* (1996) with *Girls at Play* (1969) and *Jungle Lovers* (1971).

Antonia Saw the Oryx First
Maria Thomas 1988 (1987)
Maria Thomas had lived in Africa for twenty years and with her first novel has managed to get under the skin of it, understanding the corruption and writing satirically about its transition from colonial times. The novel is about two women: one black, one white.

General Background

People on the Edge in the Horn
Gaim Kibreab 1996
An in-depth study of land use in Africa.

The Linen Goddess
Sheila Paine 2003
Sheila Paine continues her quest for the amulet through Eritrea, Ethiopia, the Sudan & Egypt.

East and West Africa: Travel Resource Guide
Louis Taussig 1994

Guides

Bradt: East and Southern Africa: The Backpacker's Manual 2001

East Africa Handbook 2002

Lonely Planet: East Africa 2003

History

The Lunatic Express
Charles Miller 1987 (1972)
George Whitehouse arrived in Mombasa in 1895 to build a railway. The danger and folly of the enterprise soon became apparent as the railway would have to cross deserts and the Great Rift Valley as well as contend with malarial swamps and wild animals. The saga of the controversial, but extraordinary Victorian engineering feat, is written here as an exciting history. Miller is also good on general early East African history.

In the Grip of the Nyika
J.H.Patterson 1909
An account of the adventures that befell Colonel Patterson on two trips through the *nyika* (wilderness) in British East Africa. It seemed almost standard that some members of the party would die en route, nevertheless there are interesting descriptions of what a safari was like at the turn of the century.

The Man-Eaters of Tsavo; and Other East African Adventures.
J.H. Patterson 1979 (1907)
The author's terrifying adventures (which impressed President Roosevelt) with man-eating lions when he was an engineer during the building of the Uganda Railway. The chapters on construction of the railway and bridges are also interesting; well illustrated with his photographs.

East African Explorers
ed. Charles Richards 1968 (1960)
One of the World's Classics series, this is an anthology devoted to the writings of the first travellers and explorers to East Africa such as: Livingstone, Stanley, Teleki, Burton, Speke, Baker, Lugard and Emin Pasha. Rather limited in its coverage.

Leisure Activities

Trekking in East Africa. A Lonely Planet Walking Guide 2003

Natural History

A Field Guide to the Wild Flowers of East Africa
Michael Blundell 1992 (1987)
Over 1200 detailed descriptions of species and 864 colour photographs of wild flowers in Kenya, Tanzania, Uganda, Mozambique and Zimbabwe. Invaluable.

Field Guide to the Common Trees & Shrubs of East Africa
Najma Dharani 2002

Collins Pocket Guide Coral Reef Fishes
Ewald Lieske & Robert Myers 2001
A practical book which will help with the identification of the more common fishes which might be seen when diving or snorkelling; a simple key is used and the book is illustrated with colour plates and line drawings.

Insight Guide East African Wildlife 1997
The first half of the book is devoted to describing specific animals and is illustrated by 'artistic' photographs, this is followed by descriptions of the game parks and reserves. A run-down of various safaris follows.

Lonely Planet Watching Wildlife – East Africa 2001

Birds of Eastern Africa
Ber van Perlo 1996
An illustrated checklist.

Field Guide to the Birds of East Africa
J. Williams & N. Arlott 1980
This used to be the standard guide, but has been superseded partly because of its poor illustrations.

Wildlife of East Africa
Martin Withers & David Hosking 2002

59

Birds of Kenya and Northern Tanzania
Zimmerman et al 1996
A large and comprehensive tome – well illustrated. A smaller version – a *Field Guide* is also available.

Photographic

The End of the Game
Peter Beard 1988 (1963)
A documentary history of East African wildlife. Over three hundred black and white photographs show the widespread destruction of the African elephant. The text tells of the explorers, missionaries and game hunters and quotes many of them at length. A powerful and disturbing book.

East Africa
Tim Beddow 1988
A lengthy and interesting introduction by Dominic Sasse is followed by seventy eight colour photographs which do much to show the diversity of landscape and people in East Africa.

Valley of Life
Chris Johns 1991
National Geographic photographer Chris Johns spent eighteen months following the 3,500 miles of the African Rift Valley which stretches from Ethiopia to Mozambique via Ethiopia, Djibouti, Kenya, Uganda, Tanzania, Zaire and Malawi to Mozambique. The diverse country, people and animals along the rift are shown here by stunning and original photographs, many of them taken from the air.

Religion

Islam in East Africa
J.S.Trimingham 1964
Islamic history in East Africa and the extent to which it has merged with African culture and produced the mix that exists today.

Travel Literature

Travels with Myself and Another
Martha Gellhorn 1991 (1978)
Part of this entertaining and observant book about Martha Gellhorn's 'horror journeys', takes place in East Africa.

Green Hills of Africa
Ernest Hemingway 1991 (1935)
Most of Hemingway's love for Africa seems to come from big-game hunting; however there is more to it than that because his descriptions of the landscape and of smells indicate that Africa really did get into his blood. His encounter with an European in the bush and discussion of Rilke is on a par with Kinglake's encounter in *Eothen* (q.v.).

Straight on till Morning
Mary S. Lovell 1988 (1987)
The acclaimed story of Beryl Markham's life.

West With the Night
Beryl Markham 1992 (1942)
Beryl Markham was taken to Kenya by her father in 1906, when she was four. She learned to train racehorses and in 1931 started flying, regularly piloting mail for East African Airways as well as game hunting from the air. In 1936 she became the first person to fly solo across the Atlantic from east to west. This was her only book and although there is some dispute as to whether she actually wrote it, it is a riveting read.

The Ukimwi Road
Dervla Murphy 1994
Murphy rode a bike between Kenya and Zimbabwe and was shocked at how much AIDS she found.

North of South
Shiva Naipaul 1980 (1979)
A brilliant travel narrative about journeying through Kenya, Tanzania and Zambia. Naipaul was extremely observant and with a novelist's eye for detail could be

devastatingly accurate and cynical about what he saw.

Discovery of Lakes Rudolf and Stefanie
Lieut. Ludwig von Höhnel 1894
(A Narrative of Count Samuel Teleki's Exploring & Hunting Expedition in Eastern Equatorial Africa in 1887 88). This account was written for the general reading public and deals with the big game hunting aspect of the trip rather than with the scientific observations which were made; the wealth of animals that they both saw and pursued do not exist today.

A Tourist in Africa
Evelyn Waugh 1960
A slight book, but a funny one, about a short trip to Kenya, Tanganyika and Rhodesia.

DJIBOUTI

Jibuti, white and neat and empty, looked as if it had just been washed and dumped out in the sun to dry. Rosita Forbes
From Red Sea to Blue Nile 1925

General Background
Complete Works and Selected Letters 1854-1891: Arthur Rimbaud
ed. Wallace Fowlie 1975
When Rimbaud was 21 he abandoned poetry to wander eventually settling in Harar in Ethiopia where he became a gun-runner, returning to France in 1891.

Guide
Lonely Planet: Ethiopia, Eritrea & Djibouti 2000

History
Amedo
Sebastian O'Kelly 2003 (2002)
O'Kelly unearthed a remarkable story of how a young Italian aristocratic army

officer led a cavalry charge against a battalion of British tanks.

Photographic
African Ark
Carol Beckwith and Angela Fisher 1991 (1990)
The photographers spent five years in the Horn of Africa collecting material for this book which contains 320 pages of colour photographs as well as explanatory line drawings in the text. Racked by famine and war today, the region contains sophisticated Christian and Muslim cultures as well as nomads and primitive tribes.

Travel Literature
Hashish. A Smuggler's Tale
Henry de Monfreid 1994 (1935)
De Monfreid sailed from Marseilles to Djibouti and on to Suez with a dream of being completely independent. He saw smuggling hashish as a way of achieving his ambition: "I didn't know exactly what hashish was...I knew only two things - that it was grown in Greece and sold very dear in Egypt".

The Life of My Choice
Wilfred Thesiger 1987
When he was 23 he led an expedition into the Danakil territory.

When the Going Was Good
Evelyn Waugh 1951
Included in the collection is a train trip from Djibouti to Abyssinia.

ERITREA

Fiction
Towards Asmara
Thomas Keneally 1990 (1989)
A powerful novel which uses war-torn Eritrea as its focus for four people travelling under rebel escort to Asmara. Keneally travelled with the Eritrean

61

Relief Association, so much of the book reads as fact making it especially moving.

General Background

The Long Struggle of Eritrea for Independence and Constructive Peace
eds. Lionel Cliffe & Basil Davidson 1988
A collection of essays by nine contributors each of whom had a prolonged, concerned and independent interest in their subject.

Against All Odds
Dan Connell 1995
A chronicle of the Eritrean revolution

Beyond the Conflict in the Horn 1992
M. Doombos

Ciao Asmara
Justin Hill 2002
The author spent two years in Eritrea.

62

Eritrea: Revolution at Dusk
Robert Papstein 1996

Eritrea: Even the Stones are Burning
Roy Pateman 1998

Eritrea, A Colony in Transition 1941-52
G.K.N. Trevaskis 1960
The author was taken to Eritrea as a prisoner of war in 1940. On his release he was seconded to the British Administration and remained in its service until 1950. He served in most districts of the country.

The Challenge Road
Amrit Wilson 1989
Women's experiences during the revolution in Eritrea. The author shows how the revolution addressed women's issues.

Guides

Bradt: Eritrea 1996

Lonely Planet: Ethiopia & Eritrea 2003

ETHIOPIA

I saw parch'd Abyssinia rouse and sing.
John Keats *Endymion* 1818

Art & Archaeology

The Abyssinians. Ancient Peoples and Places
David Buxton 1970
The book documents the country, its people, their history, religion and way of life. The architecture, literature, painting and other arts including music and metalwork are illustrated throughout by line drawings and 128 photographs.

Abyssinie Swing
Francis Falceto 2001
A documentation of Ethiopia's rich musical heritage.

African Zion. The Sacred Art of Ethiopia
eds. Roderick Grierson & Marilyn Heldman 1994 (1993)
A magnificent illustrated catalogue with lengthy descriptions of Ethiopia's sacred art.

Archaeology at Aksum 1993-7
David Phillipson 1997
Large two-volume work.

Biography

The Pale Abyssinian
Miles Bredin 2001
A life of James Bruce and his time spent in what was still medieval Ethiopia.

Fiction

The History of Rasselas, Prince of Abissinia
Samuel Johnson 1986 (1759)
The story of how Rasselas and his companions escape from their valley in Abyssinia and flee to Egypt to find out how people live. Dr Johnson's moral tale which is really asking 'what is happiness, and how can we find it?' includes discussions on a wide range of subjects including greatness, marriage, solitude and astronomy. A wise and thought-provoking book.

The Emperor
Ryszard Kapucinski 1994 (1983)
"The only book I've read about Ethiopia, but I can't imagine that had I read a library it would have been any less memorable." (Jeremy Paxman)

The Abyssinian
Jean-Christophe Rufin 2000 (1997)
A novel set in 1700 about an apothecary who is talked into leading an embassy from Cairo to Ethiopia.

Firebrands
Sahle Sellassie 1979
A political novel culminating in 1974 and showing the massive corruption that existed in pre-revolutionary Ethiopia, portrayed through the eyes of one family. Also *Warrior King* (1974) based on the life of Emperor Tewodros II and *The Afersata* (1968).

A Season in Abyssinia
Paul Strathern 1972
A novel based on Rimbaud's life in Africa.

Black Mischief
Evelyn Waugh 1992 (1932)
The Emperor Seth and his Minister of Modernization, Basil Seal are pitted against the cruelty, treachery and cannibalism in the mythical country of Azania, (loosely based on Abyssinia) which is racked by civil war; but they find it a losing battle. Cynical and funny.

Scoop
Evelyn Waugh 1969 (1938)
William Boot, Countryman, mistakenly gets sent to Ishmaelia by Lord Copper to cover the war. As Boot blunders through Ishmaelia the novel becomes an hilariously funny satire on Fleet Street and war reporting.

The Thirteenth Sun
Daniachew Worku 1973
This was his first novel which came out just before the fall of Haile Selassie. Sophisticated.

General Background

At War with Waugh
W.F.Deedes 2003
The real story of Scoop.

Pastoralists, Ethnicity and the State in Ethiopia
ed. Richard Hogg 1997
Many contributors write about refugees, trans-border conflicts, humanitarian intervention and civil strife.

Guides

Bradt: Ethiopia 2002

Lonely Planet:Ethiopia & Eritrea 2003

Ethiopia the Unknown Land
Stuart Munro-Hay 2002
An historical and cultural guide to the monuments. Comprehensive and packed with information.

History

Beyond the Throne: the Enduring Legacy of Emperor Haile Selassie I
Indrias Getachew 2001
Well-written and well-illustrated.

63

Eritrea's War
Paul Henze 2001
Written by a former diplomat and expert on Ethiopian politics. Also *Layers of Time: A History of Ethiopia* (2001) -

A History of Ethiopia
Harold Marcus 1994
A readable general history.

The Blue Nile
Alan Moorehead (see Egypt)

The Ethiopians
Richard Pankhurst 2001
A reissued introduction to Ethiopia's varied cultures and social history. Also *The Ethiopian Borderlands.*

The Making of Modern Ethiopia 1896-1974
Teshale Tibebu 1995
Excellent and original overview.

A History of Modern Ethiopia 1855-1974
Bahru Zewde 1991
Aimed at the general reader.

Photographic

Journey Through Ethiopia
M. Amin, A. Matheson & D. Willetts 1997
Good general coffee-table book about Ethiopia.

African Ark
Carol Beckwith and Angela Fisher (see Djibouti)

The Beauty of Historic Ethiopia
Graham Hancock 1994

Religion

Islam in Ethiopia
J.Spencer Trimingham 1952
The account of the impact of Islam upon the nomadic and settled peoples of Ethiopia, the reaction of indigenous cultures and the way the converts to Islam moulded it into their lives.

Travel Literature

Treacherous Journey
Amhuel Avrahamis 1986
The account of a Felasha's escape from persecution under the Dergue.

The Nile Tributaries of Abyssinia and the Sword Hunters of the Hamran Arabs
Sir Samuel Baker 1867
Baker spent twelve months exploring every river that is a tributary to the Nile from Abyssinia. During the journey he managed to find time to learn Arabic and to study the character of the peoples he encountered; his wife, Florence, accompanied him throughout this tough trip which was beset by every kind of problem, but which ultimately led to his success in reaching the 'Albert N'yanza.' Although this book was written after *The Albert N'yanza* (q.v.), the part of the expedition it describes actually took place before.

The Sacred City of the Ethiopians
J.Theodore Bent 1893
A record of four months of travel and research in Abyssinia in 1893 to Aksum, the sacred city of the Ethiopians. The author was the first to find Sabœan inscriptions in a temple proving a connection between the peoples of South Arabia and of Abyssinia mentioned in the 10th chapter of Genesis and alluded to by Greek authors.

Travels to Discover the Source of the Nile
James Bruce 1964 (1790)
Bruce wanted to discover the Ethiopian source of the Nile. He set off in 1768 and in 1769 arrived at Massawa in Ethiopia. His second attempt to reach the source was successful. On returning to England he was initially acclaimed, but his travels were subsequently disbelieved. His account of his own travels is lively and

accessible to the general reader, whereas his volume on the history of Ethiopia is somewhat confused.

The Fountain of the Sun
Douglas Busk 1957
The author was posted to the embassy in Addis Ababa and from there made many trips into Ethiopia and the Ruwenzori. His main love was for the mountains, but he found so much else in Ethiopia to interest him that mountains are given less coverage than he had anticipated.

Travels in Ethiopia
David Buxton 1949
The author, a biologist, worked for mosquito control and travelled throughout Ethiopia in the 40's.

Ethiopia off the Beaten Track
John Graham 2001
The author is travel correspondent for the Addis Tribune.

The Sign and the Seal. A Quest for the Lost Ark of the Covenant
Graham Hancock 1992
In 1983 Graham Hancock had gone to a building in the Ethiopian Highlands which was alleged to contain the Ark of the Covenant. He was unable to see it, but was fired with enthusiasm and curiosity to find out all he could about it and the Queen of Sheba.

In Quest of Sheba's Mines
Frank E. Hayter 1935
Hayter searched for gold in Ethiopia – he also wrote The Gold of Ethiopia (1936).

Ethiopian Journeys
Paul Henze 2001
Ethiopia during the last years of the Imperial era.

Journey to the Jade Sea
John Hillaby 1993 (1964)
Formerly known as Lake Rudolf, now Lake Turkana, the Jade Sea is on the borders of Kenya and Ethiopia. The lava beds which surround the lake are often too hot to touch, but the colour is a stunning green and unusually large crocodiles live in the lake. John Hillaby walked over a thousand miles to the lake and along its shores and recounts his adventures in this book.

A Far Country
Philip Marsden 1991 (1990)
A combination of travelogue and a book tracing Ethiopia's past. The author remains detached but describes the many people he meets, letting them talk. The result is a book which makes you feel you have travelled through the country.

In Ethiopia With a Mule
Dervla Murphy 1968
Dervla Murphy is an intrepid traveller and went from Massawah in the north of Ethiopia to Addis Ababa in the south. She did much of her journey on foot, or rather with a mule named Jock, about whom we hear everything. The book is written in diary form so we learn much about the habits and lifestyles of the people she meets and what the landscape looks like, as she says ' every local detail interests me'.

65

Desert and Forest
L.M. Nesbitt 1934
(The exploration of Abyssinian Danakil). Already in the 1920's people seemed to be becoming aware of the impossibility for the would-be-explorer to find a 'virgin field for his enterprise on the earth.' Nesbitt appreciated his good fortune in being one of the last to be able to experience virgin territory; his three and a half month expedition traversed the Danakil territory south to north in 1927 and he presented the scientific results of the expedition to the Royal Geographical Society in 1928.

The Mountains of Rasselas
Thomas Pakenham 1959
Thomas Pakenham found himself involved in going to Ethiopia to climb Mount Wachni, near Lake Tana, where

the King's sons had been confined (see Johnson's *Rasselas*). He would be the first to give an eye-witness account of all three summits (Bruce had only visited two of the three mountains). The unknown shape of the mountain became a fixation and when he eventually saw one of the peaks, shaped like a thumb, his stomach contracted with fear. Pakenham writes clearly blending history with the myth surrounding the area.

Eating the Flowers of Paradise
Kevin Rushby 1999 (1998)
A journey through the drug fields of Ethiopia and Yemen.

In Search of King Solomon's Mines
Tahir Shah 2002
Like many before him Shah went in search of King Solomon's mines and the gold that must have come from them. Although, if he had found the mines, Shah had vowed not to take any of the gold - the metal which leads so many to destruction – he did become obsessed with finding the mines.

Arthur Rimbaud in Abyssinia
Enid Starke 1937 (see Yemen)

The Danakil Diary
Wilfred Thesiger 1998 (1996)
Thesiger's journeys through Abyssinia 1930-34 after the coronation of Haile Selassie. Also *The Life of My Choice* (1987) includes an account of Thesiger's journey through the Danakil in 1933.

In Search of Sheba
Barbara Toy (see Algeria & Sahara)

Waugh in Abyssinia
Evelyn Waugh 1984 (1936)
Waugh went to Abyssinia in 1935 to cover the Italian-Abyssinian war for the Daily Mail and with his witty prose takes a look at the crisis and its build up. His descriptions of the lives of war correspondents and their encounters with the local people are very amusing and per-

ceptive. *When the Going Was Good* includes travels in Ethiopia

KENYA

In Kenya any eccentricity gets blamed on the altitude. Richard West *The White Tribes of Africa* 1965.

Anthropology
People and Cultures of Kenya
Andrew Fedders & Cynthia Salvadori 1981 (1979)
A tribe-by-tribe introduction.

Memories, Dreams, Reflections
C.G. Jung 1971 (1963)
Jung visited Mount Elgon in 1925 to learn about the rituals, symbolism and spirits of the Elgonyi people.

Facing Mount Kenya
Jomo Kenyatta 1962
An anthropological monograph on the Kikuyu written at the LSE under the supervision of Bronislaw Malinowski.

Being Maasai
ed. Thomas Spear and Richard Waller 1993
A collection by historians, archaeologists, anthropologists and linguists which examines how the Maasai identity has been created.

Biography
My Pride and Joy
George Adamson 1988 (1986)
George Adamson first went to Kenya in 1924 and retired from being a game warden in 1963. His autobiography tells of his life with lions (including the famous Elsa) and of the murder of his wife Joy in 1980. Especially interesting because of the long span of time he spent in Kenya.

66

Out of Africa
Karen Blixen (Isak Dinesen)
1991(1937)
In 1914 Karen Blixen went to Kenya to run a coffee farm which failed. She subsequently returned to Denmark where she wrote this unsentimental but moving and introspective account of her experiences there. The friends and animals that she came across in Kenya are vividly portrayed and we share her sense of loss both for the farm and in a wider sense for an era.

Kenyatta
Jeremy-Murray Brown 1979 (1972)
A weighty biography.

Out of Isak Dinesen in Africa: The Untold Story
Linda Donelson 1998
Blixen comes to life in this biography.

Leaves from the Fig Tree
Diana Duff 2003
The author grew up in Ireland and headed for the excitement of 1950's Kenya. She married and was in Kikuyu land at the height of Mau Mau before moving to Tanganyika & South Africa.

Tom Mboya: The Man Who Kenya Wanted to Forget
David Goldsworthy 1982
A heavy biography about Mboya – a controversial but brilliant political figure who was both admired and detested. This shows his many sides.

Nellie: Letters from Africa
Nellie Grant 1980
Nellie Grant, born in 1885, was Elspeth Huxley's mother; she married a settler farmer and lived in Kenya for most of her life. Her letters describe the domestic details of life during the pioneer period and are very illuminating.

The Flame Trees of Thika 1991 (1959)
The Mottled Lizard 1981 (1962)
Out in the Midday Sun 1987 (1985)
Elspeth Huxley
These three volumes of autobiography begin when Elspeth Huxley goes with her parents to Thika to become pioneering settlers among the Kikuyu. The memoirs of her African childhood are captivatingly written; they vividly conjure up landscapes, episodes and people from another era but make valid reading for today.

Kenya Diary
Richard Meinertzhagen 1906
The diary of a young British officer takes a cold-blooded approach to his 'punitive expeditions' as well as the endless slaughter of wild animals.

Moi: the Making of an African Statesman
Andrew Morton 1998
A rather gripping, but at times frustrating biography.

Not Yet Uhuru
Oginga Odinga 1984 (1967)
Autobiography of Oginga Odinga.

Lost Lion of Empire
Edward Paice 2002 (2001)
The biography of Ewart Grogan - a pioneer settler in Kenya who, to prove his love for an heiress, undertook the first Cape to Cairo traverse.

A Nice Place to Live
Pamela Scott 1991
Pam Scott was left a farm to run in Kenya when she was eighteen; the farm was sold forty five years later, but she stayed on and was in Kenya during the Mau Mau emergency. Her straightforward account of life during and after that time is refreshing in its honesty.

My Kenya Days
Wilfred Thesiger 1994
Thesiger's autobiography of the thirty

years that he spent in Kenya. During the 1960s he made many long expeditions on foot with camels to Lakes Turkana and Marsabit and other remote areas; he writes about these as well as giving insights into his reasons for travelling and his love of Kenya.

The Life of Isak Dinesen
Judith Thurman 1984 (1982)
A biography of Isak Dinesen (Karen Blixen).

The Lives of Beryl Markham
Errol Trzebinski 1995 (1994)
The suggestion in this book is that Beryl Markham could not have written *West with the Night*.

Fiction

The Slums
Thomas Akare 1981
Rather rambling book set in the Nairobi slums, but which nonetheless does nothing to sentimentalize the reality of slum life.

Maasai Dreaming
Justin Cartwright 1993
A novel which juxtaposes a film-maker's view of Maasai-land with the Holocaust.

Moon
Jeremy Gavron 1997
A white boy growing up on a farm during the Emergency.

Alan Quartermain
H. Rider Haggard
The sequel to *King Solomon's Mines* in which the hero goes in search of a lost white race north of Mount Kenya.

Murder on Safari
Elspeth Huxley 1938
A detective story written around a big game safari which gives an accurate portrayal of the reality of such an event.

Flight to Juba – Short Stories
Sam Kahiga
Crazy and infuriating stories. Also *Lover in the Sky* (1975) and *When the Stars are Scattered* (1979).

Urban Obsessions, Urban Fears: the Postcolonial Kenyan Novel
J. Roger Kurtz 1999
An exploration between Kenyan fiction in English and of Nairobi. Plus a comprehensive bibliography of all Kenyan novels in English.

The Way to the Town Hall
Bramwell Lusweti 1984
A satire directed at small-town politicians and businessmen.

Master and Servant
David Mulwa 1987 (1979)
A novel which explores Kenyan society at the end of the colonial period through the eyes of an adolescent sent to a Dickensian type school by a cruel father. A good balance to the normal colonial literature from Kenya.

Going Down River Road
Meja Mwangi 1976
Other books by Mwangi who writes easy to read rather hip novels, include *Bread of Sorrow* (1987), *Cockroach Dance* (1979), *Weapon of Hunger* (1989) and *Striving for the Wind* (1992/1990)).

Something of Value
Robert Ruark 1955
Peter McKenzie grew up on his father's farm in Kenya. His closest friend and playmate was Kimani who later became a Mau Mau leader. Also *Uhuru* (1962).

Girls at Play
Paul Theroux 1983

Petals of Blood 1977
Secret Lives and Weep Not Child
(1964)
Ngugi Wa Thiong'o
Weep not Child was the first novel to be

68

published in English by an East African writer. It begins with the period just before the Emergency and rise of the Mau-Mau and continues through into the Emergency. *Petals of Blood* is a long and complex and much praised novel which is political, didactic and full of passion.

Come to Africa and Save Your Marriage

Maria Thomas 1995 (1989)
A collection of tales set in Kenya and Tanzania.

Food

More Specialties of the House from Kenya's Finest Restaurants

collected by Kathy Eldon 1989
Recipes from various hotels, restaurants and chefs in Kenya.

Kenya Traditional Dishes

A.B.N. Wandera 1983
A pamphlet of traditional Kenyan recipes.

Guides

Bradt: Kenya 2004

Insight: Kenya 1999

Lonely Planet: Kenya 2003

Rough Guide: Kenya 2002

History

When We Began, There Were Witchmen

Jeffery Fadiman 1993
An oral history from Mount Kenya.

White Mischief

James Fox 1988 (1982)
The 'Happy Valley' set in Kenya was thrown into confusion when Lord Erroll, founder of the set, was murdered in 1941. Much upper class decadence was revealed in the scandal that ensued, but the culprit was never found. James Fox

has written a social history/detective story which makes very exciting reading.

Mau Mau: An African Crucible

Robert B. Edgerton 1990 (1989)
An account based on the testimony of guerrillas.

The East African Coast

G.S.P. Freeman-Grenville 1975
A series of accounts from the first to nineteenth centuries.

Zanzibar Chest

Aidan Hartley 2003
Four generations of a British family's secrets & memoirs were discovered in the 'Zanzibar Chest' in Kenya.

The Hunt for Kimathi

Ian Henderson 1958
The author spoke Kikuyu fluently and writes very interestingly about the Mau Mau emergency. He was a Superintendent in the Special Branch.

A Modern History of Kenya

William R. Ochieng 1989
A very accessible book aimed at students which is based on lectures the author gave at Kenyatta University and UCLA. It goes from pre-history to the present and is well illustrated with maps and photographs. It was the first book to deal with the period.

Themes in Kenyan History

ed. William R. Ochieng 1990
Each chapter is about a theme in Kenyan history: migrations, population growth, food production, agriculture, pastoralism, urbanisation, industrialisation, religion, government and trade. The contributors all teach at Kenyan universities and create a good mix, as some are historians and others academics.

The Kenya Pioneers

Errol Trzebinski 1991 (1985)
Using letters, diaries and interviews, Trzebinski amasses an interesting record

of what it was like to be an early pioneer in Kenya. The life was exceptionally tough but as one settler said "Why should I retire to England? In this country I am somebody; in England I would only be a number on a door.". She has also written *The Life and Death of Lord Errol.*

Leisure Pursuits

Guide to Mount Kenya and Kilimanjaro
(ed.) Ian Allan 1991 (1959)
A guide for walkers and climbers published by the Mountain Club of Kenya. A convenient size with a large fold out map at the back.

Mountain Walking Kenya
David Else 1991 (1990)
Designed for the recreational walker as opposed to the serious climber, there is much practical information on the different walks and hikes as well as health and supplies. Maps and routes of the various treks are scattered throughout the book.

70

Natural History

Born Free
Joy Adamson 2000 (1960)
Joy Adamson rescued Elsa as an orphaned lion cub – the book of the story was an instant success and was made into a film starring Virginia McKenna and Bill Travers.

Birds of Kenya and Uganda
Frederick Jackson 1938 (3 vols.)
Frederick Jackson was Governor of Uganda from 1911-1917 and while he was there became an expert on the birds of the area.

The Beautiful Plants of Kenya
John Karmali 1988
A small book with many colour illustrations of plants and trees but with rather scanty text.

Elephant Memories
Cynthia Moss 2000 (1988)
The author is director of the Amboseli Elephant Research Project and has written this book of her experiences spanning the twenty years she has spent in Africa. The majesty of elephants and her love for them, shine through this book with its combination of personal experience and scientific material

Coming of Age with Elephants
Joyce Poole 1997 (1996)
A study of elephants in Amboseli.

Photographic

On God's Mountain
Mohamed Amin, Duncan Willetts and Brian Tetley 1991
A photographic history of the story of Mount Kenya which was once one of the world's highest mountains but which has now shrunk as a result of wind, sun and rain. It is now much climbed and this makes an interesting record for climbers and non-climbers alike. Also *Cradle of Mankind* (1989).

Maasai Mara
Karl Ammann 1990
A large format paperback with pictures of one Kenya's most famous game reserves. There are some wonderful close ups of animals in over two hundred pages of full colour; there is no text and minimal captions.

Kenya From the Air
Yann Arthus-Bertrand 1994

Maasai
photographs by Carol Beckwith; text by Tepilit Ole Saitoti 1991 (1980)
The author is a Maasai and in the text describes the ancient legends, songs, prayers and daily lives of his people. The text is accompanied by line drawings and beautifully descriptive photographs.

Vanishing Africa
Mirella Ricciardi 1984 (1971)
A stunning black and white photographic book showing the traditional customs of some of the Kenyan peoples which are fast disappearing making this an important historical document as well as a book which is visually pleasing.

Travel Literature

The Desert's Dusty Face
Charles Chenevix Trench 1964
A district commissioner's account of life with the Turkana just before independence; he writes about the problems on the borders with Ethiopia and Somalia as well as about the politics of Kenya at the time.

My African Journey
Winston Churchill 1990 (1908)
In 1907 Churchill made a tour of East Africa during the autumn recess. It remains readable as both a travel book and work of literature and shows extraordinary foresight.

Letters from Africa 1914-1931
Isak Dinesen 1981
These letters which were written to various members of her family during the time that she spent in Kenya portray the often very lonely life that Isak Dinesen led among the other European settlers

Shadows on the Grass
Isak Dinesen 1961 (1990)
Episodes of her life in Africa, written twenty five years later under the chapter headings of Farah, Barua and Soldani, the Great Gesture and Echoes from the Hills. These everyday incidents are an evocative portrayal of the life that she led.

I Dreamed of Africa
Kuki Gallmann 1992 (1991)
A book of tremendous courage and spirit which conveys a true love of Africa. The author has many tragedies in her life, but nevertheless manages to come through them and write about them upliftingly,

with her father's words helping her "The most important thing you can ever learn in life, Kuki, is to be able to be alone". She has set up a conservation project and does much work in helping to conserve the black rhinoceros. *African Nights* (1995) continues the story.

Journey to the Jade Sea
John Hillaby (see Ethiopia)

Travel and Missionary Labours in Africa
J. Ludwig Krapf 1968 (1860)
The first missionary to Mombasa.

The Frozen Leopard
Aaron Latham 1991
As much a search for himself as a straight travel book, Latham suffering from "the rainy season in the soul" travels through Kenya to Rwanda observing the wild life and trying to pull himself out of his depression. A fascinating odyssey which follows paths set by ancient man.

No Man's Land
George Monbiot 1994
A journey through Kenya and Tanzania which shows a shocking exposé of Maasai dispossession.

Another Land, Another Sea: Walking Round Lake Rudolph.
Stephen Pern 1979
Pern walked round the lake, now called Lake Turkana, with two companions and three donkeys. Lake Rudolph was the last of the great lakes of East Africa to be discovered in 1888 and Pern's journey contains elements of real adventure as well as good descriptions of the country he was passing through.

The Land of Zinj
C.H. Stigland 1912
An account of East Africa, its ancient history and present inhabitants.

71

*Through Maasailand: To the
Central African Lakes and Back*
Joseph Thomson 1968 (1885)

*A Small Town in Africa. Kenyan
Journal*
Daisy Waugh 1994
Daisy Waugh spends six months in a
remote and poor Kenyan town, Isiolo,
describing well the feelings of loneliness
and frustration as well as the happiness
she feels about being there.

SOMALIA

*British Somaliland is the only country I
know where you see camels walking in
the sky and goats climbing trees. This of
course, is the effect of the mirage, and
not the result of exposing your head to
the sun.* Geoffrey Harmsworth *Abyssinian
Adventure* 1935.

Autobiography/Biography

72 *Warriors. Life and Death among
the Somalis*
Gerald Hanley 1993 (1971)
Gerald Hanley spent several years in
Somalia where he got to know the local
people well: "Of all the races of Africa,
there cannot be one better to live among
than the most difficult, the proudest, the
bravest, the vainest, the most merciless,
the friendliest: the Somalis." The book
was originally published under the title
Warriors and Strangers.

Fiction

A Long Dry Season
Omar Eby 1988
Also *The Sons of Adam*. Eby was born in
the US, but spent four years teaching in
Africa.

From a Crooked Rib
Nuruddin Farah 1970
The first work of fiction to be published
by a Somali writer in English, the title is
from a Somali proverb "God created
woman from a crooked rib; and any one

who trieth to straighten it, breaketh". The
novel, set in pre-independence Italian
Somaliland is about a girl from the country who survives the transition to city life
by learning to cheat when she is cheated.
Also *Gifts and Sardines.*

Leopard Among the Women
Hassan Sheikh Mumin 1974
Mumin was born in the Borama District
in north-western Somalia, the son of a
local religious leader.

History

First Footsteps in East Africa
Richard F. Burton 1987 (1856)
The account of Burton's epic and brave
journey into the forbidden East African
Muslim city of Harar (in present day
Ethiopia) is an extraordinary story.
Burton spoke fluent Arabic and so was
able to enter the city disguised as an
Arab, becoming the first European to do
so without being executed. His observations about Muslim beliefs and customs
make this an invaluable historical document, but it is also a very readable book.

Stoics Without Pillows
John Drysdale 2000
An account of the history & traditions of
the Somali people.

Two Dianas in Somaliland
Agnes Herbert 1908
The record of a shooting trip. The author
was aware of the glut of 'hunting' books
being published, but she had decided to
write this one because 'simply - I want to
write'. She embarked on the four month
trip with a female cousin and had many
alarming adventures which she recounts
with a great sense of humour.

Natural History

Lone Dhow
Adrian Conan Doyle 1963
Conan Doyle was sent by the Natural
History Museum of Geneva to find an
adult tiger shark off the Somali coast. He

used a Somali crew and gives good descriptions of the Somali coastal area.

Somaliland
C.V.A. Peel (reprint 1986)
A study of the natural history of Somaliland by a Victorian writer, traveller and big-game hunter – with photographs.

Photographic
African Ark
Carol Beckwith and Angela Fisher
(see Djibouti)

Travel Literature
The Prophet's Camel Bell
Margaret Laurence 1963
The author's husband went to what was then the Somaliland Protectorate as an engineer to construct thirty earth dams over an area of 6500 miles. This involved a great deal of travel and Margaret Laurence wrote a perceptive account of their travels and life.

SUDAN

It has the intense virility of something newly born and its vibrant will to live derives from sound old roots. John Gunther *Inside Africa* 1955.

Autobiography/Biography
An Arab Tells His Story
Edward Atiyah 1946
Several chapters are devoted to the author's life and work in the Sudan; he has many interesting observations about Khartoum between the wars and his feelings towards the British are vividly portrayed.

The Camel's Back
Reginald Davies 1957
The author was in service for twelve years in rural Sudan at the beginning of the century. He writes about the people he encountered in his day to day life, as

he reckoned that there had been very little written about the Sudanese as individuals.

Traveller Extraordinary. The Life of James Bruce of Kinnaird.
J.M.Reid 1968
A biography of the Scottish explorer James Bruce (1730-94) who travelled in the Sudan at the end of the eighteenth century.

Fiction
The Songlines
Bruce Chatwin 1988
For part of the book Chatwin went to Sudan to expand his horizons where he meets someone who wants to convert him to Islam.

Their Finest Days
Sir Hassan El-Fadl 1969
Two long short stories; the first is based on the Sudanese revolution of 1964 when the military regime was overthrown, the second portrays the revolution through the eyes of a young partisan.

Season of Migration to the North
The Wedding of Zein
Tayeb Salih 1980 (1969)
Salih, a Sudanese, is one of the leading Arab writers of today who knows Europe well. In the first story a student returns to his village after having experienced 'the mysterious west', where he met women who were obsessed by 'the mysterious east'. In the second, a village buffoon marries a sought-after girl from a Sudanese village.

History and Politics
The Wind of Morning
Hugh Bousted 1974
Bousted was a soldier and administrator in the Sudan during the Condominium period at the turn of the century.

The River War. An Account of the Reconquest of the Soudan
Winston Churchill 1899
The Anglo-Egyptian conquest of the Sudan described here by Winston Churchill in his readable style.

The Journals of Gordon at Kartoum
C.G. Gordon 1984 (1885)
The journals record the day-to-day events during the final months of the siege of Khartoum.

A History of the Sudan
P.M. Holt & M.W.Daly 2000
The making of modern Sudan from the coming of Islam to the present day.

Behind the Red Line
Human Rights Watch 1996
Political repression in Sudan

The Blue Nile and The White Nile
Alan Moorehead (see Egypt, History)

74

Fire and Sword in the Sudan. A Personal Narrative of Fighting and Serving the Dervishes 1879-1895
Colonel Sir R. Slatin Pasha 1895
Slatin Pasha, an Austrian, having held high posts in the Sudan, was then held in captivity for many years. He was unable to take any notes during his imprisonment so he relied entirely on his memory to write this book which describes the events leading up to his captivity as well as his time as a prisoner.

My Sudan Year
E.S. Stevens 1985
An account of life in Sudan during the first decade of the twentieth century.

Natural History
The Cry of the Fish Eagle
Peter Molloy 1957
Most of the travelling that Peter Molloy did with his wife, in his capacity as Game Warden of the Southern Sudan, was on foot. His love of nature, skill as an observer and ability to communicate make this an unusually sympathetic book.

Elephantoms: Tracking the Elephant
Lyall Watson 2002
Watson saw his first elephant as a child and has retained a life-long fascination with them. The book is a meditation and evocation into their mystery.

Photographic
Last of the Nuba 1973 (1995)
People of Kau
Leni Riefenstahl 1978 (1976)
The Nuba of Kau live in South East Nuba. Riefenstahl focuses on what makes them different from other peoples in the area; they are a wild and passionate people and show this by the way they paint their faces and bodies and by the kind of dances they do. Riefenstahl spent about four months living with them gathering material for this book.

Village of the Nubas
George Rodger 1999 (1955)
Rodger's classic photographs with text.

Sudan
Nick Worrall 1980
A selection of colour photographs taken all over the Sudan.

Religion
Turabi's Revolution. Islam and Power in Sudan
El-Affendi 1991
An historical and political look at Islam in the Sudan.

Islam in the Sudan
J.Spencer Trimingham 1949
The classic book on Islam in the Sudan which aims to help those interested in the Sudanese to understand the significance of Islam in their lives. It gives a broad background on which to base a deeper

knowledge of the country through its religion.

Travel Literature

In Search of the Forty Days Road
Michael Asher 1986 (1984)
Michael Asher determined to follow an ancient trade route through the Sudan by camel. He encountered much danger and hardship, but it is the variety of people he met, who became his friends and that he felt it was a privilege to know that make this an interesting book.

Travels in Nubia
J.L.Burckhardt 1822
Burckhardt, who was Swiss, visited the Sudan in 1812-14 and wrote this account of his travels; it is still relevant today as his powers of observation were acute.

African Calliope
Edward Hoagland 1981 (1979)
The Sudan covers such a diverse range of territory and peoples: an Arab north, a black south, rain forests and desert. There are over one hundred and fifteen languages spoken across the country and it is this diversity which appealed to Edward Hoagland who specifically wrote this as a 'travel book, not a book of history'. However Hoagland weaves the richness of Sudanese history and culture into his narrative making this an ideal travel book.

Till the Sun Grows Cold
Maggie McCune 2000 (1999)
The very moving account about McCune's daughter Emma who fell in love with a Sudanese warlord and who eventually died in mysterious circumstances in Nairobi.

TANZANIA

How can one convey the power of Serengeti? It is an immense, limitless lawn, under a marquee of sky ... The light is dazzling, the air delectable Cyril Connolly *The Evening Colonnade* 1973

Anthropology

Being Maasai
eds. Thomas Spear and Richard Waller 1993 (see Kenya)

Biography

Stanley – the Making of an African Explorer
Frank McLynn 1989
The first of two volumes about Stanley ends with Stanley's arrival at Boma on the lower Congo in August 1977 after his epic journey down the uncharted Congo River. The second volume *Stanley: Sorcerer's Apprentice* (1991) begins with the arrival of food and an incongruous banquet laid out for him. It includes his second big expedition across Africa from West to East 1887-89.

Fiction

The Wicked Walk
W.E. Mkufya 1977
Set in contemporary Dar-es-Salaam, the novel deals with the themes of prostitution and corrupt management and the attempts to deal with them.

75

Three Solid Stones
Martha Mvungi 1975
Twelve oral tales from the traditions of the Wahehe and the Wabena which are recounted here in a simple and direct style.

Dying in the Sun
Peter K. Palangyo 1968
A son alienated from his father tries to piece together a new life after his father's death. Set in post-independence Tanzania, the novel is more about the universal suffering of man.

Village in Uhuru
Gabriel Ruhumbika 1969
The author was born in Tanzania. Uhuru (independence) comes to Tanganyika and this is the story of what that meant to the

people of an island village in a remote district.

The Gunny Sack
M.G. Vassanji 1989
Winner of the Commonwealth Writer's Prize. Also *Uhuru Street* and *The Book of Secrets.*

Guides

Bradt: Tanzania 2002

Cadogan: Tanzania & Zanzibar 2001

Insight: Tanzania & Zanzibar 2003

Lonely Planet:Tanzania 2002

Rough Guide: Tanzania 2003

History

Kilimanjaro and its People
Charles Dundas 1968 (1924)
A history of Wachagga – their laws, customs and legends with some account of Kilimanjaro.

Serengeti Shall Not Die
Bernard Grzimek 1965 (1959)
Dr Grzimek was a director of Frankfurt Zoo; he saw that if the Serengeti Reserve was to be saved, he had to know it properly so he bought a plane and learned to fly, with his son Michael, who was tragically killed in a plane accident in 1959.

A Modern History of Tanganyika
J.A. Iliffe 1979
A fully documented history of Tanganyika (mainland Tanzania); attention is paid to the consequences of small scale societies with their incorporation into the international order.

Natural History

In the Shadow of Man
Jane Goodall 1971
Account of the early years of her studies

with chimpanzees in Tanzania. Also the sequel *Through a Window – My Thirty Years with the Chimpanzees of Gombe* (1990).

Photographic

Journey Through Tanzania
Mohamed Amin, Duncan Willetts and Peter Marshall 1988 (1984)
Tanzania is the largest country in East Africa: it has the Indian Ocean, the natural beauty of Mount Kilimanjaro, Lake Tanganyika, Lake Victoria, the Serengeti and Ngorongoro. This book shows a cross section of all of these as well as the people and the way they live.

Maasai
photographs by Carol Beckwith; text by Tepilit Ole Saitoti. (see Kenya)

Serengeti
Mitsuaki Iwago 1987
Wonderful scenes and portraits from Serengeti.

Kilimanjaro
John Reader 1982
Large-format, well-illustrated book with lots of text about the author's 'discovery' of Kilimanjaro. Good on history.

Ngorongoro
Reinhard Künkel 1992.
A magnificently lavish photographic book.

Travel Literature

The Lake Regions of Central Africa: a picture of exploration.
Richard Burton 1961 (1860)
A description of Burton's journey with Speke in 1857-8 to Lake Tanganyika. He was an acute observer and writes in detail about the areas they crossed; since he was such an extraordinary linguist, he was able to record many of the conversations that he had with Arab traders.

Sand Rivers
Peter Matthiessen 1981

Filosofa's Republic
Thursday Msigwa (pseud. Anthony Daniels) 1992
Banned in Lambeth, Anthony Daniels only revealed that he is the author of this controversial book about Tanzania, after it was published. The book is written as if by a white visitor to Ngombia, a mythical republic, which has adopted Human Mutualism as its philosophy.

The Shadow of Kilimanjaro
Rick Ridgeway 1999 (1998)
A walk through the bush from Kilimanjaro to Mombasa.

Journal of the Discovery of the Source of the Nile
John Hanning Speke 1864
Speke played an important role in the British exploration of Tanganyika; he thought he had found the source of the Nile when he made his journey with Burton to Lake Victoria but the two men never agreed on the issue. Speke returned in 1860-2 to pursue the matter, following the Nile right up to the Mediterranean, but still failing to convince Burton. On the morning that Speke and Burton were going to debate the matter, Speke shot himself; it is not known whether this was suicide or an accident.

How I Found Livingstone
Henry Morton Stanley 1872
Stanley was given lavish support by his newspaper to find Livingstone in Central Africa in 1871-2. He set out from Zanzibar and crossed Tanganyika before encountering him and uttering the famous phrase "Dr Livingstone, I presume?"

Through the Dark Continent
Henry Morton Stanley 1878
This is the account of Stanley's second journey which began in 1874. He started in Zanzibar and crossed to Victoria Nyanza and into Uganda and to Lake

Tanganyika before going into Zaire. Stanley encountered Tippu Tip, an important Arab trader, who eventually wrote his autobiography in Swahili; as a result of this meeting much new information came out of the expedition.

UGANDA

But the forests of Uganda, for magnificence, for variety of form and colour, for profusion of brilliant life - plant, bird, insect, reptile, beast - for the vast scale and awful fecundity of the natural processes that are beheld at work, eclipsed, and indeed effaced, all previous impressions. Sir Winston Churchill *My African Journey* 1908.

Fiction
The Last King of Scotland
Giles Foden 1999 (1998)
A thriller recounting how a young Scottish doctor became Idi Amin's personal physician.

Abyssinian Chronicles
Moses Isegawa 2001 (2000)
Through the narrator, Mugezi, we witness the everyday richness, wildness and humour of Ugandan life.

The Sobbing Sounds
Omunjakko Nakibimbiri 1975
By an anonymous author.

Return to the Shadows
Robert Serumaga 1969
The idealistic Joe Musizi encounters many difficulties in the tough new world of independent Africa.

General Background
Changing Uganda
ed. by Holger Bernt Hansen & Michael Twaddle 1991
A series of articles by a team of Ugandan and international scholars which analyse the situation in Uganda today from many different angles.

77

Kalasanda
Barbara Kimenye 1965
A village in Buganda.

Fixions and Other Stories
Taban lo Liyong 1969
The author was born near the border of Uganda and Sudan and went to university in the US. *The Last Word* is a book of criticism.

In Search of Amin
Patrick Marnham
In *The Best of Granta Travel* (1991).

Guide
Bradt: Uganda 2003

Uganda Handbook 2002

History & Politics
The Albert N'yanza. Great Basin of the Nile and Explorations of the Nile Sources
Samuel White Baker 1866
An account of the equatorial lake system from which the Egyptian Nile derives its source. Baker discovered that the lake-sources of Central Africa support the life of Egypt by supplying a stream throughout the year, but that this source unaided could never overflow the banks of the Nile creating the fertile delta that it does.

Uganda
Harold Ingrams 1960
In a series called the 'Corona Library' the book contains descriptions of how the people live and the way they are governed and has many maps and photographs illustrating the text.

A Political History of Uganda
S. Karugire 1980
Readable and acutely observed with a chapter on pre-colonial events.

Uganda's Age of Reforms
J. Mugaju 1999 (1996)
A collection of essays dealing with the economic, political and social transformation of Uganda since 1986.

Uganda Since Independence
P. Mutibwa 1992
Good for an understanding of post-colonial politics.

Kakungulu and the Creation of Uganda
M Twaddle 1993
Concentrates on the build up to colonialism.

Natural History
Birds of Kenya and Uganda
Frederick Jackson 1938 (see Kenya)

Travel Literature
The White Nile
Alan Moorehead 1960 (see Africa general)

Touching the Moon
John Preston 1991 (1990)
Inspired by a childhood dream, John Preston went to Uganda to see the fabled Mountains of the Moon. Inevitably, in post-Idi Amin Uganda, what he found was incredible poverty and corruption not the romance he was looking for. However he manages to turn his experiences into an extremely funny and informative book.

Journal of the Discovery of the Source of the Nile
John Hanning Speke 1864 (see Tanzania)

Through the Dark Continent
Henry Morton Stanley 1878 (see Tanzania)

CENTRAL & SOUTHERN AFRICA

Art

Contested Images
eds. Thomas A. Dowson & David Lewis-Williams 1994
Diversity in Southern African rock art research.

Southern Africa During the Iron Age. Ancient Peoples and Places
Brian M. Fagan 1965
A book dealing with the last two thousand years of the prehistoric period in South Africa, when farmers and metalworkers first settled there. Descriptions of the Iron Age peoples of Rhodesia, South Africa and Zambia. When the book was written much of Southern Africa had not been explored by archaeologists or ethnohistorians making this a somewhat patchy appraisal. Illustrated throughout by line drawings.

Biography

Livingstone
Tim Jeal 2001 (1973)
Livingstone is considered one of the great explorers. Jeal explores the man behind the myth.

The Many Lives of Laurens van der Post Storyteller
J.D.F. Jones 2001
A controversial biography.

David Livingstone: The Dark Interior
Oliver Ransford 1978
A good read.

Fiction

She
H. Rider Haggard 1989 (1887)
Ayesha - 'She Who Must Be Obeyed' - is the white queen of a central African tribe.

Collected African Stories
Doris Lessing
Vol 1 *This Was the Old Chief's Country* 1992 (1951) and vol. 2 *The Sun Between Their Feet*. Doris Lessing was brought up in Southern Rhodesia and she writes her stories from childhood hand experience; many of them are set in Zimbabwe and South Africa. She writes in the preface that she really enjoyed writing the stories and that enjoyment shines through her prose.

A Bend in the River
V.S.Naipaul 1979
Salim, whose forebears had come to the east coast of Africa, is offered a business in central Africa, which he accepts realising that it is up to him to make what he can of his life. He travels to the town on a bend in the river and this is the story of his life as a trader in that town, a town which comes vividly alive in Naipaul's prose.

Penguin Book of Southern African Stories 1985
This diverse and varied anthology seeks to compare the different literatures of Southern Africa and includes stories from Botswana, Lesotho, Malawi, Namibia, South Africa, Swaziland and Zimbabwe.

General Background

The Siege States
Jan Morris
About South Africa and Rhodesia – in *Destinations* (1982)

Central and Southern Africa. Travel Resource Guide
Louis Taussig 1995

Guides

Bradt:East and Southern Africa: The Backpacker's Manual 2001

Bradt: Southern Africa by Rail 1998

Lonely Planet: Southern Africa 2003

History

The Remarkable Expedition
Olivia Manning 1947
When Emin Pasha arrived in Khartoum in 1875, he said he was a Turk, but he was soon found out to be a Prussian doctor named Schnitzer who spoke Arabic, Turkish, Albanian, French, Italian, Latin and Greek, who played good chess and excellent piano. He was disillusioned by his early life and eventually found his way to Central Africa. Olivia Manning tells his story and his rescue from Equatorial Africa by Stanley.

History of Central Africa
P. Tindall 1985
A book for schools.

Natural History

Field Guide to the Snakes and other Reptiles of Southern Africa
Bill Branch 1993
There are almost four hundred species of reptile in Southern Africa and this guide describes each, with a physical description, habitat and range and information about the biology and breeding habits. There are distribution maps and numerous colour plates. Comprehensive and useful.

Guide to the Sharks and Rays of Southern Africa
L.J.V. Compagno, D.A.Ebert and M.J. Smale 1989
The authors write reassuringly about the low instance of shark attacks, but when you see the immense variety of sharks and rays illustrated in this guide you would inevitably feel wary about venturing into the sea. However, an informative and useful book.

Lonely Planet Watching Wildlife Southern Africa 2001

Roberts' Birds of Southern Africa
Gordon Lindsay Maclean 1988
The standard and definitive work on the birds of Southern Africa, but too heavy to take on a trip.

Newman's Birds by Colour
Kenneth Newman 2000
Southern Africa's common birds arranged by colour.

A Field Guide to the Trees of Southern Africa
Eve Palmer 1977

Southern Africa Birds: A Photographic Guide
Ian Sinclair 1997 (1990)
A reliable guide.

Field Guide to the Mammals of Southern Africa
Chris and Tilde Stuart 1995
Colour photographs, identification pointers and detailed descriptions of each animal make this an extremely useful and easy to use handbook.

Photographic

Beyond the Endless Mopane
Chris Harvey 1997
A photographic safari through Livingstone's Africa.

Travel Literature

Explorations in South-West Africa
Thomas Baines 1864
Baines accompanied Livingstone on his travels.

Blood on the Tracks
Miles Bredin 1994
A rail journey from Angola to Mozambique.

Zanzibar to Timbuktu
Anthony Daniels (see West Africa)

Travels and Researches in Southern Africa
David Livingstone 1857
Fascinating to read such a classic.

The Ukimwi Road
Dervla Murphy 1993
Dervla Murphy made a 3000 mile bicycle journey from Kenya through Uganda, Tanzania, Malawi and Zambia to Zimbabwe. 'Ukimwi' of the title is AIDS and Dervla Murphy discussed the implications of this devastating disease almost everywhere she went; she also discovered that some communities in Africa are reverting to traditional ways of organising village life.

Congo Journey
Redmond O'Hanlon 1996
Travels through the jungles and swamps of the northern Congo by the author of *Into the Heart of Borneo*.

Journey to the Vanished City
Tudor Parfitt 1992
A fascinating journey in which Tudor Parfitt attempts to track down the origins of the Lemba tribe, who claim to be Jewish, and their lost city of Sena. His journey takes him through South Africa, Zimbabwe, Malawi and Tanzania. No one knows who were the architects and builders of Great Zimbabwe; interesting theories as to its origins abound and Parfitt adds others.

Travel and Adventure in South East Africa
Frederick Courtenay Selous 1984 (1893)
Selous was in Zimbabwe before, during and after colonisation. Also *African Nature Notes and Reminiscences.*

Through the Dark Continent
Henry M.Stanley 1988 (1878)
This was the expedition in which Stanley explored the great lakes of Central Africa, searched for the sources of the Nile and traced the unknown Congo River to the sea. His followers were decimated by disease but he persevered, being nicknamed Bula Matari 'the rock breaker'. The book is packed with exciting accounts of his exploits but also detailed descriptions of the people, flora and fauna that he encountered.

Following the Equator
Mark Twain 1990 (1897)
Twain started a lecture trip which took him round the world from Paris via America. He sails from Ceylon to Mauritius via Mozambique to South Africa. His funny and acute observations and anecdotes make you wish that he had written more about South Africa. He tells one story of a famous doctor in Cape Town who was wild but well respected and for some odd reason never got into trouble despite endlessly misbehaving. It was only on the doctor's death that it was discovered that he was a woman in exile from a scandal in England.

ANGOLA 81

The Countrie is Champain plaine, and drie blacke earth, and yeeldeth verie little Corne. Anthony Knivet, 1601, in *Purchas his Pilgrimes* 1625

Fiction
Creole
José Eduardo Agualusa 2002
A love story translated from the Portuguese.

South of Nowhere
Antonio Lobo Antunes 1983 (1979)
The narrator leaves Portugal for Angola on a ship full of troops and in the process 'becomes a man'. Good descriptions of the torpor, lassitude and heat felt in Africa.

A Lonely Devil
Sousa Jamba 1993
Jamba was born in Angola, left and returned to join UNITA. Also *Patriots* (1992).

Sacred Hope
Agostino Neto 1974
Neto was a medical doctor and writer who became the first president of Angola; his collection of poems which are very politically committed speak of love, harmony and freedom and the humiliations caused by colonialism.

Luuanda
José Vieira 1980
The author was born in Portugal and emigrated to Angola when he was three. He was imprisoned for disclosing secret army lists. Also *The Real Life of Domingos Xavier* (1978).

Travel Literature
Another Day of Life
Ryszard Kapucinski 1988 (1976)
Kapucinski went to Angola during the last months of Portuguese rule, when many internal factions were fighting for power and both South Africa and Cuba were involved in propping up their protegés. His observations of what he terms 'the incommunicable image of war' are as enlightening as it is possible to be about the evil of war.

BOTSWANA

The miraculous thing about the Kalahari is that it is a desert only in the sense that it contains no permanent surface water. Otherwise its deep fertile sands are covered with grass glistening in the wind like fields of gallant corn. Laurens van der Post *The Lost World of the Kalahari* 1958

Autobiography/Biography
Before the Knife
Carolyn Slaughter 2003 (2002)
In this autobiography the stark beauty of the Kalahari emerges through the horror of what happened.

Fiction
When Rain Clouds Gather 1995 (1968), Maru (1971), A Woman Alone (1990)
Bessie Head
Novels which examine the relationship between the Bushmen and the African villagers.

The Elephant's Child
Rudyard Kipling 1987 (1902)
From *Just So Stories.*

Whites
Norman Rush 1987
Short stories by a US Peace Corps worker about the lives of whites in Botswana.

Love on the Rocks
Andrew Sesinyi 1981
Pule Nkgogan is driven from home by family conflicts and tries to start a new life in the city, only to discover the difficulties of breaking with the past.

The Number 1 Ladies' Detective Agency
Alexander McCall Smith 2003 (1998)
The books about the detective agency set up by Precious Ramotswe have developed a cult following. Also *Tears of the Giraffe* (2000), *Morality for Beautiful Girls* (2001), *The Kalahari Typing School for Men* (2002) and *The Full Cupboard of Life* (2003).

A Story Like the Wind
Laurens van der Post 1987 (1972)
A bushman is rescued from a horrible death and life for Francois immediately changes dramatically as he meets and becomes friends with many new people; all this within the context of the African bush. A novel which highlights the conflicts between African and European cultures.

Food

Cooking in Botswana
Pauline Cuzen 1983
Recipes compiled by different people and brought up to date so that they can be made using current ingredients.

General Background

Images of Africa
Naomi Mitchison (1980)
Also *The Africans: A History* (1970) and *A Life for Africa: the Story of Bram Fisher* (1973).

Guides

Bradt: Botswana 2003

Lonely Planet: Botswana 2001

History

History of Botswana
T. Tlou and A. Campbell 1984
A school textbook, but about the only history available.

Photographic

Kalahari
Jacques Gilliéron 1989
Photographs of the animals and landscape of the Kalahari. Very little text.

The Bushmen
photographs by Peter Johnson & Anthony Bannister; text by Alf Wannenburgh 1979
A record of a fast disappearing group of hunter-gatherers who are inexorably being drawn into the big cities. The book begins with sixty pages of text and is followed by photographs.

Okavango. Africa's Last Eden
F. Lanting 1993
A large and colourful photographic book.

Okavango. Jewel of the Kalahari
Karen Ross 1992 (1987)
A book based on the three part television series which shows the mass of wildlife in the Okavango Delta; the fragile environment is fast disappearing and this book explains why.

Travel Literature

The Healing Land: A Kalahari Journey
Rupert Isaacson 2001
Part travel writing and part history of the Bushmen whose stories Isaacson had heard in his childhood.

Cry of the Kalahari
Mark and Delia Owens 1988 (1984)
In 1974 the authors sold everything they possessed in America in order to go and study wild-life in the Kalahari. They spent seven years living and researching there before returning to the States where they published scientific papers. This is the account of their everyday existence, which was often very hard, in the desert and among the animals.

The Lost World of the Kalahari
Laurens van der Post 1992 (1958)
The Bushmen had been driven by successive invaders of South Africa into the waterless Kalahari desert. Van der Post rediscovers the Bushmen with their cave art, music-making and hunting skills and records what he found of what is a fast disappearing culture. *The Heart of the Hunter* is a sequel and goes into much more detail about the life and lore of the Bushmen as well as much soul searching about how badly the Bushmen were treated. Also *The Voice of Thunder* (1993) and *Testament to the Bushmen* (with Jane Taylor 1984.)

83

BURUNDI

The Last Elephant. An African Quest
Jeremy Gavron 1993
There has been one solitary elephant left to wander round Burundi for the last several years. No one knows where it came from, but it is left alive since killing it

would be taboo; by killing the last of a species, an African would lose a fragment of his belief system. Only the first part of this book is about Burundi.

CENTRAL AFRICAN REPUBLIC

It was the only place in the world where I have seen almost the entire French community drunk at 10 o'clock in the morning (Bangui) Negley Farson *Behind God's Back* 1940

General Background
Central African Republic: The Continent's Hidden Heart
Thomas O'Toole 1986
The author spent a Fulbright Year at the University of Bangui. Useful but rather dry approach.

Travel Literature
Behind God's Back (see Africa general)
Negley Farson

Travels in the Congo
André Gide (see Chad)

CONGO

In the management of a bargain I should back the Congolese native against Jew or Christian, Parsee or Banyan, in all the round world. Henry Morton Stanley *The Congo* 1885

Fiction
The Catastrophist
Ronan Bennett 1999 (1998)
An Irishman, Gillespie goes to the Congo in pursuit of his beautiful Italian lover Inès.

Brazzaville Beach
William Boyd 1991 (1990)
A woman lives on a beach somewhere in post-colonial Africa.

The Poisonwood Bible
Barbara Kingsolver 1999 (1998)
The Congo seems to drive some white people mad - the Price family headed by Nathan, a Baptist preacher, go to live there in 1959. Things go horribly wrong for them as they have for so many. A family saga told through the eyes of the wife and four daughters of Nathan Price.

Myths and Legends of the Congo
collected Jan Knappert 1971

The Laughing Cry
Henri Lopes 1982
Lopes was born in Kinshasa and educated in Paris; he later became Prime Minister. The Laughing Cry is about an African tyrant. He also composed the Congolese National Anthem and wrote *Tribalques*.

History
The King Incorporated
Neal Ascherson 1999 (1963)
The causes of the failure of the Congo go back to the traumas inflicted by Leopold II, King of the Belgians.

Travel Literature
Corsairville
Graham Coster 2001 (2000)
How the Imperial Airways flying boat Corsair, which was rescued from the Belgian Congo over sixty years ago, gave its name to a village in Central Africa – Corsairville.

Travels in the Congo
André Gide 1986 (1927) (see Chad)

East Along the Equator
Helen Winternitz 1987
The author travelled east along the Congo river by boat to Kisangani in Zaire, before striking out over land through the

84

Ituri rain forest, visiting the Pygmies and travelling past the Mountains of the Moon and into the Great Rift Valley. She contrasts well the abundance of nature with the greed of mankind and her book contains politics, history and ecology.

DEMOCRATIC REPUBLIC OF CONGO

Anthropology

The Forest People
Colin Turnbull 1994 (1961)
The Bambuti, the pygmies, who live in the forest in north-east Zaire are an ancient people who were mentioned by both Homer and Aristotle. Turnbull spent a long time living in the forest with them writing this book for the lay reader as well as his more serious anthropological studies. Turnbull conveys the pygmies love of the forest as well as his intense love and friendship for them.

Fiction

Heart of Darkness
Joseph Conrad 1967 (1902)
Conrad went to the Belgian Congo in 1890 to command a river steamer, an event which physically weakened, but psychologically strengthened him. In Conrad's words "*Heart of Darkness* is experience, too; but it is experience pushed a little (and only very little) beyond the actual facts of the case for the perfectly legitimate, I believe, purpose of bringing it home to the minds and bosoms of the readers. There it was no longer a matter of sincere colouring. It was like another art altogether. That sombre theme had to be given a sinister resonance, a tonality of its own, a continued vibration that, I hoped, would hang in the air and dwell on the ear after the last note had been struck".

A Burnt Out Case
Graham Greene 1992 (1960)
Greene went to what was then the Belgian Congo with an idea for a novel in mind but on his return to England found the writing of *A Burnt Out Case* very depressing. Querry, a famous but disillusioned architect arrives at a leper colony and is diagnosed as the mental equivalent of a 'burnt out case'. However as he throws himself into work with the lepers he begins to get better, but then his identity is discovered by the white community. Full of thought provoking ideas.

Before the Birth of the Moon
V.Y. Mudimbe 1989
Psychological novels which reflect the social situation. Also *Between the Tides*.

General Background

The Return of Eva Peron
V.S.Naipaul 1988 (1980)
The last two essays in this book are called *A New King for the Congo: Mobutu and the Nihilism of Africa,* and *Conrad's Darkness.* Having examined Mobutu's society and the legacy left by colonialism, Naipaul reflects on Conrad's reactions to a similar society.

History

King Leopold's Ghost
Adam Hochschild 2000 (1999)
The harrowing story of King Leopold's ruin of the Congo, beautifully told.

Travel Literature

In Search of a Character
Graham Greene 2000 (1961)
Graham Greene's two African journals – *Congo Journey* and *Convoy to West Africa.*

Back to the Congo
Lieve Joris 1992 (1987)
The Amsterdam based author's uncle had been a missionary in the Belgian Congo. She was intrigued by his experiences and travels to Zaire: she visits his old mis-

85

sionary haunts and embarks on journeys of her own. Much has changed, but much, including the attitudes of many of the white colonials she encounters, has stayed the same.

A Congo Diary
V.S.Naipaul 1980
A well-observed short essay on the Congo, published in a limited edition.

In Southern Light
Alex Shoumatoff 1988 (1986)
The second half of Shoumatoff's book tells of his trek into the heart of the Ituri Forest where the Bambuti and Efe pygmies live.

Through the Dark Continent
Henry Morton Stanley 1878 (see Tanzania)

Facing the Congo
Jeffrey Tayler 2000
A reckless journey up the Congo River from Kinshasa towards Kisangani.

East Along the Equator
Helen Winternitz (see Congo)

LESOTHO

Basutholand is the Switzerland of South Africa, and very appropriately, is the part of South Africa where the old inhabitants, defended by their hills, have retained the largest measure of freedom. James Bryce *Impressions of South Africa* 1897

Fiction
Wrath of the Ancestors and other plays
Bob Leshoai 1972
The writer is believed to be his people's first writer in English. He has also published a collection of freely adapted traditional tales *Masilio's Adventures and Other Stories* (1968)

Chaka
Thomas Mofolo 1981
Mofolo was the first great fiction writer from Lesotho. About the Zulu king Shaka.

General Background
Basali 1995
Stories by and about women in Lesotho.

Guide
Lonely Planet: South Africa, Lesotho and Swaziland 2002

Rough Guide: South Africa, Lesotho & Swaziland 2002

History
A Short History of Lesotho
Stephen Gill 1993
Written by the Morija Museum's chief archivist – a well-informed history.

MALAWI
Autobiography/Biography
I Will Try
Legson Kayira 1967
The author walked 2500 miles across Africa in search of an American education, eventually ending up at the University of Washington.

Banda
Philip Short 1974
The latter years of Banda's presidency aren't covered – yet good on the early years.

Fiction
The Looming Shadow (1968), *The Detainee* (1974)
Legson Kayira.
A novel of village life and feuding and a novel about dictatorship.

Of Chameleons and Gods
Jack Mapanje 1981
A volume of poetry written by a Malawi prisoner-of-conscience during his 10 years spent in jail.

Jungle Lovers
Paul Theroux 1982 (1971)
A comedy about love and guerrilla war set in Malawi. Calvin Mullet of Homemakers International is taken prisoner by the ruthless Marais and inevitably his life gets intertwined with theirs. Also *My Secret History.*

General Background

Land of Fire: Oral Literature from Malawi
Matthew Schoffeleers & Adrian Roscoe 1985
Traditional Malawi beliefs.

Guides

Bradt: Malawi 2003

Malawi Handbook 1999

Lonely Planet: Malawi 2000

History

Livingstone's Lake
Oliver Ransford 1966
A general easy-to-read - but somewhat dated - background and history about the drama of Nyasa. Livingstone was the first to furnish an accurate account of Lake Nyasa. The author was Government Medical Officer in Angoni Highlands at Dedza.

Photographic

Malawi: Lake of Stars
Frank Johnston & Vera Garland
Good photographs – but only available in Malawi.

Travel Literature

Venture to the Interior
Laurens Van Der Post 1992 (1952)
After the war Van Der Post was sent by the British to what was then Nyasaland to explore the region around Mount Mlanje and the Nyika plateau area to obtain information about these remote areas. As in his later books he is introspective and questions his own motives for wanting to go; this inner journeying is accompanied by interesting descriptions of what he sees. The book starts with a quote by Sir Thomas Browne "We carry with us the wonders we seek without us: there is all Africa and her prodigies in us".

MOZAMBIQUE

Mozambique is a curious mixture - Shangri La with a bullwhip behind the door. John Gunther *Inside Africa* 1955

Fiction

The Returning Hunter
Mario J. Azevedo 1978
The author was born in Mozambique and set his novella there. Bento, a Portuguese African has his confidence in his colonial government shattered.

General Background

Assignments in Africa
Per Wästberg 1986
The Swedish writer and journalist talked to Mozambique's leading poet.

Guides

Bradt: Mozambique 2002

Globetrotter Mozambique 2001

Lonely Planet: Mozambique 2003

Vacation Work: Travellers Survival Kit Mozambique 1999

87

Natural History
A Natural History of Inhaca Island
ed. Margaret Kalk 1995 (1958)
Inhaca Island is off the southern coast of Mozambique. Many line drawings and colour illustrations.

Politics
Mozambique: São Tomé and Principe
Jens Erik Torp and L.M.Denny and Donald I. Ray 1989
There is so little on Mozambique that this has been included; a book which is in the Marxist Regimes series of politics, economics and society; it is a serious introduction to the country by people who know the areas well.

Travel Literature
Kalashnikovs and Zombie Cucumbers
Nick Middleton 1994
Two trips to Mozambique, before and after the peace accord in 1992.

88

NAMIBIA

This hilly capital [Windhoek] is God's gift to the picture postcard industry. Its sky is just that incredible blue. Negley Farson *Behind God's Back* 1940

Fiction
Born of the Sun
Joseph Diescho 1988
Diescho was born into a poor family in the north of Namibia – the novel is autobiographical.

Guides
Bradt: Namibia 2003

Footprint: Namibia 2001

Insight Guide: Namibia 2001

Lonely Planet: Namibia 2002

Rough Guide: Namibia 2004

History
The Devils are Among Us
Denis Herbstein and John Evenson 1989
The story behind the eventual South African withdrawal from Namibia. The book exposes the brutality of the occupation and the extraordinary resistance of the Namibian people to the occupying army.

Photographic
Namib
David Coulson 1991
A wonderful record of Namibia's wilderness.

Journey Through Namibia
Tahir Shah & Mohamed Amin 1994

Travel Literature
The Skeleton Coast
Benedict Allen 1997
A journey through the Namib desert.

Lake Ngami
Charles John Andersson 1850s
This and *The River Okavango* are a record of Namibia in the 1850s through the eyes of traders and hunters.

Sheltering Desert
Henno Martin 1957
The story of two German geologists who hid in the Kuiseb Canyon in World War II.

Lost World of the Kalahari (see Botswana)
Laurens Van der Post

RWANDA

Anthropology

The Dark Romance of Dian Fossey
Harold Hayes 1992 (1990)
Hayes gets to the core of what Dian Fossey was really like. He describes her early life in Kentucky and her turbulent love life as well as her work with the gorillas. The film *Gorillas in the Mist* was largely based on Hayes' article published in Life magazine, but in this book he has uncovered much more material.

Woman in the Mists
Farley Mowat 1987
Fossey's own journals are widely used in this biography.

Fiction

A Sunday at the Pool in Kigali
Gil Courtemanche 2003
A novel set around a hotel in Kigali - a magnet for the Kigali residents during the Rwanda genocide.

General Background

We Wish to Inform You that Tomorrow we will be Killed With Our Families
Philip Gourevitch 2000 (1998)
Compelling journalism and stories about the Rwandan genocide.

Land of a Thousand Hills
R. Halsey Carr & A.H. Howard Halsey 1999
Rosamond Halsey Carr, newly married, moved to Rwanda in 1949 and stayed for fifty years. She was evacuated during the genocide but returned after four months opening a home for genocide orphans.

The Soccer War
Ryszard Kapucinski 1990
Kapucinski was held prisoner at Bujumbura airport in Burundi.

Guide
Bradt: Rwanda 2001

History

History of a Genocide
Gerard Prunier 1998 (1995)
Prunier believes that the genocide in Rwanda is on a par with the Nazi holocaust. The author is an African scholar, journalist and French political analyst who believes the genocide was part of a deadly logic. Also *From Genocide to Continental War* (2002).

Travel Literature

Gorillas in the Mist
Dian Fossey 1983
Readable and informative and invaluable for anyone gorilla tracking in the Parc Des Volcans.

Season of Blood – a Rwandan Journey
Fergal Keane 1995
Beautifully written prose – part narrative and analysis combined with spontaneous emotion.

The Frozen Leopard
Aaron Latham (see Kenya)

Visiting Rwanda
Dervla Murphy 1998
Much more than a travel book - Murphy had intended to trek in the mountains, but after being warned of the dangers, she spent her time talking to local people.

SOUTH AFRICA

The light in South Africa ... replaces architecture. Cyril Connolly *The Evening Colonnade* 1973

Autobiography/ Biography

Nelson Mandela
Mary Benson 1994
The man and the movement.

True Confessions of an Albino Terrorist
Breyten Breytenbach 1984
The author returned to South Africa in 1975 and was immediately arrested and jailed for seven years.

Trevor Huddleston. A Life
Robin Denniston 2000 (1999)
Huddleston worked among the urban blacks in Johannesburg in the 1950s and later founded the Anti-Apartheid Movement.

White Boy Running
Christopher Hope 1991 (1988)
Christopher Hope returned to his native South Africa in 1987 to cover the May election. He tried to make sense of what he saw but the more he saw the more nonsensical it all seemed; he traces his childhood and describes the South Africa of the 1950s and using straight reporting writes about the madness of the modern South Africa which he found in the 1980s

Let My People Go
Albert Luthuli 1962
The memoirs of the former leader of the ANC explains the struggle for majority rule compellingly.

My Traitor's Heart
Rian Malan 1990
An extraordinarily powerful book about the reality of being brought up in South Africa. Malan left South Africa for America, but returned after eight years to face up to what he had left. He is extremely tough on his conscience and on himself with the result that he has produced an honest, moving and instructive book. "I'm bored with the torrent of travel books about gimmicky journeys, and much prefer to read a book that attempts to get into the heart of a place. Such a book is *My Traitor's Heart* - brilliantly paced, beautifully written, and a revelation about both black and white South Africa" (John Hatt).

Long Walk to Freedom
Nelson Mandela 1995
Mandela's autobiography. Very evocative about his early years and moving about his many years in prison.

Down Second Avenue
Es'kia Mphahalele 1959
The archetypal black male autobiography of the time.

Island in Chains
Indres Naidoo 1982
His years on Robben Island.

The Seed is Mine
Charles van Onselen 1996
Life of Kas Maine – a South African share-cropper 1894-1985. The book concerns the disenfranchised blacks who shaped the destiny of South Africa.

Journey Continued
Alan Paton 1989 (1988)
This volume of autobiography begins in 1948, the year that *Cry the Beloved Country* (q.v.) was published. Paton died before it was published but he writes about literature and politics, both of which played such an important part in his life, in a direct and simple style which shows a deep understanding of South Africa.

Cecil Rhodes
William Plomer 1984 (1933)
A critical account which portrays Rhodes as immature.

Jail Diary
Albie Sachs 1966
Records his detention without trial. Also *The Soft Vengeance of a Freedom Fighter* written when he was in exile in Mozambique.

Mandela
Anthony Sampson 2000 (1999)
The authorised biography of this extraordinary man.

Rhodes. The Race for Africa
Antony Thomas 1966
At the centre of this biography is the story of Britain's race for Africa.

Yet Being Someone Other
Laurens van der Post 1984 (1982)
Episodes of autobiography.

The Long Way Home
Annmarie Wolpe 1994
The author's husband was arrested in 1963. He escaped from prison and fled to England where he was joined by his family. They returned to South Africa in 1991.

Fiction

Mine Boy
Peter Abrahams 1989 (1946)
One of the first novels to show the condition of black South Africans under a white regime. Also *The Path to Thunder* (1948) *A Night of Their Own* (1965) and *Tell Freedom* (1978).

The Smell of Apples
Mark Behr 1996 (1995)
A small white boy grows up in a military family under apartheid.

A Bekkersdal Marathon
Herman Charles Bosman 1971
Wry and amusing short stories about Afrikaner life in the then Western Transvaal where he was a teacher in 1925.

A Dry White Season 1989 (1979)
Rumours of Rain 1984 (1978) *An Instant in the Wind* (1976) and *On the Contrary* (1993)
Andre Brink
Andre Brink was born in South Africa and now teaches modern literature and drama at Rhodes University. His novels are all set in South Africa and he uses real events making his fiction seem very true to life. Also *A Chain of Voices* about 18th-century Cape life.

Prester John
John Buchan 1956
Set at the turn of the 20th century – Crawfurd is sent to work as a storekeeper in South Africa because of his father's death. On the voyage from Scotland he encounters the Zulu minister John Laputa.

In the Heart of the Country
J.M. Coetzee 1982 (1977)
A powerful novel set on a farm in South Africa. *Waiting for the Barbarians* (1980) is allegorical, and *Disgrace* (winner of the 1999 Booker prize) is an extraordinarily powerful novel which captures the white dilemma in South Africa. His first novel was *Dusklands* (1974); *Age of Iron* (1990) is deemed by some to be one of the finest South African novels of the last ten years.

Elegy for a Revolutionary
Jonty Driver 1969
Written during the years of repression.

Ladysmith
Giles Foden 1999
A novel set in 1899 when Boer forces have surrounded the small South African town of Ladysmith.

Occasion for Loving
Nadine Gordimer 1994 (1963)
Set against a background of South Africa in the 1960s. Also among others *The Lying Days* (1953) which explores the growing political awareness of the lead character, *The House Gun* (1999), *Burger's Daughter* (1981) and *July's People* (1991) set in post-revolutionary South Africa.

King Solomon's Mines
H. Rider Haggard 1989 (1885)
The adventures of Allan Quartermain, Sir Henry Curtis and Captain John Good who go in search of Sir Henry Curtis's younger brother who was searching for King Solomon's mines.

91

The Cardinals
Bessie Head 1993
An exploration of apartheid; one of the few books published by a black woman journalist who turned to fiction.

The Trap and A Dance in the Sun
Dan Jacobson 1988 (1955)
Although these novels were written in the 1950's, they are as relevant today as they were then; Jacobson was inspired by the bleak and forlorn landscapes around his home town of Kimberley in the Northern Cape and uses this setting to describe the issues between blacks and whites living uneasily together.

Love Themes for the Wilderness
Ashraf Jamal 1996
One of the first magical realism novels from South Africa.

The Heart in Exile
eds. Leon de Kock & Ian Tromp 1996
South African poetry in English 1990-1995.

The Devil's Chimney
Anne Landsman 1999
Two women each trying to take control of their lives in the days of the ostrich-feather boom.

Call Me Not a Man
Mtutuzeli Matshoba 1987 (1979)
A collection of short stories.

The Party is Over
James Matthews 1997
An autobiographical novel which recounts the frustrations of a black writer in a white-dominated world of arts and letters.

Ways of Dying
Zakes Mda 1997
The story of a professional mourner. Magical and funny.

92

God's Stepchildren
Sarah Gertrude Millin 1924
Shows the stark contrast between Europe and Africa. Her notion was about 'good' and 'bad' blood.

Triomf
Marlene van Niekerk 2000 (1999)
An Afrikaans novel about a family of poor whites living in the Johannesburg suburb of Triomf.

Cry, The Beloved Country
Alan Paton 1988(1948)
Even today this book remains one of the classics to be written about racial tension in South Africa. In Johannesburg a father looking for his delinquent son encounters the worlds of murder, prostitution, racial hatred and eventually reconciliation. The simplicity and compassion of the prose make it an extremely moving book. Also Too Late the Phalarope (1953).

Sol Plaatje. Selected Writings
ed. Brian Willan 1996
Plaatje was a founder member of the ANC. He also wrote Mhudi (1930) the story of an African society in transition and Native Life in South Africa (1916) which deals with the terrible effect on Africans of the 1913 Land Act.

Turbott Wolfe
William Plomer 1985 (1925)
A novel which is a record of the struggles of the few against the forces of prejudice and fear. When it was published it was a landmark in both English and South African literature.

Iron Love
Marguerite Poland 2000 (1999)
A novel set in 1913 in a boy's school in South Africa.

Mittee
Daphne Rooke 1991 (1951)
A best seller when it was published, this novel set in late nineteenth-century Transvaal describes the intense love-hate

relationship between Selina, a young servant girl and Mittee her mistress who both vie for the love of the same man.

The Story of an African Farm
Olive Schreiner 1883
Regarded as the first novel set in South Africa, It was published under a male *nom de plume.*

The Betrayal
Gillian Slovo 1992 (1991)
A political thriller set in the secret world of ANC activists where loyalty is the code. The story of Alan, a white ANC member who is suspected of betrayal.

The Beadle
Pauline Smith 1926
Also *The Little Karr* (1925) – books which foster the myth of the Boer as a landless and culturally oppressed victim.

The Stooping of Aquila
Tony Spencer-Smith 1999
An erotic thriller set in Cape Town which focuses on environmental issues.

Trekking to Teema
Pieter-Dirk Uys 2001
The story of a South African man who returns home to find his nanny Fatima.

Flamingo Feather
Laurens Van der Post 1992 (1955)
A story of international intrigue about how a rich white South African foils a Soviet plot to flame a co-ordinated tribal revolution.

In a Province
Laurens van der Post 1984 (1934)
His first novel written with fire and fury but tempered by wisdom and human understanding.

Missing Persons
Ivan Vladislavic 1989
A collection of short stories which give a good insight into the troubled psyche of white South African males. Also *The*

Folly (1993) and *Propaganda by Monuments and Other Stories* (1996).

General Background

Zulu Thought Patterns and Symbolism
Axel-Ivar Berglund 1976
An account of rural Zulu world views.

I Write What I Like
Steve Biko 1978
A collection of non-fiction written between 1969-72.

Return to Paradise
Breyten Breytenbach 1993
The author's latest exploration of his African and South African identity.

Naught for Your Comfort
Father Trevor Huddleston 1971 (1956)
A description of his 12 year ministry in Sophiatown, outside Johannesburg, between 1944-56. He later became Bishop of Stepney.

Drum: An African Adventure and Afterwards
Anthony Sampson 1994 (1956)
Sophiatown in Johannesburg was the last area where Africans had freehold property rights. The 'Drum' generation wrote about it.

A Snake with Ice Water
Barbara Schreiner 1992
A collection of interviews, stories and poems by women about their prison experiences.

Living and Working in South Africa
Matthew Seal 2000

Feather Fall
Laurens van der Post 1995
A collection of Van der Post's writings which includes two chapters on Africa - edited by Jean-Marc Pottiez.

93

A Walk With a White Bushman
Laurens van der Post 1988 (1986)
A mixture of Van der Post's thoughts, philosophy and in part biography.

Guides

Bradt: South Africa 2001

Culture Shock South Africa 1999

Eyewitness: South Africa 2003

South Africa Handbook 2002

Insight Guide South Africa 2003

Lonely Planet: South Africa, Lesotho and Swaziland 2002

Rough Guide: South Africa, Lesotho & Swaziland 2002

History

Twentieth Century South Africa
William Beinart 1994
The emphasis is on economic history but it manages not to get tedious.

Hidden Lives, Hidden Deaths
Victoria Brittain 1990 (1988)
The author has travelled as a journalist over much of Africa; in this book she exposes the reality of how the South African government really behaves and how so much of what it does is covered up by the United States and Britain.

The Kruger National Park: A Social and Political History
Jane Carruthers 1995
An examination of the broad issues of nature and conservation approached through the Kruger National Park.

Born in Soweto
Heidi Holland 1994
Inside the heart of South Africa.

The Politics of Race, Class and Nationalism in 20th century South Africa
eds. Shula Marks and Stanley Trapido 1987
A left-leaning collection of essays.

The Washing of the Spears
Donald Morris 1994 (1966)
Described by Colin Legum in New Society as 'enormously readable and tremendously exciting', *The Washing of the Spears* describes how Zulu power rose and fell in a period of just fifty years. "But my own favourite book about the place is Donald Morris' *The Washing of the Spears*, about the Zulu Wars." (Jeremy Paxman)

The Boer War
Thomas Pakenham 1995 (1979)
A well-researched full-scale history of the Boer War.

Shaka Zulu
E.A.Ritter 1992 (1955)
Shaka Zulu who founded the Zulu nation was a contemporary of Napoleon; within the space of twelve years he organised an army and conquered an area larger than Europe. His exploits had been handed down by word of mouth, but are recorded here by an author who grew up with the Zulus and gained their trust and respect.

A Concise History of South Africa
Robert Ross 1999
An ideal introduction to the history of South Africa.

The Mind of South Africa
Alistair Sparks 1991 (1990)
The author was formerly editor of the Rand Daily Mail and in this book surveys the rise and fall of apartheid. He analyses the history, culture and warped mythology of apartheid and the reasons why it still has such a powerful hold. "The best shortish and easily comprehensible history of that country." (Jeremy Paxman)

A History of South Africa
Leonard Thompson 1996
A new and fresh look at South African history written by an eminent professor at Yale; it is objective and focuses primarily on the black majority rather than the white minorities. Authoritative and full of insight.

White Tribe Dreaming
Marq de Villiers 1990 (1987)
The history of South Africa traced through the author's Afrikaner ancestors and family who arrived in South Africa in 1688. It is a compassionate and illuminating attempt by a white liberal to understand the roots of apartheid; the book won the Alan Paton prize.

A History of South Africa
Frank Welsh 2000 (1998)
A remarkable and readable history.

Leisure
Best Walks in the Cape Peninsula
Mike Lundy 1995
Well-researched guide.

The Wines of South Africa
James Seely 1997
Arranged region by region with tasting notes.

Natural History
Kruger National Park
L.E.O. Braack 1996
The Kruger National Park

Jock of the Bushveld
Sir Percy Fitzpatrick 1925 (1907)
Life could be very lonely in the South African Bush at the turn of the century; one way of dealing with this loneliness was to have a dog. In this case 'Jock' became the narrator's best friend and his exploits are recounted here in a lively way. The original illustrations were by E.Caldwell.

Kwazulu/Natal Wildlife Destinations
Tony Pooley & Ian Player 1995

South African Eden. The Kruger National Park
James Stevenson-Hamilton 1993 (1937)
The story of the founding of the Kruger National Park, told by the man who was its first warden.

Marine Shells of South Africa
Douw Steyn and Markus Lussi
Full colour photographs of all the shells which occur along the coast of South Africa.

Field Guide to the Wild Flowers of the Witwatersrand and Pretoria Region
Braam van Wyk and Sasa Malan 1988
The 763 species in the guide are divided into colour groups and within the colour groups into families. Each species is illustrated by a colour photograph and line drawings of the leaves accompany the concise text. A glossary to the terms used and indexes to both the scientific names and Afrikaans names complete this useful guide.

Photographic
This Is South Africa
Peter Borchert 1993
An illustrated book covering some of the scenery and natural history of South Africa.

South Africa in Focus
ed. Willem Drechsel 1993
A well illustrated book full of text, accompanied by small photographs, showing the many faces of South Africa.

95

Travel Literature

Alone Among the Zulus
Catherine Barter 1995
Written in 1855, Catherine Barter was the first woman to write about the Zulu kingdom.

Somewhere Over the Rainbow
Gavin Bell 2001 (2000)
As a foreign correspondent Bell had reported on the last days of apartheid. He returns to find out what has happened.

Impressions of South Africa
James Bryce 1897
Bryce travelled from Cape Town to Fort Salisbury in Mashonaland in 1895. The book is not a narration of his journey but is divided into various sections: the physical character of the country, the characteristics of the people, the history of the natives and of the European settlers, the present conditions and the economic resources.

96

Diary of an African Journey
H. Rider Haggard 2001 (1914)
Rider Haggard returned to South Africa in 1914 for the first time in over 20 years.

The Electric Elephant
Dan Jacobson 1994
The author, who had left South Africa in the 1950s returned in 1994 and travelled from Kimberley to Victoria Falls.

South from the Limpopo: Travel Through South Africa
Dervla Murphy 1998 (1997)
One of Murphy's classic bike journeys.

Innocents in Africa
Drury Pifer 1994
The author's father, a young, idealistic newly-married mining engineer went to South Africa in the 1930s. He was soon caught between the hostility of the Afrikaners and the arrogance of the British, and the new 'apartheid', however he persisted and brought up his family there.

SWAZILAND

In all Africa there is no more vividly African place than Swaziland. James Morris *Swaziland Places* 1972

Fiction

Tell Me No More
Senzenjani Lukhele 1982
The story of a court case and the family problems that ensue because of Gugu interfering in a village affair and subsequently being banished by her adoptive father.

Guide

Lonely Planet: South Africa, Lesotho & Swaziland 2002

Rough Guide: South Africa, Lesotho & Swaziland 2002

History

Kings, Commoners and Concessionaries
Philip Bonner 1983 (1982)
The (to date) definitive history of Swaziland.

The Swazi, A South African Kingdom
Hilda Kuper 1986 (1952)
A mixture of anthropology and history.

ZAMBIA

The capital, Lusaka, looks like a Wild West set in early, shabby movies. John Gunther *Inside Africa* 1955

Fiction

The Tongue of the Dumb
Dominic Mulaisho 1971
A symbolic novel about the struggles by the new elite against the traditional powers of the chiefs, written from a very Westernised viewpoint. In his second novel *The Smoke That Thunders* (1979),

the author had become economic advisor to President Kaunda and he sets the book in a mythical country between Rhodesia and Zambia.

General Background

Tales of Zambia
Dick Hobson 1990
Sections on mining, legends and the country's flora and fauna. Very readable.

Guides

Bradt: Zambia 2004

Lonely Planet: Zambia 2002

History

The Africa House
Christina Lamb 2000 (1999)
The story of Stewart Gore-Browne who built himself a feudal paradise in what was Northern Rhodesia during the British Empire.

A History of Zambia
Andrew Roberts 1976
From pre-history to 1974.

Natural History

A Guide to the Wildlife of the Luangwa Valley
Norman Carr 1997 (1985)
Written by the area's most famous guide.

Survivor's Song
Delia and Mark Owens 1993 (1992)
The authors were expelled from Botswana after writing *Cry of the Kalahari*. They went to the North Luangwa Valley in Zambia where they discovered that the locals lived by poaching elephants. This is their account of how they tried to change the villager's attitude to poaching.

Photographic

Zambia
photographs Ian Murphy ed. Richard Vaughan nd.
A cross section of the whole country showing as many urban scenes as rural ones; the photographs were taken over a four year period by Ian Murphy who travelled the length and breadth of the country. So little has been written about Zambia that the text in this book is important as reference

Travel Literature

Kakuli: A Story about Wild Animals
Norman Carr 1996
A collection of tales from the time the author spent in the Luangwa Valley.

Pole to Pole
Michael Palin 1999
A very good section on Zambia, visited by Palin on one of his epic journeys.

97

ZIMBABWE

Art & Archaeology

Zimbabwean Stone Sculpture
M. Arnold 1981
A thorough but not very well-illustrated book.

The Painted Caves
Peter Garlake 1987
An illustrated look at San rock art in Zimbabwe. And *The Hunter's Vision* (1995) – a new interpretation of Southern African rock art.

Shona Sculpture
F. Mor 1987
Good colour photography.

Autobiography/Biography

Mukiwa
Peter Godwin 1997 (1996)
Godwin grew up in Rhodesia in the

1960s and returned to Zimbabwe as an adult.

Under My Skin
Doris Lessing 1994
The first volume of her autobiography which goes up to the year 1949.

Cecil Rhodes
William Plomer 1984 (see South Africa)

Fiction

Nervous Conditions
Tsitsi Dangarembga 1988
About growing up in colonial Rhodesia.

African Ark
Leonard Ashford Hughes 1995
A novel set in Zimbabwe.

Bones
Chenjerai Hove 1991
Experiences of the war; also by Hove is *Shadows,* a story of lovers who choose death, and *Red Hills of Home.*

A Son of the Soil
Wilson Katiyo 1989 (1976)
A first novel which tells of the stresses and struggles of growing up in colonial Zimbabwe.

The Grass is Singing
Doris Lessing 1973
A depiction of white Rhodesia with powerful descriptions of the physical landscape. Also *This Was the Old Chief's Country* – a collection of short stories.

Zenzele. A Letter for My Daughter
Nozipo Maraire 1996
A letter written to her daughter who is leaving Zimbabwe for the first time to go to university overseas.

The House of Hunger
Dambudzo Marechera 1978
This collection of short stories won the

1979 Guardian Fiction Prize. Angela Carter wrote: "But it is rare to find a writer for whom imaginative fiction is such a passionate and intimate process of engagement with the world". Also *The Black Insider* (1992), *Black Sunlight* (1980) and *Mindblast* (1984).

The Coming of the Dry Season
Charles Mungoshi 1982
His first collection of short stories. Also *One Day Long Ago* (1991) and *Waiting for Rain* (1975)

The Mourned One (1975), Year of the Uprising (1978)
Stanlake Samkange
History and fiction are melded together. *Year of the Uprising* is set in 1896, the time of the uprising between the Matabele and the Mashona. *The Mourned One* is the narrative written by 'Ocky' (Muchemwa) looking back over his life while awaiting execution in a Salisbury jail in the 1930's.

Food

A Zimbabwean Cookery Book
ed. by Yvonne Hayward 1984 (1967)
A collection of eighty-seven recipes.

General Background

African Laughter
Doris Lessing 1993 (1992)
Doris Lessing visited Zimbabwe four times between 1982 and 1992 and interviewed many people, some of whom had recently returned disillusioned from South Africa. An excellent introduction to the country.

Guides

Lonely Planet: Zimbabwe 2002

Zimbabwe Handbook 1999

Rough Guide: Zimbabwe 2000
Includes Okavango Delta & Chobe National Park

History

Zimbabwe: A New History for Primary Schools
David Beach 1986 (1982)
A readable history spanning 15,000 years. Also *The Shona and Zimbabwe 900-1850: An Outline of Shona History* (1980) and *War and Politics in Zimbabwe 1840-1900* (1986).

None But Ourselves. Masses vs. Media in the Making of Zimbabwe
Julie Frederikse 1988
Interviews, quotes and photographs from the media.

Guns and Rain: Guerrillas & Spirit Mediums in Zimbabwe
David Lan 1985
The book demonstrates how important spirit mediums are in fostering the liberation struggle in the remote Dande region along the eastern Zambezi river.

Voices from the Rocks: Nature, Culture and History in the Matopos
Terence Ranger 1999
The history of the Matopos Hills where Cecil Rhodes is buried.

Photographic

Journey Through Zimbabwe
Mohamed Amin, Duncan Willetts and Brian Tetley 1990
Over one hundred and fifty colour photographs of the wilderness and the animals that inhabit it, Lake Kariba (at 280 kilometres long the largest manmade lake), flora, botanical parks and the cities. Ample text accompanies the glossy pictures.

Zimbabwe
photographs by Ian Murphy; text Richard Vaughan 1991
The book covers every aspect of life in Zimbabwe. Scenes of wildlife and scenery are of course included but there is a great emphasis on showing how the country works, by including many photographs of people and their work. This makes it a much more interesting than most other 'coffee table' books.

Travel Literature

Songs to an African Sunset
Sekai Nzenza-Shand 1997
Personal stories intertwined with a picture of contemporary Zimbabwe.

A Tourist in Africa
Evelyn Waugh (see East Africa)

AFRICAN ISLANDS
General
Pirates of the Eastern Seas 1618-1723
Charles Gray 1971 (1933)
Piracy in the Indian Ocean was rife at this period; crews of pirates from Réunion, the Comoro Islands, Mauritius and Madagascar preyed on ships which were engaged in trade with India and the spice-producing islands of South Asia.

Empires of the Monsoon – A History of the Indian Ocean and its Invaders
Richard Hall 1998
The exploration and exploitation of the Indian ocean.

Hunting Pirate Heaven
Kevin Rushby 2002 (2001)
A search for the lost pirate settlements that once existed on the islands and atolls of the Indian Ocean.

Natural History
Birds of the Indian Ocean Islands
Ian Sinclair and Olivier Langrand 1998
Concise descriptions in field guide form with features for easy diagnosis.

99

MADAGASCAR

Magastar, one of the greatest and richest Isles of the World, three thousand miles in circuit, inhabited by Saracens, governed by foure old men. Marco Polo in *Purchas his Pilgrimes* 1625

Anthropology/Ethnology

Madagascar: Island of the Ancestors
J. Mack 1986
Published by the British Museum – a scholarly account.

Freedom by a Hair's Breadth
P.J.Wilson 1993
A readable anthropological study of the Tsimihety people.

Guides

Bradt: Madagascar 2002

Lonely Planet: Madagascar 2001

Vacation Work: Madagascar, Mayotte & Comoros 2000

History & Politics

Madagascar Rediscovered
Mervyn Brown 1978
Mervyn Brown traces the history of Madagascar from its origins to the recovery of independence in 1960 in a clear and objective manner. After the French conquest in 1895 most contacts with non-French speaking countries were severed and the opening of the Suez Canal meant that Madagascar was no longer on major shipping routes meaning that there was very little written in English; Mervyn Brown here rediscovers the past and varied history of the island.

Madagascar: Politics, Economics and Society
M. Covell 1987
In the Marxist regimes series – a look at the Marxist past.

History of Madagascar
Rev. William Ellis 1838
Comprising also The Progress of the Christian Mission Established in 1818; and an Authentic Account of the Persecution and Recent Martyrdom of the Native Christians.
Originally conceived as a history of the missions in Madagascar, it was then decided to include a history of the island from the earliest times. This made it a much more comprehensive book which contains chapters on the climate, natural history and native customs. Also *Madagascar Revisited* (1867).

The Drama of Madagascar
Sonia E. Howe 1938
The author approached the writing of this book from a different viewpoint to most other histories written about the island in that she writes about the role that Madagascar has played in history - the interrelation between it and Britain, France and Portugal. Madagascar owes its economic and historical interest solely to its geographical situation; it lay on the route to India and was therefore of vital importance to mariners of all nations.

Natural History

Zoo Quest to Madagascar
David Attenborough 1961
One of the trips that Attenborough did which was sponsored by the BBC to collect animals for the London Zoo. Many of the creatures that he returned with had never been seen alive in England before; he also did a great deal of filming and recording of animal sounds on the trip.

Madagascar Wildlife
Hilary Bradt 2001

The Aye-Aye and I
Gerald Durrell 1993 (1992)
Durrell's task was to capture some aye-ayes to take back to Jersey for breeding.

Mammals of Madagascar
N. Garbutt 1999
Comprehensive with good photographs.
Too heavy to travel with.

A World Like Our Own
Alison Jolly 1980
(Man and Nature in Madagascar). Alison
Jolly is a biologist and she travelled the
thousand mile length of Madagascar
recording what she saw. Madagascar
broke away from Africa 100 million
years ago and managed to preserve many
of the species which eventually became
extinct on the mainland.

*Birds of Madagascar: a
photographic guide*
Peter Morris 1999
Comprehensive but bulky.

Madagascar A Natural History
Ken Preston-Mafham 1991
Madagascar has many species of flora
and fauna which do not exist anywhere
else; this large format book with ample
text and over three hundred colour photographs shows many of them in their natural habitats.

The Song of the Dodo
D. Quammen 1996
The island's biogeography.

A Naturalist in Madagascar
James Sibree 1915
*A Record of Observation Experiences and
Impressions made during a period of over
Fifty Years' Intimate Association with the
Natives and Study of the Animal &
Vegetable Life of the Island.*
Sibree was a missionary in Madagascar,
but this book is an account of the natural
history of the island rather than about his
missionary work, which he considered
had had enough written about it; the
author was rare for his time in that he
admits that he takes "more delight in
silently watching the birds ... than in
shooting them to add a specimen to a

museum". Also *Madagascar Before the
Conquest* (1896).

Photographic

Madagascar
Gian Paolo Barbieri 1995

Madagascar
ed. Hilary Bradt 1988
A collection of colour photographs and
text by a number of experts on
Madagascar, the world's fourth largest
island.

Madagascar. The Red Island
Arlette Kouwenhoven Photos:
Toussaint Raharison 1995
An introduction to the history and flora
and flora.

Madagascar, a World Out of Time
F. Lanting 1991
Photographs of landscape, people and
wildlife.

Travel Literature

*Distant Shores: by Traditional
Canoe from Asia to Madagascar*
S.Crook 1990
The 4000 mile Sarimanok Expedition by
outrigger canoe across the Indian Ocean
from Bali to Madagascar.

Madagascar Travels
Christina Dodwell 1996 (1905)
Travels throughout the island.

Dancing with the Dead
Helena Drysdale 1991
Helena Drysdale's journey to Madagascar
was made more interesting because she
discovered that her family had had trading connections with the island in the
nineteenth century. She and her husband
travel from Zanzibar to the Comoro
Islands and all over Madagascar by a
variety of different kind of transport
which often seems very uncomfortable.
They attend the fascinating death ritual

famadihana, whereby ancestors are exhumed, in the middle of Madagascar.

Muddling Through in Madagascar
Dervla Murphy 1990 (1985)
Dervla Murphy travelled through Madagascar with her fourteen year old daughter Rachel; they encountered many disasters and mishaps on their journey, but maintained a curiosity about what they saw and who they met, so that you do get some idea of what the country is like.

The Great Red Island
Arthur Stratton 1965 (1964)
A mixture of personal anecdote and history which jumps backwards and forwards in time in an opinionated way. A badly edited book which nonetheless contains some interesting information.

Lemurs of the Lost World
Jane Wilson 1990
The 'Lost World' is the Ankàrana Massif in northern Madagascar which is hidden behind vertical cliffs and dense, thorny shrubs. Jane Wilson penetrated this area through sixty miles of caves and canyons and discovered a wealth of wildlife including lemurs, chameleons, blind fish, twenty-foot long crocodiles and six-inch hairy spiders. Good descriptions of the animals, the people, the trip and the realities of ecological fieldwork.

MAURITIUS

This is, by heavens, a Paradise, and not without angels. Theodore Hook, Letter to Charles Mathews. 24th March 1814

Art and Architecture

Living in Mauritius. Traditional Architecture of Mauritius
photographs by Christian Vaisse 1990
A lavishly illustrated book showing the traditional architecture of Mauritius in colour photographs.

Fiction

The Hell-Hot Bungalow.
Azize Asgarally 1967
A play about a family quarrel; it was originally banned but when it was eventually performed was a great success.

Mauritius through the Looking Glass
Sir Satcam Boolell 2000
A collection of short stories.

The Rape of Sita
Lindsey Collen 2001 (1993)
A novel which echoes myths, folk tales and religious prophecies.

King's Garden
Fanny Deschamps 1986
There is a long (350 page) chapter called *Love's Progress* about life in Mauritius after the 1760 cyclone.

George; or the Planter of the Isle of France. A tale of the land and the sea
Alexandre Dumas 1853
Set in Mauritius

The Mauritius Command
Patrick O'Brian 1997 (1986)
Captain Jack Aubrey is ashore on half-pay without a command until Stephen Maturin arrives with secret orders for Aubrey to take a frigate to the Cape of Good Hope. A must for O'Brian's many fans.

Paul and Virginia
J.H.B. Saint-Pierre 1989 (1799)
Set in a well-described Mauritius. The novel tells the story of a girl and boy of French parentage, their idyllic childhood, their sexual awakening and the tragedy that prevents their reunion.

102

Food

Genuine Cuisine of Mauritius
Guy Félix 1988
African, European and Asian recipes are combined to make up the Creole and Indian Ocean dishes.

General Background

Mauritius – an Island of Success
Edward & Bridget Dommen 2000
Mauritius has become a model island for successful development. The book shows how other islands could benefit.

Culture Shock Mauritius
Roseline Lum 1997

Not a Paradise: I Love You Mauritius
A. Cader Raman 1991
Letters from Mauritius, England and Libya. The author, a psychiatrist was born in Mauritius and spent many years in England as a medical student. This is his autobiography in the form of letters.

Festivals of Mauritius
Ramesh Ramdoyal 1990

Journey to Mauritius
Bernardin de Saint-Pierre (1775) (ed. Jason Wilson) 2002
A survey of Mauritius done as a series of letters with detailed descriptions of the island's geography, flora and fauna. Also chilling descriptions of plantation life and slavery.

Guides

Bradt: Mauritius, Rodrigues & Reunion 2002

Globetrotter: Mauritius 2000

Insight: Mauritius, Réunion & Seychelles 2002

Lonely Planet: Mauritius, Réunion & Seychelles 2001

History

New History of Mauritius
John Addison 1984

Servants, Sirdars and Settlers: Indians in Mauritius 1834-1874
Marina Carter 1995
A scholarly book. Good bibliography.

History of Mauritius
Charles Grant 1995
The Isles of France and the neighbouring islands - their history from their first 'discovery'.

Natural History

Last Chance to See
Douglas Adams & Mark Carwardine 1990
A journey round the world in search of lost species. A section on endangered Mauritian birds.

Golden Bats and Pink Pigeons
Gerald Durrell 1996 (1979)
Durrell's expedition to Mauritius to rescue several species from extinction. He took some to his zoo in Jersey for later release back into the wild.

103

Photographic

Mauritius – a Visual Souvenir 2000

Mauritius from the Air
Genevieve Dormann 1996

This is Mauritius
Alan Mountain 1996
An exploration of all aspects of Mauritius in a series about exotic places.

Travel Literature

Journey to Mauritius
Jacques-Henri Bernardin 2003
First published in 1773. The author spent two years in Mauritius and describes and

denounces slavery. He was fascinated by the new genre of 'travel-writing'.

Island of the Swan
Michael Malim 1952
The Portuguese were the first to call Mauritius the 'Island of the Swan', although the origin of the name is unknown and it is thought unlikely that they ever went there. Following the Dutch withdrawal, the French rechristened it 'L'Isle de France', and held it until 1810 when it became British; the British returned La Réunion to France in 1816 but held on to Mauritius. The book is an account of a trip through the island as well as having some fairly detailed historical background.

Darwin and the Beagle
Alan Moorehead 1969
Darwin landed and collected specimens at Mauritius and the Bourbon Islands (Réunion) and kept detailed diaries of what he saw and found.

Baudelaire
Claude Pichois 1989
Baudelaire arrived in Réunion in 1841 and wrote about his arrival at Saint-Denis.

Mauritius
Carol Wright 1974
An account of the island's geology, early history, wildlife, people and landscape written in a straightforward way.

SEYCHELLES
Guides
Bradt: Seychelles 2001

Insight: Mauritius, Réunion & Seychelles 2002

Lonely Planet: Mauritius, Réunion & Seychelles 2001

Travellers Survival Kit: Mauritius, Seychelles & Réunion 2000

Natural History
Birds of Seychelles
Adrian Skerrett, Ian Bullock & Tony Disley 2001

Photographic
Journey Through Seychelles
Mohamed Amin & Duncan Willetts 1994
Exotic photographs.

Seychelles
Peter Vine 1992
Accompanied by text.

Travel Literature
Beyond the Reefs
William Travis. 1990.
Beyond the Reefs (1959) and *Shark for Sale* (1961) are accounts of diving and sailing in the Indian Ocean. Travis left the RAF and flew small planes round the world before deciding to make his living by diving and shark fishing. He now lives in Samoa where he runs a fishing business.

ZANZIBAR
Autobiography/Biography
Memoirs of an Arabian Princess: an Autobiography
Emily Ruete 1907
The author was daughter of one of the rulers of Zanzibar; she married a German and left for Europe. The book gives an interesting insight into the lives of women in Zanzibar at the time.

Paradise
Abdulrazek Gurnah 1994
Set around Zanzibar in the early years of European involvement. Yusuf, a young Muslim boy, is taken into the service of

his merchant uncle and we see Europeans, as colonizers, through his eyes. Also *Admiring Silence.*

Fiction

Zanzibar
Giles Foden 2002
A novel set in 1998 (and mostly written before 9/11). Nick Karolides is a marine biologist working on coral reef protection off Zanzibar. On a visit to Dar-es-Salaam he meets an American working at the US Embassy and together they become embroiled in a terrorist conspiracy.

Guides

Bradt: Zanzibar 2002

Cadogan: Tanzania & Zanzibar 2001

Insight: Tanzania & Zanzibar 2003

Lonely Planet: Tanzania, Zanzibar & Pemba 1999

Rough Guide: Zanzibar 2002

History

Princes of Zinji: the Rulers of Zanzibar
Genesta Hamilton 1957
The reign of Seyyid bin Sultan and background information on what life was like under Omani influence.

Zanzibar: its History and its People
W.H. Ingrams 1967 (1931)
A detailed and comprehensive history of Zanzibar. The author discovered that early Zanzibar traders dealt with the City of London in the twelfth century and also found fossils which were reputedly the remains of Stone Age meals.

The History and Conservation of Zanzibar Stone Town
ed. Abdul Sheriff 1998
The problems of conservation in its most acute forms.

Photographic

Images of Zanzibar
photographs Javed Jafferji 1996

Travel Literature

Zanzibar: city, island and coast
Richard Burton 1967 (1872)
Burton gives an account of the main coastal towns as well as the islands and describes his visit to Usambara.

Pemba, the Spice Island of Zanzibar
J.E.E. Craster 1913
The author undertook the survey of Pemba Island for the Zanzibar government. An account of his stay plus the history.

Heaven Has Claws
Adrian Conan Doyle 1953
Conan Doyle and his wife went sailing in the Indian Ocean in search of freedom. They started in the Red Sea and sailed to Mombasa before moving on to Zanzibar and getting a boat in which they sailed through the Mafia Channel and visited the east coast of Tanzania, Kilwa Kisiwani and the ruins of Songa Manra.

Isle of Cloves
F.D. Ommanney 1955
Ommanney was sent to Zanzibar by the Colonial Office to improve local methods of fishing, but here he mixes what he saw on the land with history and observations of Islam. He visited the leper colony on the island of Pemba and describes the rich sea life on the coral reefs.

105

Middle
East

Turkey

Lebanon

Syria

Israel Jordan

Iraq

Iran

Kuwait

Saudi
Arabia

Bahrain

Qatar

United Arab
Emirates

Oman

Yemen

MIDDLE EAST - GENERAL

Anthology

Night and Horses and the Desert
Robert Irwin 2000 (1999)
The Penguin anthology of Classical
Arabic Literature.

Art, Architecture and Archaeology

Islamic Ceramics
James Allan 1991
A clear, straightforward well-illustrated
introduction to Islamic ceramics.

Islamic Art
Barbara Brend 1991
This easy to read book really takes over
from where the Ettinghausen/Grabar
book finishes, as it gives the history of
Islamic art from the 7th to 19th centuries

Art of Islam: Language and Meaning
Titus Burckhardt 1976
A superb overall view of Islamic art and
architecture.

Persian Painting
Sheila Canby 1993
A good, well-illustrated introduction to
Persian painting from 1300 to 1900.

Gods, Graves and Scholars
C.W. Ceram 1984 (1949) (see Egypt)

The Art and Architecture of Islam 650 - 1250
Richard Ettinghausen and Oleg
Grabar 1991 (1987)
History, culture and arts of the period are
shown in relationship to each other
throughout the Islamic world: the Arab
countries, Turkey, Iran and Central Asia.
The book has over 400 illustrations and
maps and line drawings.

Middle Eastern Mythology
S.H.Hooke 1991 (1963)
Professor Hooke explains how mythology
plays a role in ritual and customs
throughout the Middle East; he demonstrates this with myths from the Assyrians
to the Hebrews and shows how they
throw new light on the Hebrew scrip-
tures and the Gospels.

Kilims: the art of tapestry weaving in Anatolia, the Caucasus and Persia
Yanni Petsopoulos 1979
A beautifully-illustrated and comprehensive book which deals with the history of
kilim weaving in each of the localities
separately.

Islamic Art
David Talbot Rice 1993 (1965)
A concise, well-illustrated chronological
survey of Islamic art with ample descriptions of objects and buildings.

Islamic Metalwork
Rachel Ward 1993
A good general, well-illustrated introduction to the many forms of Islamic metalwork.

Biography

Lawrence – the Uncrowned King of Arabia
Michael Asher 1999 (1998)
A re-examination of all the evidence
about Lawrence.

The Wilder Shores of Love
Lesley Blanch 1993 (1954)
Biographies of four women: Isabel
Burton, Jane Digby, Aimee Dubucq de
Rivery and Isabelle Eberhardt: "Four
variations on the theme of the nineteenth-
century woman who turns to the East for
her adventurous life and love ... an odd
quartet, well selected, and fully deserving
Miss Blanch's lively and expressive por-
traiture". (*The Times*)

109

The Jewish People. Their History and Their Religion
David Goldberg and John Rayner
1995 (1987)
The book is divided into two parts; the first is a survey of Jewish history and literature and the second is an analysis of the teachings and practices of Judaism.

Solitary in the Ranks
H. Montgomery Hyde 1987
Lawrence of Arabia as airman and private soldier.

The Golden Warrior
Lawrence James 1995 (1990)
A controversial biography of T.E. Lawrence which included new material.

A Pilgrimage of Passion. The Life of Wilfred Scawen Blunt.
Elizabeth Longford 1982 (1979)
Blunt who lived between 1840 and 1922 was the embodiment of a past era; he combined being a poet, diarist, politician and explorer with a strong romantic streak which made him very attractive to women. He was full of energy and travelled, with his wife Lady Anne Blunt (q.v.), to remote and unmapped parts of Central Arabia.

110

Glubb Pasha. A Biography
James Lunt 1984
Lunt traces the life and fascinating career of Sir John Bagot Glubb; Glubb was a Special Services Officer in Iraq, Officer Commanding the Desert Areas in Transjordan and commander of the Arab Legion, which he transformed into a modern army before he was dismissed by King Hussein of Jordan in 1956.

The Arabs
Peter Mansfield 1992 (1976).
An introduction to the modern Arab world from both political and historical aspects; the second half of the book looks at each Arab state separately.

Philby of Arabia
Elizabeth Monroe 1980 (1973)
Elizabeth Monroe embarked on her biography of H. St. JB Philby anticipating that she would get enormous pleasure from the 'hunt'. She found her task both geographically and intellectually rewarding as he had left mountains of papers. But since he found difficulty in seeing a point of view which was not his own, most of the papers were entirely subjective. Ironically for him, he was thought to be overwhelmingly English by the Arabs and considered out of touch with England by the English. "My ambition is fame, whatever that may mean and for what it is worth. I have fought for it hard ... If my ambition had been to make money, it would have been easier to understand."

Coming of Age in the Middle East
Trevor Mostyn 1987
The author - who later went on to become a journalist writing about Middle Eastern affairs - felt that he had finally come of age whilst living in the Middle East.

Mohammed
Maxime Rodinson 2002 (1971)
As well as being a fascinating biography of Mohammed, this book shows the tremendous impact that the ideology that grew around him had on a society which was evolving from a nomadic to a settled economy.

The Prophet Muhammad
Barnaby Rogerson 2003
An extremely readable introduction to the life and legacy of Muhammad.

Out of Place
Edward Said 2000 (1999)
A memoir of Said who was born in Jerusalem but spent much of his youth in Cairo and Lebanon. Arab but Christian, Palestinian but the holder of a US passport, with a very British first name all combined to make him feel increasingly an outsider.

Desert Traveller: the Life of Jean Louis Burckhardt
Katherine Sim 1969
A biography of the Swiss traveller who spent so much time in Arabia. He learnt Arabic in Aleppo in preparation for travelling, in disguise, to Mecca.

Traveller's Prelude 1893 1927
(1950)
Beyond Euphrates 1928-1933
(1951)
The Coast of Incense 1933-1939
(1953)
Dust in the Lions Paw 1939-1946
(1961)
Freya Stark
The four volumes of Freya Stark's autobiography span a fascinating and changing time in the Middle East. The text is interspersed with letters and extracts from her diaries. *Traveller's Prelude* begins with Freya Stark's childhood which was spent between France, Italy and England; she began to learn Arabic in 1921. *Beyond Euphrates* is mainly about her life in Baghdad, Damascus and Persia; *The Coast of Incense* includes her first journey to Southern Arabia and travels in Iraq and Syria; *Dust in the Lion's Paw* begins in Syria and continues with Aden, the Yemen and includes the siege of the embassy in Baghdad.

The Life of My Choice
Wilfred Thesiger 1992 (1987)
Thesiger's autobiography explains how he got the yen for travel and who it was that influenced him. "He is, unquestionably, one of the greatest travellers the British have ever produced, the last of our recognizable primitives. He also writes with much distinction and honesty" Geoffrey Moorhouse (*The Daily Telegraph*).

Playing the Game
Penelope Tuson 2003
Gertrude Bell and Freya Stark, as well as many lesser-known women, are included

in this wide-ranging look at women's lives in Arabia.

Lawrence of Arabia. The authorised biography.
Jeremy Wilson 1990 (1989)
Extremely detailed account of Lawrence's life (although there is an abridged version). Jeremy Wilson, the acknowledged expert on Lawrence spent ten years researching this book and uncovered much new material. He gets to grips with the odd, eccentric, obsessive and intensely private Lawrence, ironically now a household name.

Lady Anne Blunt
H.V.F. Winstone
Lady Anne Blunt was Byron's granddaughter and the first woman to make a recorded journey to Central Arabia.

Fiction

Opening the Gates: a Century of Arab Feminist Writing.
eds. Margot Badran and Miriam Cooke 1990
An anthology which is divided into three sections: 'Awareness', 'Rejection' and 'Activism'; it includes both fact and fiction and has a long explanatory introduction.

Bedouin Poetry - from Sinai & the Negev
Clinton Bailey 2002
The Bedouin have a strong tradition of oral poetry collected here by Clinton Bailey who has spent more than 30 years among them.

Coming up Roses
Michael Carson 1991 (1990)
King Fadl wants to acquire an imaginary Arab kingdom, Zibda; GCHQ is listening to his conversation and sends Charlie Hammond to gather information.

Palestine Twilight
Edward Fox 2001
An American archaeologist gets murdered on the West Bank and Fox, by using the techniques of detective fiction, enlightens us about the current conflict.

The Arabian Nights
trans. Husain Haddawy 1992 (1907)
The Everyman edition of the translation by Haddawy of the Mahdi edition of the Arabian Nights, the definitive Arabic edition which is in the Bibliothèque Nationale in Paris. The stories told by the Princess Scheherazade and collected from Arabia, Persia and India were first published in the West in 1700.

The Arabian Nightmare
Robert Irwin 1998 (1983)
A brilliant and original work which weaves fantastical tales about sleep with oriental twists.

Arabic Short Stories
112
trans. Denys Johnson-Davies 1983
A collection of twenty four stories from Saudi Arabia, the Yemen, Iraq, the Lebanon, Syria and other countries of the Arab world.

Journey to the Orient
Gérard de Nerval 1973 (1851) (see Egypt)
A journey made in 1843.

The Relic
Eca de Queiroz 1994
Raposo, the novel's anti-hero escapes his life and embarks on a journey to the Holy Land in search of a holy relic.

The Persian Boy
Mary Renault 1974
A young Persian boy is taken on as an attendant to Alexander as he pushes his conquests eastwards.

'Antar and 'Abla. A Bedouin Romance
ed. Diana Richmond 1978
A short selection from the original work which was transcribed into thirty two volumes by a courtier of Haroun ar Rashid. The stories were from the 'time of ignorance' (before the birth of the prophet); this collection concentrates on 'Antar's love for 'Abla and his success in gaining his rightful place in the tribe, something which was of extreme importance to the Bedouin.

Food
Traditional Arabic Cooking
Miriam Al Hashimi 1993

New Book of Middle Eastern Food
Claudia Roden 1986 (1965)
A classic book on Middle Eastern food which revolutionised the West's attitude. Paul Levy wrote in the *Literary Review*: "This is one of those rare cookery books that is a work of cultural anthropology and Mrs Roden's standards of scholarship are so high as to ensure that it has permanent value".

General Background
Arabs: The Myth and Reality
Gerald Butt 1997
A hard and thought-provoking look at the origins of Arab-Western conflict in the Middle East.

New Jerusalems
Daniel Easterman 1992
A collection of essays, articles and lectures about Islamic fundamentalism, the Iranian revolution, the Rushdie affair and other topics pertaining to the Islamic world which show how pervasive is the Western myth of Orient and the Islamic myth of the decadent west.

A Blood-Dimmed Tide
Amos Elon 2001 (1997)
Dispatches from the Middle East. Elon, a

liberal-minded commentator on the Middle East, gives the background to the Arab-Israeli conflict and looks at the possibilities of peace.

Walking the Bible
Bruce Feiler 2001
A journey by land through the five books of Moses.

The Arab World: Forty Years of Change
Elizabeth Warnock Fernea and Robert A. Fernea 1985
The anthropologist authors recount the story of their forty years spent in the Middle East and the people they met.

Middle Eastern Muslim Women Speak
Elizabeth Fernea 1977
A collection of writings by and about women.

From Beirut to Jerusalem
Thomas Friedman 1990 (1989)
The author delved deep into the complex history of the recent conflicts in the Middle East and has produced an analysis and understanding of the situation which is well worth reading.

The Epic of Gilgamesh
Trans. Andrew George 2000 (1999)
The earliest fragments date back over 4000 years – so it can truly claim to be the 'world's first truly great work of literature'.

Price of Honour
Jan Goodwin 1996
A controversial look at Muslim society in which Muslim women speak out.

Bright Levant
Laurence Grafftey-Smith 2002 (1970)
The author was a member of the Levant Consular Service.

Dictionary of the Middle East
Dilip Hiro 1996
A general-purpose dictionary with over 1000 entries.

The Modern Middle East
ed. Albert Hourani, Philip S. Khoury and Mary C. Wilson 1993
Key writings of the modern history of the Middle East from 1789 up until the present day. There is an introductory essay by Hourani, followed by twenty seven articles arranged in four sections:
'Reforming elites and changing relations with Europe 1789-1918'
'Transformations in society and economy 1789 - 1918' 'The construction of nationalist ideologies and politics up to the 1950s' 'The Middle East since the Second World War'.

A Middle East Mosaic
Bernard Lewis 2001 (2000)
Fragments of life, letters and history which give a wonderful overview of the Middle East.

Veiled Half-Truths
Judy Mabro1996
An anthology of Western travellers' perceptions of Middle Eastern women.

Beyond the Veil
Fatima Mernissi 1991 (1975)
A look at the tensions experienced by modern Muslim women.

The Arab World Handbook
James Peters 2000
Background to Bahrain, Kuwait, Qatar, Oman, Saudi Arabia, United Arab Emirates and Yemen.

Orientalism
Edward Said 1978
A dismissal of established Western images of the Middle East.

113

A Modern History of the Islamic World

Reinhard Schulze 2002
After September 11th, the importance for the West to understand Islamic culture has become far more important.

Sinai and Palestine

A.P. Stanley 1986 (1896)
A study of the region looking at the links with biblical references.

The Prize

Daniel Yergin 1993 (1991)
A history of the oil industry throughout the world.

Guides

Lonely Planet: Middle East 2003

The Drinkers' Guide to the Middle East

Will Lawson 1997
Humorous introduction to the Middle East.

History & Politics

The Clash of Fundamentalism

Tariq Ali (2003) (2002)
Subtitled crusades, jihads & modernity - in this book Ali puts the events of 9/11 into perspective.

The Arab Awakening

George Antonius 1938
The classic study of the Arab national movement with its origins, development and problems taken from European and American sources as well as from first hand Arab evidence.

The Arabs

Edward Atiyah 1955
An analysis of the Arabs as a people, their world and how it came into being and what is happening to it and what are its future prospects. All of which is useful for understanding the politics and events in the Middle East today.

Rome in the East

Warwick Ball 2000
The social and cultural interaction between the Roman empire and the civilizations of the Near and Middle East.

Islam: The View from the Edge

Richard Bulliet 1994
A concise account of the historical evolution of Islam.

A Peace to End all Peace. Creating the Modern Middle East 1914 - 1922

David Fromkin 1991 (1989)
A history of what happened from the time of the Allies destruction of the Ottoman Empire in 1914, up until the emergence of eight separate states in 1922.

Arab Historians of the Crusades

Francesco Gabrieli 1984 (1957)
Extracts from seventeen Arab authors who wrote about the crusades.

Britain and the Arabs

John Bagot Glubb 1959
A study of the fifty years between 1908 and 1958.

A Soldier with the Arabs

John Bagot Glubb 1957
"The self-portrait of an honest man, as true as steel, marvellously unembittered, and sustained through all these anxieties and disappointments by an unyielding spiritual faith." (James Morris in *The Manchester Guardian*)

The Story of the Arab Legion

John Bagot Glubb 1948
"Glubb Pasha tells his exhilarating story of adventure and achievement - a story made more vivid by a real gift for the portrayal of the desert scene, by excellent illustrations and by many revealing little anecdotes and excursions into history. I find it entrancing." (General Sir John Burnett-Stewart in *The Sunday Times*)

Inside the Middle East
Dilip Hiro1982
In the late 1970s Hiro spent much time travelling in the Middle East (a term he defines as the Arab East which includes the countries of Lebanon, Jordan, Syria, Iraq, Saudi Arabia, the Yemen, Oman, the UAE, Qatar, Bahrain, Kuwait and Egypt (and, geographically, Israel). Born in Pakistan, he felt at home in an Islamic environment and was able to get under the skin of the countries he visited.

History of the Arabs
Philip K.Hitti 1970
A very readable book about the history of the Arabs.

A History of the Arab Peoples
Albert Hourani 2002 (1991) (ed. Malise Ruthven)
A large and readable, yet scholarly, book which sums up the whole history of the Arab peoples from the seventh century and the rise of Islam until the present day.

Crusades
Terry Jones & Alan Ereira 1996 (1994)
Short, pithy and to the point.

Paradise and Power
Robert Kagan 2003
The recently much-cited essay on American hegemony by the ex-state department analyst.

The Bedouin
Shirley Kay 1978
A comprehensive well-illustrated overview of the Bedouin, their roles, and the changes that wealth and education has brought to them. She questions whether the Bedouin will be able to survive in contemporary society.

Politics in the Middle East
Elie Kedourie 1992
An historical analysis which attempts to explain why ideological politics, such as nationalism and fundamentalism, have

triumphed in the Middle East and why constitutional governments have not worked in Islamic countries. Also *England and the Middle East: the Destruction of the Ottoman Empire 1914-21.*

Crusader Castles
Hugh Kennedy 1995
An illustrated history of the castles.

The Muqaddimah. An Introduction to History
Ibn Khaldun 1987 (see Morocco)

A History of Islamic Societies
Ira M. Lapidus 1988
An authoratative, clear and comprehensive history of Islamic societies from the seventh century to 1983.

The Essential T.E. Lawrence
A Selection of his Finest Writings
ed. David Garnett 1992 (1951)
Extracts both by and about Lawrence which include many of his letters.

The Letters of T.E. Lawrence
selected and edited Malcolm Brown 1991 (1988)
A collection of letters, written by Lawrence between 1905 and 1935, which gives interesting insights into Lawrence the man, as well as the political and historical situation of the time.

Seven Pillars of Wisdom
T.E.Lawrence 1962 (1935)
Seven Pillars of Wisdom has been criticised for its historical inaccuracy as it is a very personal account of the Arab Revolt, but Lawrence's lively prose ensures that this book will remain a classic; it is essential reading for anyone interested in the Middle East. "It's a great, great book - a heady mixture of war, politics and history - despite its author's detractors." (Peter Hopkirk)

115

The Arabs in History
Bernard Lewis 1993 (1988)
Lewis traces Arab history from pre-Islamic times to the present day. The central question is who are the Arabs and what has been their place in history.

The Assassins – a Radical Sect in Islam
Bernard Lewis 2001 (1967)
A reasonable look at the sect which is often surrounded by myth.

The Middle East
Bernard Lewis 1996
200 years of history from Christianity to the present day.

The Crusades through Arab Eyes
Amin Maalouf 1984
The author has used contemporary Arab chronicles to retrace Middle Eastern history.

A History of the Middle East
Peter Mansfield 1992 (1991)
Peter Mansfield's book is the history of the turbulent last two hundred years in the Middle East. It starts with Napoleon in Egypt and follows the collapse of the Ottoman Empire which brought with it the emergence of new nations. He explains how the discovery of oil affected the whole region and ends with what he considers the prospects for the twenty first century. The Arabs (q.v.), an earlier book by Mansfield, is an introduction to the politics, economy and history of the modern Arab world.

Islam and Democracy
Fatima Mernissi 1993 (1992)
A look at why democracy hasn't taken root in the Middle East - written by a leading Arab feminist.

Islamic Politics in Palestine
Beverley Milton-Edwards 1999 (1996)
The author draws on extensive interviews with Palestinian and Jordanian Islamists.

The Cambridge Encyclopaedia of the Middle East and North Africa
eds. Trevor Mostyn and Albert Hourani 1988
An invaluable reference work to the culture, history and geography of the Middle East; the background economy, peoples, history, culture and religion of each country are described as well as contemporary history and politics.

The Crusades
Zoe Oldenbourg 2001 (1966)
A large book about the first three crusades between 1095 and 1192. Good on the structure of feudal society.

The Background of Islam
H.St J.B Philby 1947
A sketch of pre-Islamic Arabian history which attempts to cover most of the area affected by Islam rather than just the northern countries which at the time of Philby's book were the only ones written about.

A History of the Crusades. Vol.I The First Crusade and the Foundation of the Kingdom of Jerusalem, Vol.II The Kingdom of Jerusalem and the Frankish East 1100-1187. 1990 (1952) and vol.III The Kingdom of Acre and the Later Crusades 1978 (1954)
Steven Runciman
The classic trilogy of books on the Crusades. Volume I starts at the beginning, through the preaching of the First Crusade up to the triumphant establishment of the Kingdom of Jerusalem. The main theme of volume II is warfare and tells the story of the Frankish states of Outremer from the accession of King Baldwin I to the reconquest of Jerusalem by Saladin. Volume III describes the revival through the Third Crusade of the Frankish Kingdom of Jerusalem and its fall a century later with the accompanying degeneration of Crusading ideals.

The End of the Peace Process
Edward W. Said 2000
A collection of essays covering six years
of the peace process.

The British in the Middle East
Sarah Searight 1979 (1969)
The author concentrates on the social and
cultural aspects of British interest in the
Middle East with vivid descriptions of
four hundred years of visitors and travellers.

*The Arabs: the Life-story of a
People who have left their deep
impress on the world*
Bertram Thomas 1937
Thomas travelled into unknown places
and got to know the Middle East so well
that his account of the culture and history
of the Arabs became a classic. He begins
by describing the Arabs of antiquity and
continues with the birth of Muhammad;
he then goes on to describe Arab civilization, its arts and sciences before writing
about the disintegration of Arabia and the
effect of the West on Arab culture.

Heart Beguiling Araby
Kathryn Tidrick 1989 (1981)
Kathryn Tidrick explores two themes in
her book: firstly the idea that the Bedouin
were a pure race and as such were independent, noble, honourable and led simple lives until spoilt by contact with the
outside world, an idea which came to
fruition in the work of Niebuhr and
Burckhardt. Her second theme is the idea
that there is a natural affinity between the
English and the Arabs; many of the early
explorers to Arabia were misfits in their
own culture and she traces the origin of
this illusory idea to the inequality of
power "those who lie under the power of
another are always conscious of it, while
those who possess power may be
unaware of it".

Arabia - Cradle of Islam
Rev. S.M. Zwemer 1986 (1900)
A scholarly account of the Arab people,
their lives and customs.

Leisure Activities

Falconry in Arabia
Mark Allen 1980
Beautifully illustrated book which
describes falconry in Arabia.

*Lonely Planet: Diving and
Snorkelling: the Red Sea 2001*

Natural History

In Unknown Arabia
R.E.Cheesman 1926
Descriptions of the flora and fauna of
Arabia.

*A Photographic Guide to the
Birds of Israel and the Middle
East 2000*

*The Birds of Britain and Europe
with North Africa and the Middle
East*
Hermann Heinzel, Richard Fitter and
John Parslow 1992 (1972)
A field guide which aims to describe and
illustrate every bird in the regions cov-
ered.

Birds of Arabia
Richard Meinertzhagen 1954
This was the first serious book about
birds in Arabia and as a result, has
become extremely sought after on the
second-hand market by anyone taking an
interest in the subject.

Flowers of the Mediterranean
Oleg Polunin and Anthony Huxley
1990
A well-illustrated guide to the flowers of
the Mediterranean, which includes the
parts of the Middle East which border the
Mediterranean. Over 700 species are

117

described and 300 are illustrated with colour photographs.

Photographic

Bedouin. Nomads of the Desert
Alan Keohane 1994
Colour photographs taken all over the deserts of the Middle East, with ample text.

Desert, Marsh and Mountain
Wilfred Thesiger 1995
A selection of some of the sixty volumes of photographs that Thesiger took during his many years of travelling. He quotes extensively from *Arabian Sands* and *The Marsh Arabs,* but the prologue includes an account of his childhood in Abyssinia. "The urge to travel and explore probably originated in my childhood. Certainly it was an unusual childhood."

Visions of a Nomad
Wilfred Thesiger 1993 (1987)
A collection of Thesiger's black and white photographs from Africa, the Arab World and Asia: "These photographs capture the total confidence and naturalness of the subject created by long and trusting relationships". Stephen Haggard (*Literary Review*).

Arabia and the Gulf: in Original Photographs 1880-1950.
Andrew Wheatcroft 1982
The book is divided into six parts and through these divisions, it is possible to get a fairly comprehensive historical overview of what life was like in Arabia and the Gulf.

Religion

The Koran
trans. A.J. Arberry 1991 (1964)
The Koran is a fusion of prose and poetry, and in its 114 Suras (chapters) comprises the revelations believed to have been communicated to Muhammad by God, between 610 -632 AD.

The Battle for God
Karen Armstrong 2000
A look at fundamentalism in Judaism, Christianity and Islam. Also *Islam: A Short History.*

Islam: The Straight Path
John L. Esposito 1998
A clear explanation of what Islam really means.

The Quran: A Modern English Version
Majid Fakhry (trans.)
A comprehensible translation.

Islam
Alfred Guillaume 1990 (1956)
Professor Guillaume deals with the massive influence that Islam has had on the culture of the Arab peoples; he begins with its historical background and writes about Muhammad and the Quran before describing the evolution of Islam and its different schools as systems of faith, law, religion and philosophy.

Islam & the Myth of Confrontation
Fred Halliday 1999 (1996)
A well-balanced look at religion and politics in the Middle East.

Judaism
Nicholas de Lange 1991 (1986)
A short book which explains what Judaism is and defines its history, ethics and code.

Beyond Belief
V.S.Naipaul 2001 (1998)
The second part of Naipaul's journey through the Islamic world, the first being *Among the Believers.*

Islam in the World
Malise Ruthven 2000 (1984).
The author tries to get behind the reason why Islam has become such a powerful political force in the modern world.

The Sufis

Idries Shah 1984 (1964)

Sufi literature and preparatory teaching is designed to help bridge the gap between the 'secret tradition' and the 'scientific'. Idries Shah attempts to provide the bridge.

Travel Literature

Travellers in Arabia

Robin Leonard Bidwell 1976

A collection of some of the travels and explorations that were undertaken by Europeans in the Middle East. The book includes chapters on Niebuhr, Burckhardt, Burton, Palgrave, Doughty, and Philby. Bidwell reckons that there is probably more written on Arabia than on any other part of the world, so he chose what he thought was interesting, amusing or important; inevitably he had to miss out much of value, but the end result is a good brief introduction.

Far Arabia: Explorers of the Myth.

Peter Brent 1977

The myth of Arabia was often promulgated by what the explorers and travellers wrote; this book discusses these unrealities and the effect they had, while also describing various journeys. *From the Holy Mountain*

William Dalrymple 1998 (1997)

A witty, learned and scholarly journey in the Shadow of Byzantium inspired by the journey of John Moschos' *The Spiritual Meadow.*(q.v.)

Tribes With Flags

Charles Glass 1992 (1990)

Charles Glass lived in Lebanon from 1972-6 and from 1983-4 and has travelled throughout much of the Middle East. Here he recounts some of his many journeys leading up to his capture and subsequent escape from Hizballah.

Baghdad Without a Map

Tony Horwitz 1992 (1991)

A very entertaining book written with a journalist's desire for 'hot stories' about the author's travels through Yemen, the Persian Gulf, Egypt, Iraq, Iran, Libya, Sudan and the Lebanon, with an additional epilogue on Iraq, written after the Gulf War, where Horowitz was sent as a reporter.

Eothen

Alexander Kinglake 1991 (1844)

One of the classic travel books; written by the young Kinglake in 1844; after the book's publication, Kinglake became known as 'Eothen' Kinglake, which means 'from the East.' He travelled at a time when the European wars had ended and 'gentlemen' were able to resume the Grand Tour, but Kinglake wanted travel that would take him to the heart of the country and that might involve danger. He travelled over fifteen months to Turkey, Beirut, Jordan, Palestine and Egypt, visiting Lady Hester Stanhope in a convent near Sidon.

Crusader Castles

T.E.Lawrence 1992 (1936)

Lawrence walked eleven hundred miles through Palestine and Syria visiting every Crusader Castle of importance: this was his first introduction to the Middle East. He described the great Krak des Chevaliers as 'the most wholly admirable castle in the world,' but noted that in terms of scientific defence it could not begin to compare with Coucy in France or Caerphilly.

The Spiritual Meadow

John Moschos 1992

Moschos entered monastic life near Bethlehem and withdrew to a remote site in the Judaean desert. He died in Rome in 619 AD.

The Travels of Sir John Mandeville

trans. C.W.R.D.Moseley 1983

Little is known about Sir John

Mandeville and where he actually travelled between 1322 and 1356 - some critics maintain that he never got further than the nearest library. Nevertheless it is known that Leonardo and Columbus both possessed his book, which is written with wit and skill.

The Market of Seleukia
James Morris 1957
This is an impression of the Muslim Middle East written at a crucial and changing time in its history, "frozen for a moment in all its varied attitudes, before the hot breath of history melted the tableau". Morris writes about Egypt, the Sudan, Syria, Jordan, the Arabian Peninsula, Iraq and Persia, in a down-to-earth yet evocative manner.

The Afghan Amulet
Sheila Paine 1994
Sheila Paine spent over two years searching for a particular amulet pattern which was relevant to her work as a textile expert. She was constantly told that it was 'in the next valley', so her trip took her to Makran, Iran, Baluchistan, Afghanistan, Iraqi and Turkish Kurdistan, ending up in eastern Bulgaria.

Arabia
Jonathan Raban 1987 (1979)
Jonathan Raban was living in Earls Court in the 1970s when it began to fill up with Arabs; he decided to go and see for himself their countries of origin and produced "one of the most delightful travel books in thirty years" (*New York Times*). He travelled through much of the Middle East and the book "in its ingenious understanding...should do a great deal to dispel the easiest and therefore the most prolific paranoid deception which the Western imagination has now fabricated in its desperate attempt to avoid facing reality". (Angus Wilson.)

To War With Whitaker
Countess of Ranfurly 1996
The war-time diaries of the Countess of Ranfurly between 1939-45; she vowed not to return to Britain while her husband was a prisoner-of-war.

Beyond Ararat
Bettina Selby 1994 (1993)
Bettina Selby cycled from the Black Sea coast of Turkey through the mountains to Ani and to Mount Ararat and through Kurdistan, near the borders of Iran, Iraq and Syria at the end of the Gulf War.

Riding to Jerusalem
Bettina Selby 1994 (1989)
Bettina Selby bicycled across Europe and through Turkey and Syria to Israel.

East is West
Freya Stark 1991 (1945)
At the outbreak of war in 1939, Freya Stark travelled to the Middle East to start work as an official in the Diplomatic Corps. She travelled through Arabia, Egypt, Palestine, Syria, Iraq and Persia. The book is a combination of personal anecdote and descriptions of what she was observing.

Incidents of Travel in Egypt, Arabia Petrœa, and the Holy Land
John Lloyd Stephens 1996 (1837)
Stephens is best remembered for his discovery of Mayan ruins in the Yucatan, but this record of his year long journey through the Middle East has detailed observations of such diversions as how to catch a crocodile, the wardrobe of a Nubian damsel and a night in a tomb.

Sandstorms. Days and Nights in Arabia
Peter Theroux 1991
Peter Theroux was stationed as a journalist in Saudi Arabia and travelled throughout the region.

Alarms and Excursions in Arabia
Bertram Thomas 1931
Thomas was a political officer in Mesopotamia and Trans-Jordan before becoming Financial Adviser in Muscat

and Oman. Owing to his good relationship with several Arab leaders, he was able to make several important journeys into previously unknown territory.

ARAB GULF STATES -GENERAL

General Background

The Merchants
Michael Field 1984
A good overview of big business families, life, business and culture in the Gulf.

The Turbulent Gulf. People, Politics and Power
Liesl Graz 1992
A country-by-country account of the Gulf in the post-Cold War era with an account of the Gulf War and its consequences: "Liesl Graz is a sharp-eyed observer and probably the best European correspondent working in the area ... Excellent". Malise Ruthven (*Sunday Telegraph*)

The New Arabians
Peter Mansfield 1981
An introduction to the history and society of the Gulf with an emphasis on Saudi Arabia.

History

The Gulf: Arabia's Western Approaches
Molly Izzard 1979
Molly Izzard describes the history and culture of the Gulf, including the arrival of the British, as well as writing about her own life in the area. An excellent introduction and survey to the area when "Arabia proper was still a poor country".

Arabia, the Gulf and the West
J.B.Kelly 1980
An overview of the economy of oil in the Gulf: the author is very critical of the political and British military withdrawal from the area, and remarks that when the British relinquished their responsibilities

the rest of the world paid little attention. Kelly attempts to offer a new interpretation of the recent history of Arabia which tries to dispel any complacency about what happened.

Guardians of the Gulf
Michael A. Palmer 1992
One of the many books written about the first Gulf War this book is better than most because it traces the US and British involvement back to the late 18th century.

Natural History

The Wild Flowers of Kuwait and Bahrain.
Violet Dickson 1955
An illustrated guide to the flora of Kuwait, north-east Arabia, Dubai and Bahrain. Violet Dickson was the wife of Col.H.R.P. Dickson who had been Political Agent in Bahrain and Kuwait. She was still living in Kuwait when it was invaded by Iraq.

Mammals of the Arabian Gulf
David L.Harrison 1981
Fifty different kinds of animals found in the Gulf and others found in neighbouring areas are described.

121

BAHRAIN

And here are the best Pearles, which are round and Orient. Joseph Salbancke, Letter to Sir Thomas Smith, 1609 in *Purchas his Pilgrimes* 1625

Art and Archaeology

Looking for Dilmun
Geoffrey Bibby 1972 (1970)
An account of the Danish excavations in Arabia between 1953 and 1965, in search of the ancient civilisation of Dilmun. Much was discovered about the pre-history of Bahrain.

Arabian Fantasy
Herbert Chappell 1976
The author went to Bahrain to film a

musical score by David Fanshawe which had been combined with traditional music. The book of the project is a good introduction to the country with particular emphasis on its music and famous pearl fishing.

Guides

Lonely Planet: Bahrain, Kuwait & Qatar 2000

Bahrain. A Travel Guide
Philip Ward 1993
Bahrain deserves more than the short airplane stop-overs which people usually give it as it has over 5,000 years of history. Philip Ward's guide describes some of that history and also lists hotels and useful information. The map of the State of Bahrain is supplied by the Ministry of Information and is extremely hard to fathom.

Travel Literature

Ibn Battuta. Travels in Asia and Africa 1325-1354. 1984 (1929) *(*See North Africa, Travel Literature)
Ibn Battuta describes Bahrain in his book of travels "a fine large city with gardens, trees and streams...The city has groves of date-palms, pomegranates, and citrons, and cotton is grown there".

The Pirate Coast
Charles Belgrave 1966
The book is based on the diaries of Francis Erskine Loch written between 1818 and 1820. Bahrain is mentioned many times, especially in connection with Portuguese activity in the area and the relocation in 1946 to Bahrain of the British Residency in the Gulf.

Arabia Phoenix
Gerald de Gaury 1946
Included in this book of his travels, De Gaury discusses the fall of Bahrain to the Wahabbis at the beginning of the nineteenth century.

Ben Kendim. A Record of Eastern Travel
Aubrey Herbert 1924
Herbert provides a summary of Bahrain's history and an account of the kind of life he found there on his visit.

KUWAIT

Biography
Forty Years in Kuwait
Violet Dickson 1971
Violet Dickson was the wife of the British Political Agent in Kuwait. Although this is her personal account of the years between 1922 and 1962 she also includes profiles of the various Arab leaders.

General Background
The Evolving Culture of Kuwait 1985
An illustrated introduction to the country.

Kuwait. A Nation's Story
Peter Vine 1992
A large-format illustrated book with good general background information.

Guide
Lonely Planet: Bahrain, Kuwait & Qatar 2000

History
Kuwait and Her Neighbours
H.R.P. Dickson 1956
Dickson was the British Political Agent in Kuwait and therefore had first hand knowledge of all that was going on in the Saudi-Kuwait frontier problems.

OMAN

In the months of August and September, it is here so incredible hot and scorching that I am not able to express the condition strangers are in, being as if they were in boiling Cauldrons or in sweating-

tubs, so that I have known many who were not able to endure the heat would jump into the sea and remain there till the Heat of the day be over. John Struys *The Voyages of John Struys, done out of the Dutch by John Morison* 1684 - *(of 1673)*

General Background

Letters from Oman
David Gwynne-James 2001
Letters the author wrote his future wife in the early 1960s when he was on secondment from the British Army to the Sultan's Armed Forces.

Guides

Insight: Oman & UAE 1999

Lonely Planet: Oman and the UAE 2000

Travellers Survival Kit: Oman & the Arabian Gulf 2001

History

The Wind of Morning
Hugh Boustead 1971
Development in Oman under Sultan Said bin Taimur, looked at from the British point of view.

The Road to Ubar
Nicholas Clapp 1999 (1998)
The search for and discovery of the Atlantis of the Sands.

Oman. The Reborn Land
F.A.Clements 1980
It was not until 1967 and the discovery of oil that Oman started to become modernised: prior to the late 1960s, as a deliberate policy, Oman had been completely cut off from the outside world. A coup in 1970 changed this, and Clements examines the background to the coup and the emergence of the 'new' Oman.

Where Soldiers Fear to Tread
Ranulph Fiennes 1975
Ranulph Fiennes fought in Dhofar, so writes from first hand experience about this and also the changes that were taking place in Oman.

Oman: A History
Wendell Phillips 1967
A readable general history of Oman. The author was at one time economic adviser and director of general antiquities to Sultan Said bin Taimur.

Arabian Assignment
David Smiley 1975
David Smiley commanded the forces of the Sultan of Muscat and had to expel the Saudi-backed rebels from the mountainous Jebel Akhdar; he writes convincingly about what it must have felt like to have been an European in Arabia.

Travel Literature

Atlantis of the Sands
Ranulph Fiennes 1993 (1992)
Ranulph Fiennes determined to find the lost city of Ubar, which legend had it was buried under the sand dunes of southern Oman. In 1991, armed with aerial photographs from the space shuttle 'Challenger,' he began his search. The book recounts his search and eventual discovery of the city.

Sultan in Oman
James Morris 2000 (1957)
Morris accompanied Sultan Said Bin Taimur on a rushed journey through Oman in the hope of quashing a rebellion, and wrote about the incident with insight and humour. *The Times Literary Supplement* wrote that the book should have "a place on the shelf not so far from those of the great Arabian travellers, Doughty, Gertrude Bell, Lawrence and others".

Unknown Oman
Wendell Phillips 1966
Phillips wrote his two books on Oman in

conjunction with each other; this is the account of his travels, excavations and explorations throughout the country. J.R.Wellsted had remarked in his book *Travels in Arabia* (1838) "Is this Arabia, this the country we have looked on heretofore as a desert? Verdant fields of grain and sugar cane stretching along for miles, are before us; streams of water, flowing in all directions, intersect our path". Phillips also describes the landscape and has chapters on women, disease, religion and archaeology.

The Southern Gates of Arabia
Freya Stark 1990 (1936) (see Yemen)

Arabian Sands
Wilfred Thesiger 1991 (1959) (see Saudi Arabia)

Alarms and Excursions in Arabia
Bertram Thomas 1931 (see Middle East General)

124 *Travels in Oman. On the Track of the Early Explorers*
Philip Ward 1987
A compendium of all the significant travellers, explorers and adventurers who went to Oman. The book includes Bent, Cole, Cox, Eccles, Geary, Haines, Hamdani, Hamerton, ibn Battuta, Kaempfer, Loyd, Miles, Pengelley, Stiffe, Bertram Thomas, C.Ward, Wellsted and Whitelock. Their writings are quoted and Philip Ward adds his own narrative about today's Oman.

QATAR
General Background
In Defiance of the Elements: a Personal View of Qatar
John Moorehead 1977
A general introduction to the history and contemporary culture of Qatar.

If the Sun Doesn't Kill You, the Washing Machine Will
Peter Wood 1993
In 1991 Peter Wood was sent to work in Qatar and finding the way that everything was done was so completely different he wrote an amusing book about his experiences.

Guide
Lonely Planet: Bahrain, Kuwait & Qatar 2000

SAUDI ARABIA
Art and Archaeology
The Art of Arabian Costume. A Saudi Arabian Profile
Heather Colyer Ross 1981
The author compares collecting costumes in modern Arabia to an exciting treasure hunt. Spurred on by her enthusiasm in hunting down rare and exotic dress she decided to write about her discoveries; the resulting book has much interesting text and is full of photographs, artist's impressions and line drawings illustrating Arabian costume throughout the region.

Bedouin Jewellery in Saudi Arabia
Heather Colyer Ross 1978
Much of the book is based on the author's collection of Bedouin silver jewellery which she and her husband had bought in the Women's Suq in Riyadh. The different techniques, materials, types of jewellery and historical influences are illustrated with both drawings and photographs and ample text.

Biography
Desert Governess
Phyllis Ellis 2000
Ellis answered an advertisement to become governess to a Saudi royal family.

Princess
Jean Sasson 1993
The author lived in Saudi Arabia for over ten years and was asked to write *Princess* and *Daughters of Arabia* by a member of the royal family. Also *Desert Royal.*

Captain Shakespear: a Portrait.
H.V.F. Winstone 1978(1976)
Captain Shakespear, a Kiplingesque figure who combined being an explorer, diplomat, soldier, botanist and photographer was killed in battle whilst fighting with Ibn Saud against Ibn Rashid of Hail in 1915. Winstone pieced together the fragments of information he found to write this entertaining 'portrait'.

Fiction
Crash of '79
Paul Erdman 1980
A retired banker working for the Saudis observes the events of 1979 that lead to a war in the Middle East and the crash of 1979.

The Doomed Oasis
Hammond Innes 1998 (1960)
An adventure story about saving an oasis from extinction.

Eight Months on Ghazzah Street
Hilary Mantel 1989 (1988)
A horror story full of twists and suspense: a woman joins her husband in Jeddah and owing to boredom starts speculating about the empty flat upstairs. The novel keeps you gripped to the end.

The Saddlebag
Bahiyyah Nakhjavani 2001 (2000)
A Chaucerian-type fable about a group of pilgrims who travel between Mecca and Medina in the nineteenth century.

Endings
'Abd al-Rahman Munif (trans. Roger Allen) 1988 (1977)
This was probably the first translation ever made of a Saudi novel set in the desert; drought is a recurring theme, for it is the environment and climate which play such an enormously important place in the daily lives of the people who live in the desert. The author's descriptions of nature and hunting are superb.

Food
Recipe Memories of Desert Storm
Mona Gabbori
The only book in English on Saudi cooking. Recipes include: jareesh, fattush, ghraybi (butter cookies), and shredded nut pastries.

General Background
Culture Shock Saudi Arabia 2003

Death in Riyadh
Geoff Carter 2000
A look at the inter-cultural relationships between the different races and nationalities of this oil-rich peninsula.

Guides
An A-Z of Places and Things Saudi
Kathy Cuddihy 2001

Complete Idiot's Guide to Saudi Arabia 2004

How to Books: Living and Working in Saudi Arabia 2004

Living and Working in the Gulf States & Saudi Arabia 2003

History
The House of Saud
David Holden and Richard Johns 1982 (1981)
The book was started by David Holden before his murder in 1977 and completed by Richard Johns. It tells the extraordinary story of the emergence of an unknown Saudi prince, Ibn Saud, who rose from obscurity to fame and power with the discovery of oil, and of British intrigue and involvement in the kingdom.

125

The Kingdom
Robert Lacey 1981
A history of Saudi Arabia, which inevitably includes much about all the surrounding countries. The book was written after four years of living in the country.

The Queen of Sheba
H. St J.B. Philby 1981
Philby's last journey in Central Arabia was made the aim of finding out all he could about the Queen of Sheba, the Queen believed to have been loved by King Solomon. The book was published posthumously.

Flowered Men and Green Slopes of Arabia
Thierry Mauger 1988
An illustrated travel journal of a journey through the south-west of Arabia, Arabia Felix, which emphasizes the abundant richness of the traditional environment.

126 Leisure Activities

Desert Treks from Jeddah
Patricia Barbor 1996
Detailed itineraries.

Impressions of Arabia
Thierry Mauger 1996
Architecture and frescoes of the Asir region. Beautifully illustrated.

Travel Literature

A Pilgrimage to Nejd
Lady Anne Blunt 1985 (1881)
In 1878 Anne Blunt and her husband, Wilfred Scawen Blunt, embarked on a two thousand mile trek to find the Bedouins in remotest Central Arabia; she was only the second woman to travel into the inhospitable interior of Arabia. Unlike most other Victorians Wilfred and Anne Blunt travelled rough, with the minimum of fuss, and again, unusually for the time, they were interested in the details of ordinary life and insatiably curious about the places they visited.

Travels in Arabia
J.L. Burckhardt 1993
The Swiss orientalist arrived in Cairo in 1812. He travelled up the Nile to Mecca and Medina.

Personal Narrative of a Pilgrimage to Al-Madinah & Meccah
Richard Burton 1964 (1893).
Burton went to Mecca and Medina in 1853; disguised as a wandering dervish, he managed to get to the Kaabah and to the Tomb of the Prophet at Medina, joining in the Hadj. He was a very sharp observer of all that he saw and that combined with his descriptions means that his book is of great interest to the traveller today.

Travels in Arabia Deserta
Charles Doughty 1979 (1888)
"The place book I find most unforgettable is Doughty's Travels in Arabia Deserta: partly because of its sonorous prose, partly because of Doughty's own stately character, self-presented so majestically between its lines, but chiefly because it evokes so magically the strangeness, the beauty, the danger and the excitement of travel in the Arabian desert a century ago." (Jan Morris)

Arabistan: the Land of the Arabian Nights
W.M.P. Fogg 1985
Fogg travelled through Egypt, Saudi Arabia, Iran and Iraq in 1874.

Arabia of the Wahhabis
H. St J.B. Philby 1977 (1928)
The third volume in Philby's The Heart of Arabia was published in 1922. It completes the account of his experiences in Arabia in 1917 and 1918 when he was sent on missions by Ibn Sa'ud; his primary task was to prepare a campaign against Ibn Rashid, Ibn Sa'ud's northern neighbour. The mission was not a great success - something Philby found hard to concede - but his belief in Ibn Sa'ud, who

now ruled Arabia from sea to sea, was vindicated.

The Empty Quarter
H. St J.B. Philby 1933
The description of Philby's travels in the *Rub' al Khali* or Empty Quarter, the Great South Desert of Saudi Arabia. He had planned the journey obsessively for fifteen years, having been inspired by Dr D.G. Hogarth; Bertram Thomas was the pioneer, nevertheless Philby's book is important. He wrote much of the draft as he wandered around the desert, but actually completed the book in North Wales.

A Pilgrim in Arabia
H. St J.B. Philby 1946
A collection of essays collected from Philby's time in Arabia and which includes the pilgrimage he makes to Mecca.

Sheba's Daughters
H. St J.B. Philby 1939
A record of three months travel in 'unknown' Southern Arabia. Philby was constantly looking for new areas to explore and Sir Percy Cox reckoned "that this journey from Mukalla right along the hinterland, through the Western confines of great Arabian desert to Taif would be a very fine piece of travel, about the only piece of the Arabian peninsula that is entirely unexplored".

Arabian Sands
Wilfred Thesiger 1991 (1959)
Most of Thesiger's journeys described in this book, are about crossing the Empty Quarter; much of what he saw had not been seen by an European before and although he had no intention at the time of writing a book, by writing with a combination of intimate detail and anecdote he brings wherever he is very much alive, making this one of the classic works of travel. Thesiger says of the book "For me this book remains a memorial to a vanished past, a tribute to a once magnificent people".

Arabia Felix: Across the Empty Quarter of Arabia
Bertram Thomas 1932
In his foreword to the book, T.E.Lawrence explains that he had been doubtful of Bertram Thomas's achievements, but having read the draft he was assured that Thomas "has snatched, at the twenty-third hour, feet's last victory and set us free". Lawrence was reluctant to say how much he liked the book in case Jonathan Cape used what he said for the blurb, but he thinks Thomas "a master of every desert art".

UNITED ARAB EMIRATES

The United Arab Emirates are a group of seven emirates, Abu Dhabi, Dubai, Sharjah, Ras al-Khaimah, Fujairah, Ajman and Umm al-Qaiwain which stretch along the coast of the Arabian Gulf, and which were formed into a federation in 1971.

Autobiography
The Wind of Morning
Hugh Boustead 1971 (see Oman)
The author was Political Agent in Dubai and writes interestingly about his time there.

General Background
Culture Shock! United Arab Emirates 2000
A guide to the customs and etiquette.

Dubai. Gateway to the Gulf
ed. Ian Fairservice 1992 (1986)
An illustrated general introduction.

Guides
Abu Dhabi Explorer 2001

Dubai Explorer 2001

Insight Pocket Guide Dubai 2003

Insight: Oman & UAE 1999

Lonely Planet: Dubai 2002

Lonely Planet: Oman & UAE 2000

Time Out: Dubai 2004

History
Abu Dhabi: a Portrait
John Daniels 1974
Pearl fishing and oil both played an important part in making Abu Dhabi the wealthiest state in the UAE. Daniels describes the background and lead up to the formation of the federation and looks at the development projects which were happening in the 1970's.

The Trucial States
Donald Hawley 1970
Hawley deals with the seven states of the region from their earliest history, through the arrival of the Arabs and ultimately the British and their time as the Trucial States. He concludes with their formation into the UAE federation and the withdrawal of the British. He includes very useful information on each of the states, their geography and natural history.

The Gulf States and Oman
Christine Osborne 1977
The author begins by dealing generally with the birth of the federation before examining each state separately.

Photographic
The Emirates of Yesteryear
Ronald Codrai 2001
A collection of black and white photographs which show just how much conditions have changed.

Phoenix Rising: UAE Past, Present and Future
Werner Forman 1996
Photographs accompanied by text on the past, present and future of the Emirates.

IRAN

The start of a journey in Persia resembles an algebraical equation: it may or may not come out. Robert Byron. *The Road to Oxiana* 1937.

Anthropology
Nomad. A Year in the Life of a Qashqa'i Tribesman in Iran
Lois Beck 1991
Beck lived with the Qermezi, a Qashqa'i tribe, in south-western Iran for a year in 1970-1. She kept a daily journal documenting the migratory cycle of these nomadic pastoralists, but also focuses her observations on one man, the group's leader who selected pastures and mediated in disputes.

Black Tents of Baluchistan
Philip Carl Salzman 2000
The nomadic Baluch inhabit the highland Sarhad region of south-eastern Iran. The author spent 27 months living among them.

Art and Archaeology
Persian Painting
Basil Gray 1977
The author reckons that the Mongol invasion actually actively encouraged the growth of calligraphy and book illustration, the disciplines which he emphasises in this book.

Tribal Rugs: an Introduction to the Weaving of the Tribes of Iran.
Jenny Housego 1978
An introduction to the weaving of the nine principal weaving tribes; the short text is accompanied by black and white photographs.

Persia: an archaeological guide
Sylvia A. Matheson 1972
Obviously now out of date, it is however still interesting as a guide to what had been excavated up until 1972.

Old Routes of Western Iran
Sir Aurel Stein 1940
Stein went on an archaeological journey to southern and western Iran between 1932 and 1936. The antiquities are described in detail.

Islamic Painting: a Survey
David Talbot Rice 1971
The book goes up to the eighteenth century and is mainly devoted to book and miniature painting. Illustrated by both colour and black and white reproductions.

Persian Lustre Ware
Oliver Watson 1985
The technique of lustre ware is described: how it is made, the kinds of materials needed and the different styles. Lists of individual objects are included.

The Shah-namah of Firdausi: the book of the Persian kings.
J.V.S.Wilkinson 1931
Twenty four illustrations from the *shah-nameh* manuscript, with an in-depth analysis of their narrative power. There is an introduction by Laurence Binyon on their artistic importance.

Biography
Out of Iran
Sousan Azadi with Angela Ferrante 1991 (1987)
The author grew up in a wealthy Iranian family, but was thrown into jail after the Shah was overthrown; she finally managed to escape with her son over the Zagros mountains into Turkey.

Death Plus Ten Years. My Life as the Ayatollah's Prisoner by 'Notorious British Spy'
Roger Cooper 1994 (1993)
Roger Cooper spent over five years in the notorious Evin prison in Tehran; the story of how he coped with his imprisonment, not knowing from one day to the next what was going to happen to him, makes inspirational reading.

The Blindfold Horse
Shusha Guppy 1989 (1988)
Shusha Guppy writes movingly about her childhood in Persia where she was born and brought up. The lost life of pre-Ayatollah Persia is vividly described by using both large and small incidents and she has wonderful recall for the memories of her own childhood.

Diplomacy and Murder in Tehran: Alexander Griboyedov and the Tsar's Mission to the Shah of Iran
Laurence Kelly 2001
A biography of the literary diplomat whose life was overshadowed by tragedy.

Robert Byron
James Knox 2003
A stimulating biography of the author of one of the finest travel books of the twentieth century.

An Iranian Odyssey
Gohar Kordi 1991
The author was born in a small Kurdish village going blind at the age of four. Her family then moved to Tehran and she became involved in the struggle to get an education, finally becoming the first woman student at the university.

129

Persia & the Great Game: Sir Percy Sykes
Antony Wynn 2003
A biography of Sykes - an explorer, consul, soldier & spy. Sykes first went to Persia for Army Intelligence in the 1890s with the aim of deterring Russian expansion towards India.

Fiction
Classical Persian Literature
A.J. Arberry 1958
The chronological development of Persian literature from the ninth to fifteenth centuries by both Iranian and European scholars. The chief poets,

Sa'di, Rumi, Hafez and Jami, all have chapters devoted to them.

Sohrab and Rustum
Matthew Arnold 1853
Based on Ferdousi's original.

The Collected Persian poems: poems from the Persian.
John C.E.Bowen 1976
Fifty poems which have the Persian text and English translations taken from the major poets from the 10th to 15th centuries.

A Good Place to Die
James Buchan 2000 (1999)
John Pitt a young Englishman is teaching English to young Iranian girls in Isfahan in 1974. He falls in love with one of them and they have to escape.

Persian Myths
Vesta Sarkhosh Curtis 1993
A short, illustrated edition of the most important Persian myths.

130

Savushun
Simin Daneshvar 1991 (1969)
About modern Iran. The story follows basic cultural themes and metaphors: sensitive and imaginative, it goes straight to the emotions. 'Savushun' is a pre-Islamic folk tradition from Southern Iran that conjures up hope in spite of everything.

The Legend of Seyavash
Ferdowsi (trans. Dick Davis) 1992
A section from the *Shahnameh*, Persia's national epic, which was written by Ferdowsi in the 10th century. The poem combines heroic warfare with psychological and ethical insight and is reputedly the longest poem ever written by one person.

Haji Agha. Portrait of an Iranian Confidence Man
Sadeq Hedayat 1978
Also Trois Gouttes de Sang.

Folk Tales of Ancient Persia
retold by Forough Hekmat 1974
A group of ten folk-tales from Shiraz which had been handed down in the oral tradition.

Rubaiyaat
Omar Khayyam

Samarkand
Amin Maalouf 2001 (1992)
Maalouf weaves fact and fiction using the manuscript of the *Rubaiyaat of Omar Khayyam*.

Persian Letters
Montesquieu (trans. C.J. Betts) 1973
The letters of two Persian travellers in Europe, Montesquieu's first book, was published in 1721; he uses their journey as a backdrop to air his views on every area of human interest.

The Adventures of Hajji Baba of Isphahan
James Morier 1986 (1824)
Morier was a diplomat in Tehran and wrote this satire on his return to England. It was instantly extremely popular and went into many editions: it shows a faithfully captured portrait of contemporary Persian manners and life that could only have been written by someone with a deep understanding of the Orient. The hero is a Persian adventurer, one part good and three parts knave who is always at the mercy of fortune; the book charts his various adventures and encounters and Hajji Baba is never totally implausible as a character.

The Siege of Isfahan
Jean-Christophe Rufin 2003 (2001)
Further adventures of the hero of *The Abyssinian*.

Food

The Legendary Cuisine of Persia
Margaret Shaida 1994
A glossy hardback book which explores

the long history of Persian cuisine.
Disappointingly few colour pictures.

Entertaining the Persian Way
Shirin Simmons 1991 (1988)

General Background

Behind Iranian Lines
John Simpson 1989 (1988)
Simpson was on the same flight from Paris to Tehran as Khomeini in 1979. He took full advantage of this and his invitation to return to Iran in 1987.

Guides

Bradt: Iran 2001

Odyssey: Illustrated Guide Iran 1999

Lonely Planet: Iran 2001

History & Politics

The Legacy of Persia
ed. A.J. Arberry 1968
A summary of Persian history and the many different facets of Persian culture are described here in a series of articles.

Persia and the Persian Question
George N. Curzon 1892
This is still important as a source book for nineteenth-century Persian history; there was much British interest in the area at the time and both the politics of this and other aspects of Persian life are described.

The Golden Age of Persia
Richard N. Frye 2000 (1975)
The great age of Iranian civilization occurred when Iran embraced Islam but maintained its own Persian heritage: culture flourished.

The Mantle of the Prophet
Roy Mottahedeh 2000 (1985)
Eyewitness accounts of Islam and politics in revolutionary Iran.

The Pride and the Fall: Iran 1974-1979.
Anthony Parsons 1984
The author was British ambassador to Tehran from 1973 until 1979; this personal record describes a time which he found the most interesting period of his diplomatic life.

The Shah's Last Ride
William Shawcross 1989 (1988)
Shawcross starts his book with the Shah's journey into exile in 1979 when he was denied entry into almost every country in the world and had to camp on an island in the Bahamas. He then analyses the background to the Shah's fall and, having talked to many of the doctors who treated him, is able to describe his illness in detail. A comprehensive account of the fall of a dynasty which clearly illustrates the relationship between states and leaders.

A History of Persia
Sir Percy Sykes 1969 (1915)
Sir Percy Sykes spent twenty one years living and travelling in Persia and so was well qualified to write what was to become the definitive history of the country. By the time of the third edition in 1930, Persia had changed dramatically, mainly due to the personality of Shah Riza, the founder of the Pahlavi dynasty. He had ensured that a strong national spirit had been awakened and Persia was finally competing with the west on equal terms, having shaken off the Capitulations which had been imposed by Russia. Discoveries at Ur had also taken place.

The English Amongst the Persians, during the Qajar Period 1787-1921
Sir Denis Wright 1977
Persia was considered immensely important by the British because of her geographical position on the threshold of India; they felt it imperative to protect her from Russian encroachment. This background of Anglo-Russian rivalry

with all its activity is described by Wright.

The Persian Expedition
Xenophon (trans. Rex Warner) 1972 (1949)
Xenophon joined Cyrus' army of Greek mercenaries to march into Persia in the 4th century B.C. He is observant about what he saw along the way and so we can get a very good idea of the people and the countries he and the army passed through, including Syria, Kurdestan and Armenia.

Natural History
To Persia for Flowers
Alice Fullerton 1938
The author kept a diary of her trip to Iran in 1935 in search of flowers. Twenty-four illustrations accompany the text.

Photographic
Persian Landscape: a photographic essay
Warwick Ball and Anthony Hutt 1978
A combination of black and white and colour photographs accompanied by short descriptions in a small-format book.

Isfahan, Pearl of Persia
Wilfred Blunt and Wim Swaan 1974
Blunt's text concentrates on the Safavid period, but is also a good general background to Isfahan, as he also deals with both earlier and later architecture; the text is accompanied by stunning black and white and colour illustrations.

Freya Stark in Persia
Malise Ruthven 1994
A volume of her own black and white photographs.

Travel Literature
Journeys in Persia and Kurdistan
Isabella Bird Bishop 1989 (1891)
The book was written from letters, which Isabella Bird had written over a period of two years as she was travelling. She

132

apologises for the fact that "they were written in haste at the conclusion of fatiguing marches, and often in circumstances of great discomfort and difficulty". She describes her actual travels, not wanting to go into any great detail about the antiquities in Persia, as she felt that others had done that adequately already.

Black on Black
Ana M. Briongos 2000
The author has visited Iran many times – this book is about how her friends and acquaintances there came to terms with the Islamic Revolution of 1979.

A Year Amongst the Persians. Impressions as to the Life, Character, and Thought of the People of Persia Received during Twelve Months' Residence in that Country in the Years 1887-1888
Edward Granville Browne 1926 (1893)
In his day Browne was the greatest exponent of Persian life and letters; he finally got to Persia, the country of his dreams, in 1887, already speaking the language fluently on his arrival. He had a prodigious memory and was able to recall conversations verbatim: both contributory factors in making this such an interesting book. He was a genius in conversation as well as with the written word and was well-loved by the Persians, who paid him many tributes.

The Road to Oxiana
Robert Byron 1992 (1937)
One of the classic travel books about Persia and Afghanistan. Robert Byron made this journey in 1933-4 and vividly describes the people he met and what he saw . The aim of his journey was to search for the origins of Islamic architecture; I found it very exciting to be in a building in Southern Iran in the 1970s which was then overrun by sheep and to read Byron's lyrical prose describing in marvellous detail the squinches in the roof.

Travels in Persia 1673-1677
Sir John Chardin 1988
The account of Chardin's second visit to Persia in 1673 which lasted four years. He had a great knowledge of Persia and through him we see life at the Shah's court and how he had to struggle to get paid for the jewels he had brought with him to sell.

Curzon's Persia
ed. Peter King 1986
A interesting selection, biased towards travel, from Curzon's Persia and the Persian Question which was originally published in 1892 and has remained a classic. The text is accompanied by photographs which Curzon took with his own precious Kodak.

Through Persia in Disguise
Sarah Hobson 1973
Sarah Hobson was 23 when she travelled to Persia to study designs and crafts. She would not have been able to visit many of the places she wanted as a woman, so she disguised herself as a man and was able to go almost wherever she pleased, including a men's theological college in Qum.

Eastern Approaches
Fitzroy Maclean 1991 (1949)
"A heady tale of high adventure and politics, superbly told, set in the Caucasus, Central Asia, Persia and Yugoslavia. It had a powerful effect on me as a young subaltern of 19 (and doubtless on many others of my generation) and first set my feet in the direction of Tashkent and Tbilisi, Kashgar and Kabul. I must have given away more copies of this magical book than of any other I have read." (Peter Hopkirk)

Among the Believers
V.S.Naipaul 1982 (1981)
The first part of Naipaul's Islamic journey is in Iran.

A Tower of Skulls
Gerald Reitlinger 1932
(A Journey through Persia and Turkish Armenia). A record of three months 'hurried travel' through Persia and Turkish Armenia in 1930-1. The author does not profess to be an expert on the areas he visits, but he gives good visual descriptions of what he sees.

Twelve Days
Vita Sackville-West 1928
(An Account of a Journey Across the Bakhtiari Mountains in South-Western Persia). It was some time after her journey that Vita Sackville-West was able to turn the experiences of her trip into a book. She had travelled to south-west Persia with Harold Nicolson, Gladwyn Jebb, Copley Amory (an American) and Lionel Smith to visit the Bakhtiari, a proud people, who claim that they were the only Persians not conquered by Alexander the Great.

Lords of the Mountains
Marie Therese Ullens de Schooten 1956
The author, wife of a diplomat, travelled to Southern Persia to meet the Kashkai, a nomadic tribe who had been in Persia since the 13th century. The book is the account of her journey and is also interesting archaeologically and anthropologically.

Adventures in Persia
Reginald Teague-Jones 1990 (1988)
When the book was published in 1988, the author 'Ronald Sinclair', aged 99, became famous as the oldest person to publish a first book; however it was only when he died that his true identity was revealed. For seventy years he had been in hiding from the Russians. This is the old-fashioned account of a journey from Beirut to India made in 1926 in a Model-A Ford.

Blind White Fish in Persia
Anthony Smith 1966
Four Oxford students embarked on a

133

journey to Kerman in 1950 with the aim of studying the *qanats* (underground water channels). Their adventures along the way are described in very readable prose.

Perseus in the Wind
Freya Stark 1948

Freya Stark spent several weeks one summer among the mountains of Elburz which separate the Caspian jungle from the Qazvin plain. She considered "these landscapes as among the most beautiful in the world, and [I] remember long days on stony paths, with the bells of the mules tinkling behind me as they found their steps in valleys yet unmapped, by rarely visited streams". Most nights she observed the constellation Perseus and named the book after this memory, as she felt "his stars as a friendliness and a bond in the gaiety of spaces and the cold of night".

The Valleys of the Assassins and Other Persian Travels
Freya Stark 1991 (1936)

This was Freya Stark's first book, for which she was given the Burton Memorial Medal by the Royal Asiatic Society. Her journey, which she undertook alone with a guide, was for fun. She went from north-west Luristan to the Valley of the Assassins and to the Throne of Solomon, most of which was in remote and unexplored territory.

The Land of the Great Sophy
Roger Stevens 1971 (1962)

Stevens wrote the book for those living or visiting Persia who were not experts on Asian matters. The first half of the book is devoted to background, containing chapters on geography, history, religion and art, while the second part describes his travels throughout the country. Eminently readable although now somewhat out of date.

Ten Thousand Miles in Persia or Eight Years in Iran
Percy M. Sykes 1902

The author goes into great detail about everywhere he visited during his long sojourn in Iran. The people are well described and the geography and geology of the towns and provinces are analysed in depth

Arminius Vambéry. His Life and Adventures.
Written by Himself 1884

In his autobiography Vambéry begins with his childhood, how he developed an interest in language and continues with a resumé of all his travels to Turkey, Persia and Central Asia; he ends up with his appointment as Professor of Oriental Languages in Hungary.

IRAQ

The Ark and all the rest become quite comprehensible when one sees Mesopotamia in flood time. Gertrude Bell. Letter to her family, 26th May 1916

Art & Archaeology
Ruined Cities of Iraq
Seton Lloyd 1942

Written as a guide to some of the ancient cities of Iraq, including Baghdad, Babylon, Samarra, Nineveh and Ur. The background includes an outline of Iraq's history.

Ur of the Chaldees: a Record of Seven Years of Excavation
Leonard Woolley 1950

Woolley reconstructs the past daily lives of the people who lived beside the Euphrates and describes the discoveries of the various cities which were found up until the time of Nebuchadnezzar.

Biography

Haji Rikkan, Marsh Arab
Fulanain 1927 (pseud. S.E. & Mrs Hedgecock)
Gertrude Bell suggested that this book be written, but died before she had completed her promised foreword. The central figure in the book is meant to portray an accurate picture of Arab tribal life and the changes which had occurred after the First World War.

The Life of Max Mallowan
Henrietta McCall 2001
Agatha Christie's archaeologist husband Max Mallowan was trained by Leonard Woolley at Ur and then excavated Nineveh before having his own digs at prehistoric sites in Iraq and north-east Syria.

Desert Queen
Janet Wallach 1999 (1996)
The life of Gertrude Bell who played a major role in creating the modern Middle East.

Fiction/Poetry

The Last Voyage of Somebody the Sailor
John Barth. 1992 (1991)
William Behler is shipwrecked off Sri Lanka while retracing one of Sinbad's legendary voyages; he finds himself marooned in Sinbad's house in medieval Baghdad.

Murder in Mesopotamia
Agatha Christie 1981 (1936)
A murder takes place among the members of an expedition which has gone to Mesopotamia to excavate the ruins of an ancient city. Poirot happens to be passing through Baghdad and called in to solve the diabolically clever murder. The book was written in Mesopotamia while Agatha Christie was accompanying her husband on a dig. Also They Came to Baghdad (1951) – in which Baghdad is

the chosen location for a secret super-power summit.

The Arabian Nights
Trans. Husain Haddawy 1995 (1990)
A fine new translation of the text edited by Muhsin Mahdi.

Iraqui Poetry Today
ed. Saadi Simawe 2002
Work by 40 living or recently deceased writers - includes Jewish and Kurdish as well as Arab writers.

Folk-Tales of Iraq
ed. E.S.Stevens 1931
Inevitably, folk-tales which are passed down verbally get changed and embellished over the years; this collection of forty eight fairy-tales is therefore a rich and varied assortment.

Food

The Baghdad Kitchen
Nina Jamil-Garbutt 1985

135

General Background

Baghdad Diaries
Nuha al-Radi 2003 (1998)
The artist Nuha al-Radi kept a diary through the 1991 Gulf War. In it she captures the reality of life under sanctions. She now lives in exile in Beirut.

Iraq under Siege
ed. Anthony Arnove 2000
The deadly impact of sanctions and war.

Cruelty and Silence
Kanan Makiya (Samir Al-Khalil) 1994 (1993)
War, tyranny, uprising and the Arab world. The Iraqi author wrote Republic of Fear in the 1980's about the horrors in Iraq. Cruelty and Silence was written after Saddam's invasion of Kuwait when Makiya called for a united Arab world to join together to fight him over Kuwait. Cruelty and Silence is a collection of people's stories.

Guide
Bradt: Iraq 2002

History

No Friends but the Mountains. The Tragic History of the Kurds
John Bulloch and Harvey Morris 1993 (1992)
The history of the Kurds is traced by two authors who know the area well and their hopes and disappointments, post the Gulf War, are investigated.

The Long Road to Baghdad
Edmund Candler 1919
A book which covers three stages of the Mesopotamian campaign: the first milestone was the fall of Kut, the second, the capture of Samarrah and the third, the armistice and the surrender of the Turkish Army at Shergat Ali.

Three Kings in Baghdad 1921-1958
Gerald de Gaury 1961
In 1921 Mesopotamiawas renamed Iraq by the British. The three kings de Gaury writes about are the first king of the new Iraq, Faisal 1, his son Ghazi and Ghazi's son Faisal 11 who died in 1958.

Foundations in the Dust: A Story of Mesopotamian Exploration
Seton Lloyd 1980 (1947)
A history of the lives and works of some of the better known archaeologists who worked in the region, such as: Austen Henry Layard and Henry Rawlinson.

Iraq
Stephen Hemsley Longrigg and Frank Stoakes 1958
A matter-of-fact general introduction to the history, economy, society and politics of Iraq up until 1958; the Iraqi revolution occurred in July 1958 when the book was at proof stage.

A Modern History of the Kurds
David McDowall 1997
A history of the Kurds from the nineteenth century until the present day.

Iraq - An Illustrated History
Gilles Munier 2003
A well-illustrated history of the seat of civilization.

The Shi'is of Iraq
Yitzhak Nakash 2003 (1995)
A comprehensive history of Iraq's majority group and its turbulent relations with the Sunnis.

Mesopotamia
Julian Reade 1991
A brief illustrated history.

Ancient Iraq
Georges Roux 1992 (1964)
An accessible and readable account of the early history of Iraq. The book is a compilation of articles which were originally published in *Iraq Petroleum.*

Iraq Since 1958 from Revolution to Dictatorship
Marion Farouk-Sluglett and Peter Sluglett.2001 (1987)
A political and economic history of Iraq which begins by giving an introduction to Iraq before the 1958 revolution and continues in chronological fashion to chart the rise of Saddam Husain in 1970 and the social, political and economic policies since then.

Loyalties: Mesopotamia 1914-1917
Arnold Wilson 1969 (1930)
A personal account of the events leading up to the British occupation of Iraq; Wilson was acting British Civil Commissioner in Mesopotamia. He also wrote *Mesopotamia: A Clash of Loyalties 1917-1920* (1921).

Photographic

Iraq: Land of Two Rivers
Gavin Young 1980
A photographic record of the landscape and people of Iraq showing that despite enormous industrialisation, the Iraqis are proud of their past.

Travel Literature

From Amurath to Amurath
Gertrude Bell 1911
A description of Gertrude Bell's extensive travels in Mesopotamia; she concentrates on the archaeological history of Babylon and Assyria.

The Letters of Gertrude Bell
ed. Florence Bell 1927
After leaving Cairo in 1916 Gertrude Bell wrote her second volume of letters from Baghdad. In 1923 she was involved in the founding of the national museum.

The Tigris Expedition
Thor Heyerdahl 1980
Heyerdahl built a boat of reeds in the marshes of Southern Iraq and sailed down the Tigris to the Arabian Gulf and to the sea, in search of the routes which he reckoned the ancient Sumerians must have used 5000 years before. The book begins with descriptions of the building of the boat and describes the lives and customs of the Marsh Arabs. The people who actually built the boat were from the highlands of South America The 'Tigris' was ceremonially burnt at the end of the journey.

Come, Tell Me How You Live
Agatha Christie Mallowan 1990 (1946)
The famous crime writer's light-hearted and often funny account of the time she spent in Syria and Iraq in the 1930s, with her archaeologist husband, Sir Max Mallowan. She met her husband-to-be, who was then assistant to the Woolleys, on a visit to Ur; they were soon married and she threw herself into the life of an archaeologist playing a very practical role. She wrote the book not as a task but as "a labour of love".

A Reed Shaken By the Wind
Gavin Maxwell 1994 (1957)
(A Journey through the Unexplored Marshlands of Iraq). In 1956 Gavin Maxwell accompanied Wilfred Thesiger to the marshlands of Iraq. He describes the people he met and his experiences during his travels and describes how he acquired an otter named Mijbil.

Escape from Baghdad
Carl Raswan 1938
When the Royal Commission from London were about to announce their decision in regard to Palestine, Raswan, who had lived for many years among the Bedouin, decided to go behind the scenes and see for himself what was happening.

Baghdad Sketches
Freya Stark 1992 (1937)
Eight of the short essays and sketches were written as the result of a visit to Iraq in 1937, whereas the rest tried to capture what life was like in Baghdad in 1931. Already by 1931 a veneer of westernisation was settling over Baghdad, the Caliph's City, and Freya Stark found that by 1937 this had dramatically increased.

Riding to the Tigris
Freya Stark 1959
A description of her travels in the Hakkiari and Zab Valleys in Iraq.

The Marsh Arabs
Wilfred Thesiger 1964
A book about the fast-disappearing people who live in the marshes in Iraq, around the junction of the Tigris and Euphrates. Thesiger spent eight years living among these people and visited practically every small village; the book describes in interesting detail his love for the people and his knowledge of the area. Many of the floating islands on which the Marsh Arabs lived were man-made, their houses were made of reeds and the econ-

omy was based largely on herds of water buffalo. These are one of the many groups of people who Saddam Husain virtually eliminated.

Sweet Tea With Cardamon
Teresa Thornhill 1997
A journey through Iraqi Kurdistan.

Return to the Marshes
Gavin Young 1977
Gavin Young was introduced to the marshes of Southern Iraq by Wilfred Thesiger in the 1950s. In this 'memorial to my Marsh Arab friends' he describes how much their lives had changed by the time he returned in the 1970s; and also writes about their background and history.

ISRAEL

The word Palestine always brought to my mind a vague suggestion of a country as large as the United States. I do not know why, but such was the case. I suppose it was because I could not conceive of a small country having so large a history. Mark Twain. *The Innocents Abroad*, 1869

The Bible is an obvious choice for this part of the world since as well as the religious content it's extremely helpful for the history, with good descriptions of the landscape. A small India paper edition is easy to travel with.

Art & Archaeology

Gods, Goddesses, and Images of God in Ancient Israel
Othmar Keel & Christoph Uehlinger 1998
An explanation of how male and female deities were understood in ancient Canaan and Israel.

The Bible and Recent Archaeology
Kathleen Kenyon 1987 (1978)
A serious study which summarizes the

last forty years of archaeology with its new interpretations.

The Holy Land
Jerome Murphy-O'Connor 1998 (1980)
An archaeological guide that covers sites from the earliest times up to 1700 which includes Jewish underground systems, Roman temples and Byzantine and Crusader buildings. Fairly detailed but very accessible.

Archaeological Encyclopaedia of the Holy Land 2001
ed. Avraham Negev 1972
Hundreds of entries, many illustrated, covering the Holy Land and its history from the earliest times.

Autobiography/Biography

To be an Arab in Israel
Fawzi al-Asmar 1975
The author was born in Haifa in 1937. The story of his life in Palestine up until 1970 when he was released from prison.

Ben Gurion
Michael Bar-Zohar 1978 (1967)
A biography of Israel's first leader.

The Revolt
Menahem Begin 1979 (1951)
Begin's right-wing account of his role in Israel's independence.

Crossing the Border
Kim Chernin 1994
A young American leaves her conventional life to live on a kibbutz where she becomes deeply involved emotionally.

The Yellow Wind
David Grossman 1988
Grossman, a novelist, wrote the account of his visit to the West Bank in 1987 in Hebrew. He talked to both Palestinian and Jewish settlers.

House of Windows
Adina Hoffman 2001 (2000)
A compelling evocation of Jerusalem where Hoffman has lived for 10 years since moving from the States.

My Life
Golda Meir 1975
Her - obviously biased - autobiography.

Fiction

The Lord
Soraya Antonius 1986
This and *Where the Jinn Consult* (1987) are two blockbuster novels set in Palestine at the end of the British mandate.

Children at the Gate
Lynne Reid Banks 1988 (1968)
A Jewish-Canadian divorcee is living alone in poverty in the Arab quarter of Acre; through an Arab friend she re-establishes herself and finds happiness. Lynne Reid Banks also wrote *Defy the Wilderness* (set in Jerusalem) and *An End to Running*, about life on a kibbutz.

Penguin Book of Hebrew Verse.
ed. T.Carmi 1981
An anthology with parallel texts dating from biblical times to the present day.

Dolly City
Orly Castel-Bloom 1997
An irreverent and witty satire about the Yiddishe-mamma complex.

See Under: Love
David Grossman 1991 (1989)
A wide-ranging imaginative novel which tackles the worst horrors of the twentieth century: "A brave and moving attempt by an outstandingly talented writer to redefine love, having looked the Facts of Death full in the face". Clive Sinclair, *The Independent*.

The Saturday Morning Murder
Batya Gur
This and *Literary Murder* and *Murder on*

the Kibbutz are thrillers which give a good insight into Israeli life.

The Secret Life of Saeed
Emile Habibi 2003 (1985)
A funny, wise and raw novel about an informer for the Zionist state.

The Fairest Among Women
Shifra Horn 2001 (1998)
Rosa was born a few days after her father's brutal murder in West Jerusalem and grows up to have an extraordinary life. Also *Four Mothers*.

The Little Drummer Girl
John Le Carré 1983
A spy-novel about the Israeli-Palestinian conflict.

The Silencer
Simon Louvish 1993
Louvish is a film maker who lives in London. This is a politically satirical novel. Also *The Days of Miracles and Wonders*, *The Therapy of Avraham Blok*, *City of Blok* and *The Death of Moishe-Ganef*.

139

The Source
James Michener 1993 (1965)
An extremely easy and un-put-downable read which stretches across thousands of years of life in the volatile region of the Holy Land.

The Hill of Evil Counsel
Amos Oz 1993 (1976)
Three stories which are a mixture of history and narrative which take place in Jerusalem during the last days of the British Mandate. Novels by Amos Oz include *My Michael* (1991) (1968)), a love story set in Jerusalem before Suez and *A Perfect Peace* (1993) (1985) in which Yonaton Lifshitz leaves his kibbutz and marriage to start a new life. *The Same Sea* is a novel of love and loss.

The Penitent
Isaac Bashevis Singer 1983
A rich businessman gives up his lifestyle, goes to Israel and marries a rabbi's daughter.

The Mandelbaum Gate
Muriel Spark 1967 (1965)
Barbara Vaughan visits Jerusalem and meets a diplomat, Freddy Hamilton; she ignores his warnings that she might be arrested because of her Jewish blood and promptly disappears in Jordan.

Exodus
Leon Uris 1958
A blockbuster of a novel about Palestine and Zionism.

Absence of Pain
Barbara Victor 1990 (1988)
Maggie Sommers is a journalist in the Middle East; she had assured herself that she wanted nothing more to do with love, but then meets a married Israeli general Avi Herzog. "Stark, witty, raw realism that leaves you gasping for air." (*Washington Post*)

A Lake Beyond the Wind
Yahya Yakhlif 2003
Set in 1948 - a powerful lament for a lost world by an author from Palestine.

General Background & Politics

To Jerusalem and Back
Saul Bellow 1976
Saul Bellow's personal impressions of his journey to Jerusalem.

The Fateful Triangle
Noam Chomsky 1999 (1983)
The American intellectual deals with American policy towards Israel.

Dispossessed: the Ordeal of the Palestinians
David Gilmour 1982 (1980)
Divided into three, part one looks at Palestinian society before 1948, the second with the new diaspora and the third with resistance, the PLO and international relations.

Against the Stranger
Janine di Giovanni 1994 (1993)
A weaving together of the lives and deaths of Arabs and Israelis since the Palestinian uprising in 1987: "An excellent primer on what it is like to live in one of the lousiest places on earth". (*GQ*)

Sharing the Promised Land
Dilip Hiro 1997 (1996)
A thorough and readable look at the Israel-Palestine question.

A Land Without a People
Nur Masalha 1997
'Israel, Transfer and the Palestinians 1949-96.'

In the Land of Israel
Amos Oz 1983
Amos Oz looked at his country as a tourist, in order to get to the bottom of the fears, hopes and prejudices of his fellow countrymen.

The Slopes of Lebanon
Amos Oz 1991 (1990)
A collection of pieces by Amos Oz, who is increasingly writing non-fiction. *The Washington Post* said of him "Countries need writers as their voices of conscience; few have them. Israel is one of the few. It has Amos Oz ..." This selection contains, among others, Oz's thoughts on the Israeli president's visit to Germany, Claude Lanzmann's film *Shoah: An Oral History of the Holocaust* "the most powerful film I have ever seen. It is a creation that transforms the viewer", and the Lebanon War.

The Question of Palestine
Edward Said 1992 (1980)
An excellent account of the Palestinian-Israeli conflict.

140

Tel Aviv: From Dream to City
Joachim Schlör 1999 (1996)
Tel Aviv was established in 1909 as a
modern garden suburb of Jaffa. Schlör
has interviewed many residents for this
book part of Reaktion Books Topographic
series.

Israel. Culture Shock
Dick Winter 1996
For both short and long term visitors.

Guides
*Bradt: Palestine with Jerusalem
2000*

Kibbutz Volunteer 2000

*Eyewitness: Jerusalem & the
Holy Land 2000*

Israel Handbook 1999

Israel. Pocket Insight Guide 2001

Israel Insight Guide 2002

Jerusalem Insight Guide 1998

*Lonely Planet: Israel & the
Palestinian Territories 1999*

Lonely Planet: Jerusalem 1999

*Mini Rough Guide: Jerusalem
1999*

Guide to the Holy Land
Theoderich 1986 (1897)
A guide which was written for pilgrims in
about 1172.

History & Politics
*A History of Jerusalem. One City
Three Faiths*
Karen Armstrong 1996
An attempt to establish what Jews,
Christians and Muslims mean when they
say that Jerusalem is 'holy' to them. "In

Jerusalem more than any other place I
have visited, history is a dimension of the
present."

*The Fifty Years War- Israel and
the Arabs*
Ahron Bergman & Jihan El-Tahri 1998
Based on the television series

O Jerusalem
Larry Collins and Dominique Lapierre
1972
The book is based on interviews and is
the account of the 1948 siege of
Jerusalem and the War of Independence.

Personal Witness
Abba Eban 1993 (1992)
The history of Israel as seen through the
eyes of Abba Eban who since the foundation of the state of Israel was always
close to the centre of what has happened
Also *Heritage: Civilization and the Jews*
– a history of the Jews from the time of
Abraham to the establishment of the state
of modern Israel.

Israel. A History
Martin Gilbert 1999 (1998)
Very detailed and invaluable historical
research.

The Gun and the Olive Branch
David Hirst 1984 (1977)
A clear and detailed account of the
Palestinian-Israeli conflict written by a
journalist on the *Guardian*.

The Jewish War
Josephus (trans. Paul L. Maier) 1994
An account of the Jewish revolt against
the Romans in 66AD.

Jerusalem – the Holy City
Mrs Oliphant 1985 (1891)
A scholarly history first published in
1891.

Imperial Israel
Michael Palumbo 1992 (1990)
A well researched account of the history

141

of the occupation of the West Bank and Gaza.

The Iron Wall
Avi Shlaim 2001 (2000)
"A milestone in modern scholarship of the Middle East" (Edward Said). A fresh look at Israel and the Arab world.

The Crusades and the Holy Land
Georges Tate 1996 (1991)
A well-illustrated and well-condensed book. The way the Christian army fought its way across Asia Minor, capturing Jerusalem is explored from both Arab and European viewpoints.

A History of the Israeli-Palestinian Conflict
Mark Tessler 1994
A good recent history.

Photographic
Jerusalem. In the Shadow of Heaven

A Photographic Guide to the Birds of Israel and the Middle East 2000

Religion
The Dead Sea Scrolls Uncovered
Robert Eisenman and Michael Wise 1993 (1992)
A complete translation and interpretation of fifty key documents which were withheld for thirty-five years. They show what was happening in Palestine at the dawn of Christianity.

Judaism
Isidore Epstein 1931
A good introduction.

Travel Literature
Breaking Ranks
Ben Black 2001
The author moves from Scotland to Israel, has various adventures but has a

struggle with his conscience when he gets his military call up.

Disraeli's Grand Tour: Benjamin Disraeli in the Holy Land 1830-51
Robert Blake 1982
This book is based on the diaries that Disraeli wrote about his tour of the Holy Land.

Winner Takes All. A Season in Israel
Stephen Brook 1991 (1990)
The combination of part travel and part background history and politics makes this an ideal book to take on a trip to Israel, or indeed to read as an introduction to the country.

Jerusalem. City of Mirrors
Amos Elon 1990 (1989)
A biography of Jerusalem which charts the history of the city with its violent conflicts and religious wars and shows how these conflicts are reflected in the life of the city today.

Travels with Myself and Another
Martha Gellhorn 1991 (1978)
In Eilath, Martha Gellhorn came across a group of hippies. With her wonderful ear for dialogue she condensed the conversations she had with them as to why they were travelling: "Three words sufficed for the experience of travel: great, beautiful, heavy".

In the Steps of the Master
H.V. Morton 2001 (1934)
Somewhat dated travelogue, but nonetheless interesting.

Return to the Desert
David Praill 1995
A forty-day journey from Mount Hermon to Mount Sinai.

Jerusalem
Colin Thubron 1969
A history of the city and a look at why it

became so important to so many different people as well as an account of Thubron's own time there. "The best evocation of that magical city I have ever come across." (Jeremy Paxman)

JORDAN

Match me such marvel save in Eastern clime

A rose-red city - 'half as old as time'!
J.W.Burgon *Petra* 1845.

Art and Archaeology

The Antiquities of Jordan
Gerald Lankester Harding 1967 (1959)
An invaluable guide which describes the history and archaeological sites of Jordan. The book begins with a general history and continues with chapters done as a site by site survey.

Jawa: Lost City of the Black Desert
Svend W. Helms 1981
This short lived, 4th millennium BC city, which lasted for only one generation, was phenomenal in that, to be able to function in the arid black desert of north-east Jordan, complex hydro-technology was in operation. The book demonstrates the reconstruction of the city.

Fiction

Appointment with Death
Agatha Christie 2001
The corpse of Mrs Boynton sits on the cliffs at Petra with a puncture mark on its wrist. Poirot only has 24 hours to solve the mystery.

On the Walls of My Being
Ali Tal 1995
Set in a remote village in twentieth-century Jordan.

General Background

Jewels of the Kingdom. The Heritage of Jordan
Peter Vine 1987
An illustrated book in which the contents are divided into the Past, Natural History, Traditions, Art and Artists and Modern Jordan.

Guides

Petra: The Rose Red City
Christian Auge & Jeran-Marie Dentzer 2000
Thames & Hudson New Horizons series.

Blue Guide: Jordan 2001

Jordan Handbook 2000

Insight Guide: Jordan 1999

Lonely Planet: Jordan 2003

Petra. A Traveller's Guide
Rosaly Maqsood 2000

Rough Guide: Jordan 2002

Monuments of Jordan – An Historical Guide
Rami Khouri 2002
Well-illustrated hardback with an up-to-date survey of Jordan's 200 most important historical and archaeological sites.

History

Uneasy Lies the Head
HM King Hussein of Jordan. 1962.
King Hussein writes about the ten year period between 1951, when his grandfather was assassinated, and 1961, when he married. It is interesting to read his account of Glubb Pasha's dismissal in 1956 and of the particularly turbulent period between 1956 and 1960.

The Brink of Jordan
Charles Johnston 1972
The author was British ambassador

143

between 1956 and 1960 - a time of endless coups, assassinations and plots. He has great knowledge of the area and writes with insight about those troubled times

The Hashemite Kings
James Morris 1959
Morris's book is concerned more with the history of the area and its relationship with Britain between 1916 and 1958, than with the individual Hashemite kings, although he does write about several of the Jordanian monarchs in detail. He became interested in the area after representing the *Manchester Guardian* at a press conference in Amman, at which King Hussein announced with tears in his eyes that his cousin King Feisal 11 had been assassinated.

Caravan Cities
Michael I. Rostovtzeff 1932
The ruined cities of Petra and Jerash which both featured in the caravan trade are described here and their importance on the trade route is assessed.

The History of the Crusades
Steven Runciman Vol.II. 1987 (1952)
The second volume in the trilogy is entitled *The Kingdom of Jerusalem and the Frankish East 1100-1187*. It starts with the foundation of the Kingdom of Jerusalem and ends with its reconquest by Saladin. It contains information about the crusader period in trans-Jordan after the fall of Jerusalem.

The Modern History of Jordan
Kamal Salibi 1998
A political history of Jordan which shows how the poor and sparsely-populated country became one of the most successful in the Middle East.

Leisure Activities
Trekking and Canyoning in the Jordanian Dead Sea Rift
Itai Haviv 2001

Natural History
Portrait of a Desert: the story of an expedition to Jordan
Guy Mountfort 1965
One of the aims of the expedition was to find out about the environmental situation in Jordan; the findings suggested the creation of three national parks. There are descriptions of birds and animals.

Photographic
Journey Through Jordan
Mohamed Amin, Duncan Willetts & Sam Kiley 1994

Jerash and the Decapolis
Iain Browning 1982
Jerash is the best preserved city of the Decapolis; its history, architecture and early explorers are described here and the text is accompanied by many photographs.

Petra
Iain Browning 1989 (1973)
Browning describes the importance of Petra on the trade routes, its history as the Nabatean capital, its early explorers and later scientific ones and the significance of the six major architectural periods. The text is accompanied by many photographs and line drawings.

High Above Jordan
Jane Taylor 1990 (1989)
Aerial photographs of Jordan.

Petra and the Lost Kingdom of the Nabateans
Jane Taylor 2001
A well-deserved history of the Nabateans well-illustrated with photographs by Jane Taylor who lives and works in Jordan.

Travel Literature
The Letters of Gertrude Bell
ed. Florence Bell 1927
The first desert journeys that Gertrude Bell undertook were into Jordan; she vis-

144

ited Petra in 1900 and the first volume of her two volume collection of letters are about this trip.

Kingdom of the Film Stars
Annie Caulfield 1997
A book in the series of Lonely Planet Journeys about a journey into the heart of Jordan.

The Vanished Cities of Arabia
Mrs Steuart Erskine 1925
Descriptions of the lost cities of Petra, Jerash and the Decapolis, in the days when very little archaeological exploration had taken place.

Three Journeys in the Levant
Shusha Guppy 2001
"I have nothing but praise for Shusha Guppy's excellent book on the Levant" (Patrick Leigh Fermor). Journeys in Jordan, Syria and Lebanon.

The Rob Roy on the Jordan
John Macgregor 1904
The author went in a canoe down the River Jordan to the Dead Sea.

The Lovely Land: the Hashemite Kingdom of Jordan
Ethel Mannin 1965
A personal and readable account of a trip to Jordan in the 1960's.

LEBANON

At Baalbec, as at other eastern ruins, a traveller must luxuriate on the pleasures of imagination, for he will get no luxury more substantial. John Carne. *Letters from the East* 1830

Biography
An Arab Tells His Story: A Study in Loyalties
Edward Atiyah 1946
The author was born in Lebanon, although he was educated in the West; he writes movingly about the changes that

have occurred for Lebanese Christians since the end of the Ottoman Empire of the twentieth century.

Lady Hester Stanhope: Queen of the Desert
Virginia Childs 1990
Lady Hester spent most of her life in Syria and Lebanon. She was extremely independent and was very concerned about the welfare of the people of the countries in which she lived. She died in Lebanon in 1839.

Holding On
Sunnie Mann 1990
Sunnie Man wrote this book during her husband's two year disappearance; it is a moving story of what it was like to live in post Second World War Beirut; the changes that the 1975 war brought and the struggle she was having, learning to cope with her husband's absence.

Fiction
Death in Beirut
Tawfiq Yusuf Awwad 1976
A young Shi'i Muslim girl from the south of Lebanon goes to study in Beirut. Set against the rising tension in Lebanon at the time.

Beirut Nightmares
Ghada al-Samman 1997
About everyday life while living in a war zone. The writer was born in Damascus.

The Story of Zahra
Hanan Al-Shaykh 1993
Zahra leaves the Shia community in South Lebanon where she was seduced and goes to West Africa. Later she returns to a war-torn Beirut.

The Stone of Laughter
Hoda Barakat 1995 (1990)
Hailed as the best novel set against the background of the Lebanese civil war.

145

The Return to Beirut
Andrée Chedid 1989 (1985)
Set in Beirut in 1975, when Lebanon is on the brink of civil war, an American girl, Sybil, meets her grandmother, Kalya, for the first time; Kalya recalls, through a series of flashbacks, times she spent with her own grandmother.

Kahlil Gibran: His Life and World
Jean Gibran and Kahlil Gibran 1991
The definitive biography, which draws on previously unpublished diaries and letters.

A Woman of Nazareth
Hala Deeb Jabbour 1992 (1989)
A novel set in Beirut of the 1960s and 1970s which tells the story of a Palestinian woman in exile and her struggles to come to terms with the limitations of a traditional life.

Little Mountain
146   Elias Khoury (trans. Maria Tabet) 1990 (1989).
Set in Beirut during the civil war in 1975-6, the novel examines how society disintegrates during a conflict in a mixture of surrealism and reality.

Food
Food for the Vegetarian. Traditional Lebanese Recipes
Aidda Karaoglan 1992

A Taste of Lebanon. Cooking Today the Lebanese Way
Mary Salloum 1992
The first book to be devoted entirely to Lebanese cooking. Over 200 recipes are included: pitta bread, yoghurt, hummus, tabouli, baklava and burghul.

General Background
Beirut Spy
Saïd K. Aburish 1990 (1989)
Much of the intrigue and gossip in post-war Beirut took place in the bar of the Hotel Saint-Georges, until it was blown up in 1975. The man who was general manager in the 1960s described it as "a unique, once-a-century happening. I felt as if my clients were running the Middle East, occasionally the world". Aburish recounts much of what happened there but holds back much which he reckons is still not safe to tell.

An Evil Cradling
Brian Keenan 1993 (1992)
The harrowing account of Brian Keenan's four and a half years in captivity at the hands of Shi'ite militiamen.

Ports of Call
Amin Maalouf 1999 (1996)
Aged 18 Ossyane leaves Beirut for France. In 1938 he is drawn into the Resistance and returns to Beirut as a rebel hero.

The Slopes of Lebanon
Amos Oz. 1991 (1990)   (see Israel)

Guides
Handbook Jordan, Syria & Lebanon 2001

Insight: Syria & Lebanon 2000

Lonely Planet: Lebanon 2001

Traveller's Survival Kit: Lebanon 1999

History
Pity the Nation
Robert Fisk 1992
The veteran Middle East reporter's account of the war in Lebanon and the troubled years that followed its outbreak. Fisk analyses how Lebanon is enmeshed with the Israeli-Palestinian conflict.

Lebanon: the Fractured Country
David Gilmour 1984 (1983)
Gilmour traces the conflicts in Lebanon

back to their origins, with carefully researched historical analysis and first-hand experience of the fate of the country.

A Short History of Lebanon
Philip K. Hitti 1965
The book begins with ancient Lebanon, Syria and Palestine and continues through the history of the Phoenician, Roman, Byzantine, Muslim, Crusader and Ottoman eras, up until the nineteenth century.

Natural History
The Birds of Britain and Europe with North Africa and the Middle East
Hermann Heinzel, Richard Fitter and John Parslow. 1979 (see Middle East General)

Flowers of the Mediterranean
Oleg Polunin and Anthony Huxley (see Turkey)

Photographic
Baalbek
Friedrich Ragette 1980
The history of Baalbek (which was known to the Ancient Greeks as Heliopolis) is described and illustrated. It was the centre of worship of the Sun God cult, and later had Roman, Byzantine and Arab additions.

Religion
The Prophet
Kahlil Gibran 1991 (1926)
Although Gibran emigrated to the USA, he was born in the Lebanon.

Travel Literature
The Nun of Lebanon: the Love Affair of Lady Hester Stanhope and Michael Bruce
ed. Ian Bruce 1951
When this book appeared Lady Hester

Stanhope's letters had only just been discovered. Apart from telling a wonderful story, the letters give interesting insights into nineteenth-century Lebanon and Syria.

Syria and Lebanon
Robin Fedden 1965
A very readable travelogue of post Second World War Syria and Lebanon in which the author describes the major sites and gives their potted histories.

Three Journeys in the Levant
Shusha Guppy 2001 (see Jordan)

Letters from Syria
Freya Stark 1942
These are the letters that Freya Stark wrote to her mother and friends after her arrival in the Middle East for the first time; the book begins with letters written from Lebanon.

The Hills of Adonis
Colin Thubron 1987 (1968)
The account of a walking trip that the author took into the Lebanese mountains in 1967.

147

Baalbek Caravans
Charis Waddy 1967
A history and look at some of the many travellers who have passed through the hotels at Baalbek.

SYRIA

Most perfect of medieval fortresses (and model for every sandcastle ever built).
Peter Wilsher *Sunday Times* 30 December 1979. [About The Crac des Chevaliers]

Art and Archaeology
Contemporary Art in Syria 1898-1998
Mouni Atassi (ed)
Essential reading for anyone interested in the subject.

Syria: An Historical and Architectural Guide
Warwick Ball 1997
A dense but invaluable account.

Palmyra
Iain Browning 1979
A survey of Palmyra which became famous as a trading centre in 106 AD; Browning describes many of the later travellers to the site including Lady Hester Stanhope who was there in 1813. Well illustrated with colour photographs.

Monuments of Syria
Ross Burns 2000
An invaluable guide, to the historical sites of Syria, arranged alphabetically and accompanied by maps and plans. Essential for anyone interested in Syria.

The Arts and Crafts of Syria
Johannes Kalter 1992
An overall look at what the arts and crafts mean in Syrian society.

148

Biography
In Aleppo Once
Taqui Altounyan 1969
The writer was the granddaughter of Dr Alam Altounyam who was one of the founders of Aleppo's main hospitals.

The House on Arnus Square
Samar Attar
An evocative memoir of a Damascus childhood.

Lady Hester Stanhope: Queen of the Desert.
Virginia Childs 1990 (see Lebanon)

Saladin
S. Lane-Poole 1985 (1898)
A biography of Saladin (Salah al Din 1138-1193), Sultan of Egypt and Syria who led his warrior Saracens against the Third Crusade (1189-1192) under King Richard 1.

Assad of Syria: The Struggle for the Middle East
Patrick Seale 1988
A biography of Assad which shows what the world looks like from the seat of power in Damascus.

Fiction
Sabriya: Damascus Is Asleep
Ulfat Idilbi (trans. Peter Clark) 1995
Also *Grandfather's Tale* (1998) which is about an old woman telling stories to her grandchildren about her grandfather.

Just Like a River
Muhammad Kamil al-Khatib 2003
A first novel by the intellectual Syrian. The war in Lebanon is in the background of this novel linked by blood & friendship.

Sun on a Cloudy Day
Hanna Mina
A young Syrian questions the power of the occupying French.

Said the Fisherman
Marmaduke Pickthall 1986 (1903)
The story of a corrupt Muslim fisherman who goes to Damascus to seek his fortune in the summer of 1860 at the time of a massacre of Christians by Muslims and Druze; Said takes advantage of this and abducts the daughter of a Christian merchant. He makes his fortune selling carpets and after many intrigues finally meets his death whilst upholding his faith. Pickthall's contemporaries wrote of his work; "...in imagination he goes native. And that thoroughly", D.H. Lawrence. "...the only contemporary English novelist who understands the nearer East", E.M.Forster. And ironically H.G.Wells wrote: " I wish I could feel as certain about my own work as I do of yours, that it will be alive and interesting people fifty years from now".

Daughter of Damascus
Suham Tergeman
Written in the early part of the 20th cen-

tury, originally published by the author and distributed by a sweet-seller.

Absent in the Spring
Mary Westmacott (pseud. of Agatha Christie) 1985 (1944)
The story of Joan Scudamore who finding herself alone with nothing to do on the border between Syria and Turkey confronts the person she has become.

Food
The Art of Syrian Cookery
Helen Corey 1992 (1962)
Over 250 Syrian and Lebanese recipes including kibby, shish-kebab and stuffed grape leaves.

General Background
Syria
Tabitha Petran 1972
A detailed introduction to the geography, history, economy and politics of Syria.

The Struggle for Syria
Patrick Seale 1986 (1965)
An authoritative look at the intrigues in Syria's politics and the attempt to achieve Arab unity in 1958. Very good on the 1957 Anglo-American-Iraqi attempt to overthrow the government.

Culture Shock Syria
Coleman South 1997
A guide to customs and etiquette. Very useful for anyone planning a long stay.

Guides
Handbook Jordan, Syria & Lebanon 2001

Insight: Syria & Lebanon 2000

Lonely Planet: Syria 2003

Rough Guide: Syria 2001

History
The Saracens
Edward Gibbon & Simon Ockley 1984 (1885)
The book (chapters 50-52 of *The History of the Decline and the Fall of the Roman Empire*) - traces the Saracenic history from its beginnings to its decline.

Syria: A Short History
Philip Hitti 1959
Much of the book is about the Arab Revolt and the establishment of the French Mandate.

Syria. A Modern History
Tabitha Petran 1972
Syria was much effected by the existence of Israel taken from what had been its historical south. The modern history has been one of struggle to achieve independence, national identity and socio-economic advance.

Mirror to Damascus
Colin Thubron 1986 (1967)
The history of Damascus from Biblical times until the revolution in 1966. Although James Morris wrote "Damascus is not a sophisticated city. Those westerners who do not subscribe to the brittle charm of its Arab quarters are likely to find it something of a hick town", Thubron manages to find it and describe it as a fascinating place, and calls his book "simply a work of love".

149

Natural History
Flowers of the Mediterranean
Oleg Polunin and Anthony Huxley (see Turkey)

Photographic
Syria in View
Michael Jenner 1986
Chapters on Syria's early past, the Aramaeans, Phoenicians, Greeks and Romans, Christianity, the monuments of Syria, the Umayyads and the Dawn of

Islam and the legacy of the crusades. Well illustrated.

Damascus: Hidden Treasures of the Old City
Brigid Keenan 2000 (1999)
A beautifully photographed and written book. Keenan lived for many years in Damascus.

Syria: Land of Contrasts
Peter Lewis 1980
A guide to the main sites of Syria, accompanied by many photographs.

Travel Literature

Ibn Battuta. Travels in Asia and Africa 1325-1354.
(see North Africa: Algeria and Sahara)
Ibn Battuta came from Tangier to Syria in 1325 and describes Aleppo, Antioch and Damascus.

Amurath to Amurath
Gertrude Bell 1924 (see Iraq)

The Desert and the Sown
Gertrude Bell 1985 (1907)
Gertrude Bell's life was dominated by the Arab world; she was brave, had fantastic stamina and was a good linguist. She undertook archaeological excavations, but in 1915 at the outbreak of war she was asked by the British government to join the Arab Bureau in Cairo to gather intelligence to mobilize the Arabs against Turkey. In 1916 she went to India, then to Basra and after the war to Baghdad, where in 1923 she founded the national museum. She was a great admirer of Lady Anne Blunt, wanting to follow her footsteps into unknown areas of Arabia. *The Desert and the Sown* is an account of her journey into the Syrian interior (which in those days comprised the present day Syria, Lebanon, Jordan, Israel and the occupied West Bank and Gaza strip).

Travels in Syria and the Holy Land
John Lewis Burckhardt 1992 (1822)
The Swiss explorer, Burckhardt, lived in Aleppo while he was preparing for his major expeditions, and during that time he travelled widely throughout Syria.

Syria and Lebanon
Robin Fedden 1965
A very readable travelogue of post Second World War Syria and Lebanon, in which the author describes the major sites and gives their potted histories.

Three Journeys in the Levant
Shusha Guppy 2001 (see Jordan)

The Gates of Damascus
Lieve Joris 1996
Joris is a Belgian writer who spent a year living with a woman in Damascus whose husband was a political prisoner.

Come, tell me how you live
Agatha Christie Mallowan 1990 (1946) (see Iraq)

Central and Eastern Arabia
W. Palgrave 1985
An abridged edition of Palgraves's travels in disguise through Syria and Arabia.

Giant Cities of Bashan and Syria's Holy Places
Rev. J.L. Porter 1876 (1993)
Through the Old and New Testament sites of Syria, Jordan, Palestine and Lebanon.

Letters from Syria
Freya Stark. (see Lebanon)

Cleopatra's Wedding Present
Robert Tewdyr-Moss 2001 (1997)
A fine travel book about Syria by an author who was subsequently murdered. He faces both danger and discomfort with wit and an eye for the unusual.

TURKEY

I have fallen a hopeless victim to the Turk; he is the most charming of mortals and some day, when I have a little more of his language, we shall be very intimate friends, I foresee. Gertrude Bell. Letter to her family. 21 April 1905

Anthropology

Everyday Life in Ottoman Turkey
Raphaela Lewis 1971
Interesting insights into what life was like during the days of the Ottoman Empire.

Art & Archaeology

Ancient Civilizations and Ruins of Turkey
Ekrem Akurgal 1985 (1978)
Detailed descriptions of Anatolian sites.

Aegean Turkey 1989 (1966), Turkey's Southern Shore 1989 (1968), Turkey Beyond the Maeander 1989 (1971) and Lycian Turkey 1989 (1978)
George Bean
The definitive series of archaeological guides to south-west Turkey; all include maps and plans.

The Antiquities of Constantinople
Pierre Gilles 1988 (1729)
Gilles visited Constantinople in 1544 when it was the largest and wealthiest city in the western world; his book tries to reconstruct what the city was like in the age of Justinian, as well as telling us what it was like in the 16th century.

A History of Ottoman Architecture
Godfrey Goodwin 1992.
A comprehensive guide to Ottoman architecture which covers the whole of Turkey.

The Hittites
O.R.Gurney 1990 (1952)
The Hittites, often mentioned in the Old Testament, were an advanced civilisation in Anatolia; politically well organised and with their literature inscribed on clay tablets in cuneiform writing. Their stone monuments were figurative and powerful and can still be seen on rock faces.

Caves of God. Cappadocia and its Churches
Spiro Kostof 1989 (1972)
A guide and explanation to the hundreds of monasteries and churches in Christian Cappadocia

Early Christian and Byzantine Architecture
Richard Krautheimer 1986 (1965)
A wide-ranging and overall view of the history and changing character of Early Christian and Byzantine architecture in the Pelican History of Art series.

Ancient Turkey - A Traveller's History of Anatolia
Seton Lloyd 1992 (1989)
The author was head of the British Archaeological Institute in Ankara and has written an indispensable book to the ancient sites and civilisations of Turkey.

151

Byzantine Style and Civilization
Steven Runciman 1990 (1975)
Runciman defines and describes eleven centuries of art in the Byzantine world, which culminate with the jewelled mosaics which aimed "to increase the understanding of the divine beyond the finite limits of the human mind".

Turkish Delights
Philippa Scott 2001
A gloriously-illustrated book showing paintings, drawings and decorative objects.

Turkey. A Traveller's Historical and Architectural Guide
James Steele 1990
Illustrated with plans and colour photographs.

Islamic Art
David Talbot Rice (see Middle East - General)
A good far reaching introduction to the subject.

Biography

Lady Mary Wortley Montagu
Isobel Grundy 2001 (1999)
The brilliant and beautiful Lady Mary eloped with an untitled impoverished man who was appointed British ambassador to Turkey and who later became extremely rich.

Asiye's Story
Asiye Guzel 2003
A woman's painful account of state-based violence and torture.

Atatürk: the Rebirth of a Nation
Lord Kinross 1990 (1964)
A very readable account of Ataturk's life, giving a clear picture of the birth of the Turkish Republic. "By far the most thorough study of Ataturk in English and an absorbing biography in its own right". (*The Times*)

Atatürk
Andrew Mango 1999
A thorough and well researched biography – very good on early 20th century history in Turkey.

Blood-Dark Track
Joseph O'Neill 2001
A family history which includes the author's two grandfathers – one Turkish and one Irish – who were both imprisoned during the Second World War.

Portrait of a Turkish Family
Irfan Orga 1990 (1950)
The author was born into a prosperous family under the Sultans, but with the advent of the First World War the family was ruined and Turkey transformed. Irfan Orga finally came to London in 1941 and wrote the moving story of his family's survival.

Sir Thomas Roe: A Life
Michael Strachan 1989
Biography of an Elizabethan statesman who was English ambassador to the Ottoman court and head of the Levant company.

Scenes from an Armenian Childhood
Vahan Totovents 1980
The author grew up in a town which lay on the old Roman road running from Byzantium to Babylon; his account of his childhood in the 1880s is delightful, but has an added poignancy in that we know what happens to the area.

Fiction/Poetry

George Beneath a Paper Moon
Nina Bawden 1975
A mixture of comedy, love story and thriller, set between England and Turkey.

Greenmantle
John Buchan 1916
An exciting story which is about the secret service east of Constantinople; the grand climax is set in Erzurum in Eastern Turkey.

Murder on the Orient Express
Agatha Christie 1990 (1933)
Although mostly about getting to Turkey, there are some scenes set in Turkey itself.

The Fall of an Eagle
Jon Cleary 1964
A thriller set in eastern Turkey.

The Life of the Party
Maureen Freely 1985
Set in Istanbul in 1969, the story takes place around an American college.

Count Belisarius
Robert Graves 1970 (1938)
An historical novel about Belisarius, a cavalry commander and Christian, who was born in 500 A.D. and for whom the centre of the world was Constantinople.

Stamboul Train
Graham Greene 1975 (1932)
A spy thriller set aboard the Orient Express which crosses Europe from Ostend to Constantinople.

America, America
Elia Kazan 1962
A Greek boy in Constantinople tries to save enough money from his carpet business to get to America.

Memed My Hawk
Yashar Kemal 1992 (1955)
Set in Anatolia as are its sequels: *They Burn the Thistles* and *The Lords of Akchasaz: Murder in Ironsmith's Market. The Sea-Crossed Fishermen* is set in a fishing village near Istanbul where an old man is trying to save dolphins. Also *Iron Earth, Copper Sky, The Undying Grass* and *The Wind from the Plain.*

The Book of Dede Korkut
ed. Geoffrey L. Lewis 1974
The national epic of Turkey.

Aziyade
Pierre Loti 1989 (1927)
A tale of romance and intrigue set in nineteenth-century Ottoman Turkey. Loti vividly evokes a vanished world, as Lafcadio Hearn wrote: "Constantinople and the romantic Golden Horn have never been portrayed with such elegance".

The Towers of Trebizond
Rose Macaulay 1995 (1956.)
The book opens with a much-quoted sentence: "'Take my camel, dear' said my Aunt Dot, as she climbed down from this animal on her return from High Mass". The story is about a group of people who set out with a camel to explore the possibilities of a proposed Anglican mission to Turkey. Two of the party vanish into Soviet Russia, causing a scandal.

Balthasar's Odyssey
Amin Maalouf 2003 (2002)
Before the 'Year of the Beast' in 1666, Balthasar Embriaco, a Levantine merchant sets out on a long adventure across the civilised world.

Sweet Waters
Harold Nicolson 2000 (1921)
Set on the banks of the Bosphorus this 'Istanbul thriller' takes place during the last years of the Ottoman Empire.

The Prizegiving
Aysel Özakin 1988 (1980)
The author now lives in Germany, but in this novel, written in Turkey before she left, she questions the institution of marriage. Nuray goes to Ankara to receive a prize for her first novel, but she is haunted by disturbing memories, discovering that prizes are not always what they seem.

The Black Book
Orhan Pamuk 1994
A novel which questions Turkey's shaky identity. *The White Castle* is about a captured young scholar who is put up for auction at the Istanbul slave market. *My Name is Red* is a thriller set around miniature painters.

Cages on Opposite Shores
Janset Berkok Shami 1995
Meral leaves her husband after eleven years and searches for her new identity - set against the conflicts and tensions of modern day Turkey.

Under a Crescent Moon
Daniel de Souza 1989
Vignettes from prison by a jailed foreigner; remarkable for its optimism and lack of bitterness.

Julian
Gore Vidal 1976 (1954)
Based on the life of the Emperor Julian, who attempted to suppress Christianity and revive Hellenism, Vidal has stayed

153

close to the facts found in the three volumes of his letters and essays which have survived. Much of the novel takes place in what is modern day Turkey.

Food

The Art of Turkish Cooking
Neset Eren 1993 (1969)

Lonely Planet World Food: Turkey 2000

Nevin Halici's Turkish Cookbook 1989
A selection of regional dishes from all over Turkey.

General Background

Culture Shock! Turkey
Arin Bayraktaroglu 1996
Very useful for long trips and residents.

The Owl's Watchsong
John A. Cuddon 1960
Life in Istanbul in the 1950s.

154

City of Yok
Jan Morris
About Istanbul – in *Destinations*.

Turkey Unveiled: Atatürk and After
Nicole and Hugh Pope 1997
A very good introduction by two foreign correspondents who know the country well.

Guides

Blue Guide: Istanbul 2000

Companion Guide Istanbul and Around Marmara 2000

Eyewitness Guide: Istanbul 2004

Insight Guide: Istanbul 2000

Lonely Planet: Istanbul 2002

Time Out Istanbul Guide 2004

Blue Guide: Turkey 2001

Companion Guide Southern Turkey 2002

Companion Guide Turkey 1996

Eyewitness Guide:Turkey 2002

Insight Guide: Turkey 2003

Insight Guide: Turkish Coast 2000

Lonely Planet: Turkey 2003

Rough Guide: Turkey 2003

Cultural Guides

Byzantine Monuments of Istanbul
Ahmed Akmak & John Freely 2002

Istanbul. A Traveller's Companion
Laurence Kelly 1989
An anthology of selected writings about Istanbul past and present which convey a feeling for its different periods of history.

Strolling through Istanbul
Hilary Sumner-Boyd and John Freely 1987
The classic and invaluable guide for walking around the city.

Imperial Istanbul: Iznik-Bursa-Edirne
Jane Taylor 1989
A very detailed guide to the four imperial cities.

History

The Voyage of the Argo
Apollonius of Rhodes (trans. E. V. Rieu) 1971
The account of Jason's voyage along the Black Sea coast.

The Campaigns of Alexander
Arrian (trans. Aubrey de Selincourt) 1971
Even though this was written four hundred years after Alexander the Great's death it remains probably the most reliable account of his character and achievements. Arrian himself had been a military commander.

Black Sea
Neal Ascherson 1996 (1995)
A compelling book about a great inland sea and about European history from the time of Herodotus to the fall of Communism.

Turkish Letters
Ogier de Busbecq 2001 (1927)
Originally translated into English in 1694, this is gossipy and enquiring history written by someone who was actually there.

The Alexiad of Anna Comnena
Anna Comnena. (trans. E.R.A. Sewter) 1969
A history of the reign of the Emperor Alexius 1 by his daughter, a Byzantine princess who was one of the first, if not *the* first woman historian; it includes an account of the first crusade from 'the other side'.

Inside the Seraglio
John Freely 2000 (1999)
Private lives of the Sultans in Istanbul.

Lords of the Horizons
Jason Goodwin 1999 (1998)
A readable history of the Ottoman Empire.

Gallipoli
Michael Hickey 1995
A history of the campaign.

Chronicles of the Crusades
Joinville and Villehardouin. (trans. M. R. B. Shaw) 1963
The two French chronicles were written by soldiers who took part in the Crusades. Villehardouin writes a straightforward account of the Fourth Crusade, and Joinville's Life of Saint Louis shows his close attachment to the king.

Dervish: The Invention of Modern Turkey
Tim Kelsey 1996
An analysis of modern Turkey's problems. Gloomy.

The Ottoman Centuries. The Rise and Fall of the Turkish Empire.
Lord Kinross 1977.
A thorough, all-encompassing book about the rise of the Turkish Empire with its changing fortunes and boundaries and its subsequent fall, abolition of the sultanate and declaration of a republic in 1923.

The Emergence of Modern Turkey
Bernard Lewis. 1968 (1961)
A thorough and interesting book, which is mostly about the hundred years between 1850 and 1950 and which describes the emergence of a new Turkey from the decay of the old. The first part is a chronological history and the second examines four aspects of this change: the transformation of the corporate sense of identity and loyalty among the Turks, the transformation of the theory and practice of government, of religion and the cultural life and of the economic and social order.

155

Constantinople
Philip Mansel 1997 (1995)
Impeccably researched history of the 'city of the world's desire 1453-1924'.

Sultans in Splendour
Philip Mansel 200
Full of fascinating nuggets of information.

Gallipoli
Alan Moorehead 1967 (1956)
"Essentially the great question remains: Who will hold Constantinople?"

(Napoleon). Until as late as August 1914 it was by no means obvious that Turkey was going to go into the First World War on the German side; the background to Gallipoli is examined by Moorehead along with details of the campaign itself.

Byzantium - the Early Centuries
John Julius Norwich 1990 (1988)
A narrative history about the five formative centuries and beginnings of Byzantium and the Byzantine empire. Full of detail and yet very readable: "He is brilliant ... He writes like the most cultivated modern diplomat attached by a freak of time to the Byzantine court, with intimate knowledge, tactful judgement and a consciousness of the surviving monuments". *(The Independent)*. Also *Byzantium The Apogee, Byzantium The Decline and Fall*

A Short History of Byzantium
John Julius Norwich 1997 (1988)
A condensation of the above trilogy.

The Decline and Fall of the Ottoman Empire
Alan Palmer 1992
Emphasis on Europe's involvement in the mid-nineteenth century.

War and Revolution in Asiatic Russia
Morgan Philips Price 1918
"A powerful and moving account of the war in eastern Turkey, Persia and the Caucasus in 1915-16 by the Manchester Guardian correspondent, with Russian armies fighting the Turks. Includes vivid and evocative descriptions of eastern Turkey in the terrible grip of winter and enchantment of spring." (Peter Hopkirk)

The Secret History
Procopius (trans. G.A. Williamson 1981 (1966))
Procopius, who lived in the 6th century AD, was the official historian to the emperor; however after he had written the official history he wrote this *'Secret History'* which is full of salacious gossip and tales of the murky happenings at the courts of Justinian and Theodora.

Fourteen Byzantine Rulers
Michael Psellus 1979 (1966)
The author was an advisor to several emperors between 976 and 1078.

Istanbul Intrigues
Barry Rubin
Allied-Axis activities during the Second World War.

The Fall of Constantinople 1453
Steven Runciman 1992 (1965)
Western Christendom was unprepared for the fall of Constantinople in 1453 after a siege which lasted several weeks; the plight of the city had been neglected, whereas for the Turks it meant that the survival of their empire was ensured. The classic book on the subject.

A Traveller's History of Turkey
Richard Stoneman 1993
A short and readable history of the region from Prehistory up until the present day; the book includes an historical gazetteer, a chronology of major events, historical maps and famous battles.

Armenia: The Survival of a Nation
Christopher Walker 1980
"From the earliest period to the present hour, Armenia has been the theatre of perpetual war." (Edward Gibbon *The Decline and Fall of the Roman Empire).* The dispersal of Armenians world-wide has an ancient precedent, although this 'ëspiurk' has on the whole not been voluntary, but has been characterised by invasion, massacre and misrule. Christopher Walker looks sympathetically at their history.

The Ottomans
Andrew Wheatcroft 1993
A reinterpretation of the Ottomans and their culture, and a look at the inner life

of the Ottoman world as seen through Western eyes.

Anabasis
Xenophon
The Athenian leader led the retreat from Mesopotamia to the Black Sea.

Turkey. A Modern History
Erik J. Zürcher 1997 (1993)
A new, comprehensive and scholarly guide.

Leisure Activities
The Ala Dag. Climbs and Treks in Turkey's Crimson Mountains
O.B. Tuzel 1993

Natural History
Flowers of the Mediterranean
Oleg Polunin and Anthony Huxley 1987 (1965)
Western Turkey is included in this illustrated guide to over 700 plants.

Complete Mediterranean Wildlife.
Paul Sterry 2000
Where to see birds, plants and other wildlife.

Photographic
Splendours of the Bosphorus. Houses and Palaces of Istanbul
Chris Hellier and Francesco Venturi 1993
A lavishly illustrated book showing the houses on the Bosphorus and their many architectural details.

Turkey
Roland and Sabrina Michaud 1986
A well-illustrated photographic book.

Religion
A Time to Keep Silence
Patrick Leigh Fermor 1988 (1957)
In his book about religious orders and retreats Patrick Leigh Fermor visits the Rock Monasteries of Cappadocia.

Travel Literature
On Horseback through Asia Minor
Frederick Burnaby 1985 (1877)
Burnaby travelled on a Great Game mission by horse in the winter of 1876.

A Traveller on Horseback in Eastern Turkey and Iran
Christina Dodwell 1992 (1987)
Christina Dodwell travelled from Eastern Turkey to Cappadocia, Iran and Pakistan by horse; on her way back she went up to the Russian border to Mount Ararat.

Turkey Around the Marmara
John Freely 1998
By an author who knows Turkey extremely well.

Journey to Kars
Philip Glazebrook 1985 (1984)
Intrigued by all the ancient travellers to Turkey, Philip Glazebrook made his own trip to eastern Turkey, following their routes through the ruined cities of Asia Minor.

On Foot to the Golden Horn. A Walk to Istanbul
Jason Goodwin 1993
This book records Goodwin's journey through Eastern Europe on the way to Istanbul.

Dinner of Herbs
Carla Grissman 2001
The author went to remote Anatolia in the 1960s and lived with a local peasant family.

The Histories
Herodotus. c.460 B.C.
"I wonder if you ever took a look at Herodotus - which is a wonderful travel book. It was the only book I carried with me right through the war - and I still have

some of the rags to which it was reduced." (Norman Lewis)

My Travels in Turkey
Denis Hills 1964
Wanderings in and around Turkey between 1955 and 1962. Unusually for the time, he travelled into the lesser known eastern provinces and in his words "I have tried to present Turkey in her true colours, not as a mere appendage of Istanbul and the classical coastal districts but as a country of countless small towns and villages scattered over a great area".

The Scholar and the Gypsy. Two Journeys to Turkey, Past and Present
James Howard-Johnston and Nigel Ryan 1992
This joint book uses two very different approaches to the same journey, which started in Trebizond and ranged over remote country and up to the Iranian and Soviet borders. They repeated their experience the following year, going into the interior of western Turkey.

158

Dervish
Tim Kelsey 1997
Kelsey travels through Turkey and gives us new insights into both politics and history.

Europa Minor
Lord Kinross 1956
A series of journeys made between 1947 and 1954 which ranged from Antioch and the Syrian frontier in the south-east to Adrianople and the Greek frontier in the north-west. Observant and readable.

The Crossing Place. A Journey Among the Armenians
Philip Marsden 1994 (1993)
Philip Marsden visited Armenian communities throughout the Middle East, the old Soviet Union and Eastern Europe before arriving in Armenia itself. He quickly succumbed to the beauty of Ararat and, recognising the Armenians passion for

their language, quotes Mandelstam: "These are people who jangle the keys of their language even when they are not using them to unlock any treasures".

Letters
Mary Wortley Montagu 1986
Also *Turkish Embassy Letters* (1994), written during her time in Istanbul 1716-18.

Secrets of the Bosphorus
Henry Morgenthau 1918
The US ambassador's account of the dramatic and important events in Constantinople in World War 1.

East of Trebizond
Michael Pereira 1971
Pereira's travels between the Black Sea and north-east Anatolia during the 1960s.

Fez of the Heart
Jeremy Seal 1996
Original travels through Turkey.

Beyond Ararat
Bettina Selby 1995 (1993)
The intrepid cyclist journeys to where the Tigris and Euphrates rise.

Ionia - A Quest
Freya Stark 1954
Freya Stark travelled around the Western coasts of Asia Minor during the autumn of 1952, visiting fifty five ruined sites which she describes with a mixture of history and romance; the only tourist she met during that whole trip was in Pergamum. *The Lycian Shore* (1956) is the account of a single journey by sea along the Asia Minor coast in a boat. She also wrote *Alexander's Path* (1991/1958) which traces the route Alexander took through Turkey, from Caria to Cilicia, on his way to defeat Darius.

The Innocents Abroad
Mark Twain. (see Egypt)
Many interesting observations about Istanbul.

Xanthus. Travels of Discovery in Turkey
Enid Slatter 1994
A journey with the traveller Charles Fellows who brought the collection of 'Xanthian marbles' back to Britain.

YEMEN

Aden should mean oven. Only the camels seemed baked enough to suit it. Henry Adams, In a Journal Letter to Elizabeth Cameron. 29 Sept. 1891

Art and Archaeology

Arabia Felix
Alessandro de Maigret 2002
A look at the archaeological history of Yemen.

Autobiography

The Uneven Road
Lord Belhaven 1955
The author was a British officer in Aden. He visited San'a in 1933-4.

Fiction

Treacherous Road
Simon Harvester 1967
A spy novel set between Yemen and Egypt.

The Long Lost Journey
Jennifer Potter 1991 (1989)
In 1910 Elinor Grace, an archaeologist, left Aden for Hodeidah, with James Fergusson, in order to try and discover the truth about the Queen of Sheba's legendary capital at Mareb. The expedition was ill-fated from the beginning; the intrigue has been erased from official files, but Jennifer Potter fills in the gaps: "The Long Lost Journey ... has the compelling force of a nightmare..." *(The Guardian).*

General Background

Farewell Arabia
David Holden 1966
At least half of this book is about the Yemen; it was written at the time when the Yemen entered the twentieth century from the twelfth.

Arab Tribes in the Vicinity of Aden
F.M. Hunter and C.W.H. Sealey 1986 (1909)
A compilation of detailed listings of the 20 major tribes of the region up to the end of the nineteenth century.

Qat in Yemen
Shelagh Weir 1990
A good introduction to daily life in the Yemen today.

Guides

Lonely Planet: Yemen 2004

History

The Two Yemens
Robin Bidwell 1983
A history of the Yemen Arab Republic and the People's Democratic Republic of Yemen since the Europeans arrived in the C16th.

Arabia Without Sultans
Fred Halliday 1974
The book has about 180 pages devoted to the recent history of the Yemens.

The Yemen: Imams, Rulers and Revolutions
Harold Ingrams 1963
Harold Ingrams was the British Resident Adviser in the Western Aden Protectorate, and writes predominantly about Anglo-Yemeni issues.

The View from Steamer Point
Charles Johnston 1964
The author was three years in Aden between 1960-3, as Governor and High

Commissioner. During this time Aden was merged into the Federation of South Arabia.

A History of Arabia Felix or Yemen
Sir Robert Playfair 1970 (1859)
When Aden, which was described by Ibn Batuta as "a large city without either seed, water, or tree", became a British possession, there was a sudden renewed interest in the history of the Yemen. Playfair collated the notes which he had made during a long residence in Arabia, starting his work from the beginnings of Christianity. At the time of writing there was no extant connected history of the Yemen

Arabian Assignment
David Smiley 1975
The second part of Smiley's book deals with his time in the Yemen when he supported the guerrillas in their country's fight against the Egyptians in the early 1960's. The UN chose to ignore this invasion, so it is interesting to learn what the situation was like.

160

Natural History
South Arabian Hunt
R.B.Serjeant 1976
An interesting study of the origins and meaning of the ritual ibex hunt, using anthropological fieldwork, and archaeological, epigraphical and literary evidence.

Photographic
Yemen – Jewel of Arabia
Charles & Patricia Aithie 2001
Photographs and ample text.

Yemen Rediscovered
Michael Jenner 1983
A limited amount of text, but on the whole a well-illustrated and good introduction to the Yemen and the Yemenis.

Arabia Felix: the Yemen and its People
Pascal Maréchaux 1979
Stunning photographs, mostly colour, with ample captions of the Yemen Arab Republic.

San'a - an Arabic Islamic City
R.B. Serjeant and Ronald Lewcock 1983
Vast, expensive and rare, this is the ultimate book on the Yemen, which was published by the World of Islam Festival Trust.

Yemen. Land and People
Sarah Searight. Photography Jane Taylor 2002
A beautifully-illustrated book with ample text by an expert on the area.

Queen of Sheba. Treasures from Ancient Yemen
ed. St John Simpson 2002
Published to coincide with the exhibition about the Queen of Sheba at the British Museum.

Seen in the Hadramaut
Freya Stark 1938
Photographs taken by Freya Stark, accompanied by interesting and perceptive captions.

Travel Literature
Island of the Dragon's Blood
Douglas Botting 1958
An account of the expedition to Socotra under the auspices of the Oxford University Exploration Club.

A French Doctor in the Yemen
Claudie Fayein 1958
In 1951 the author left her husband and children for a year and went to the Yemen where she was paid £100 a month. She fell in love with the country and became the first foreigner allowed into many places.

Motoring with Mohammed
Eric Hansen 2001 (1991)
A storm left Hansen and his companions shipwrecked on a deserted Red Sea island. They were rescued by smugglers and taken to the Yemeni coast.

Arabia Felix: the Danish Expedition of 1761-67.
Thorkild Hanson 1964
A readable account of the Danish expedition in which everyone lost their lives except for Carsten Niebuhr, who wrote about his experiences.

A Journey through the Yemen. Some General Remarks upon that Country
Walter Harris 1985 (1893)
A mixture of the political history of the time and a journey through the Yemen, which Harris so enjoyed, despite the hardships, that he wrote "My recollections of the country are ones that I shall always treasure, in spite of the dangers and sickness, in spite of long marches and days in prison, the Yemen will always be for me, Arabia Felix".

Yemen. Travels in Dictionary Land
Tim Mackintosh-Smith 1997
The author has lived in the Yemen for many years - a very amusing book.

Aden to the Hadramaut
D.Van Der Meulen 1947
This journey in Southern Arabia was undertaken by the author in the 1930's.

Travels Through Arabia, and Other Countries in the East
M.Niebuhr 1792 (trans. Robert Heron)
Carsten Niebuhr, one of the first European travellers, was the only survivor in the ill-fated Danish expedition to Egypt and the Yemen which reached Hodeida in 1762. He writes interestingly about the everyday life and flora and fauna that he came across. His story is recounted in *Arabia Felix* by Thorkild Hansen (q.v.).

Arabian Peak and Desert: Travels in Al-Yaman
Ameen Rihani 1930
The author was told by a Yemeni he met in New York that it was impossible for a foreigner to travel in the Yemen: firstly the British in Aden would never grant permission and secondly if permission were granted, being there would lead to almost certain death. Nevertheless, Rihani managed to travel throughout the Yemen and on reaching San'a was not disappointed: "No, San'a is not disenchanting. Unlike other cities, the nearer one gets to it the more powerful is its spell. Beautifully, uniquely situated, its atmosphere is like an Arab poet's fancy, crisp and vigorous".

Complete Works, Selected Letters
Arthur Rimbaud (edited and translated by Wallace Fowlie) 1975 (see Ethiopia, Somalia)
Several of Rimbaud's letters complaining about his life in Aden are printed in this parallel text.

161

In the High Yemen
Hugh Scott 1947 (1942)
A good background book to the Yemen. Scott was a naturalist, and this account of his travels from Aden into the Yemen and to San'a and Hodeida is full of interesting information.

The Southern Gates of Arabia
Freya Stark 1990 (1936)
Freya Stark followed the Incense Route inland from the southern shores of Arabia to Tarim in the Hadhramaut. For centuries, relays of Bedouin and camels had taken "incense of Arabia and Africa, tied pearls and muslins from Ceylon and silks from China, Malacca tortoiseshell and spikenard from the Ganges ... and from India, diamonds and sapphires, ivory and cotton, indigo, lapis lazuli, and cinnamon and pepper above all", to sell in northern markets.

A Winter in Arabia
Freya Stark 1991 (1940)
Freya Stark returned to the Hadhramaut
in November 1937 and travelled through
the desert throughout that winter; her per-
ception of people and objects is acute and
often very funny. She writes "The archaeologist was feverless in the morning and
packed our collected pots, and now alas!
is in bed again with a temperature. The
pots are so depressingly ugly that a prolonged contemplation of them would
make anyone ill".

Arthur Rimbaud in Abyssinia
Enid Starke 1937
For the last ten years of his life, Rimbaud
was a trader on the Red Sea coast, probably dealing in arms. He was as ambiva-
lent about Aden, where he often went, as
he was about Africa and the rest of his
life. He wrote to his mother and sister in
France, "Aden is the most boring place in
the world, after, however, the one where
you live" (September 22, 1880). He felt
he was like a prisoner, trapped, only earn-
ing six francs a day and thus unable to
afford to leave.

162

A Modern Pilgrim in Mecca, and a Siege in Sanaa
A.J.B. Wavell 1912
The second part of this book is an
account of Wavell's visit to Hodeidah and
Sanaa in 1911, when Yemen was under
Turkish rule.

INDEXES

PLACES

AUTHORS

165

167

169

173

174

175

177

TITLES

181

182

189

191

192

193

194